*f*P

Also by Steve Fishman

A Bomb in the Brain: A Heroic Tale of Science, Surgery, and Survival

KARAOKE NATION

OR, HOW I SPENT A YEAR IN SEARCH OF GLAMOUR, FULFILLMENT, AND A MILLION DOLLARS

STEVE FISHMAN

THE FREE PRESS
New York   London   Toronto   Sydney   Singapore

*f*P

THE FREE PRESS
A Division of Simon & Schuster, Inc.
1230 Avenue of the Americas
New York, NY 10020

For information regarding special discounts for bulk purchases, please contact Simon &
Schuster Special Sales at 1-800-456-6798 or business@simonandschuster.com

Designed by Jan Pisciotta

Manufactured in the United States of America

10 9 8 7 6 5 4 3 2 1

Library of Congress Cataloging-in-Publication Data is available.

ISBN 0-7432-2902-9

To Tina

Contents

PART THREE

KARAOKE
NATION

Preface

The Hubbub

IN SOME WAYS, this book began with an article. I'm a journalist and write about lots of subjects. For a time, my beat seemed to be people-who-blow-up-weird-things, like hometowns or waterfalls. Then, half a dozen years ago, *Details,* a magazine that once put Heather Graham on its cover dressed in gold body paint, asked me for a profile of a businessman named Ernie.

Most of the time Ernie was an accountant-for-hire. The summer I met him, he worked for three different companies in as many cities. Ernie assured himself unbroken employment through several techniques—in addition, of course, to excellent work. He learned every assistant's name and sent each one flowers on her birthday. (He married one of those assistants, though I don't believe that was an intended benefit.) Plus to stay in touch, he bought his own 800 number, 1-800-GOERNIE, and, wherever he was, answered it cheerfully.

On weekends, you might have expected Ernie to take a well-deserved break with his new wife, the former assistant. Instead, Ernie worked at a soda company, one he'd started for a few thousand dollars. Ernie had hired a bottler, a distributor, a designer, and, most important, a chemist who came up with a cola formula, the secret to which was caffeine. Ernie dosed in the legal limit. (He once delightedly told me he believed caffeine habit-forming.)

On hot summer weekends, Ernie undertook marketing himself. Once I followed him to a supermarket where he distributed samples to heavyset women whose shopping carts overflowed with giant containers of cereal, detergent, and Coke. Another weekend, this one sweltering, I joined him at a local outdoor concert where he rented a booth. I was fascinated by the misting tent. Ernie, intrigued by publicity opportunities, talked a drummer into raising a can of his soda while on stage.

When a few weeks later we met at a Kansas City bagel shop, which Ernie considered a big thing for Kansas at the time, I had just one question in mind. *Why?* Why, after a week of exhausting accounting, did Ernie pile on a weekend of what seemed, even in his own telling, grueling, half-disappointing tasks. ("I wish he'd held the can up longer," Ernie had said of the drummer.)

Ernie considered my question, looked over my shoulder, then into my eyes, which made him appear both intent and lost-in-thought, a clever trick. "I want to see how high I can fly," he said after a pause. Another time, in response to a similar question, he said, "I want to see if I can make my dreams come true."

I found these answers shocking. We all have notions of business, what it demands and what it provides. Even outsiders like me know that for most of the past fifty years, business offered a better shot at ulcers than dream fulfillment. Think of the fifties businessman, who sometimes seems the prototype of all businessmen, commuting home from the office. He caught the 5:10 out of Grand Central and pushed through the front door like an ad for open heart surgery. For him business was a rat race. When Tom Rath, hero of the fifties classic *The Man in the Gray Flannel Suit,* told his grandmother he was headed into business, she said, "I'm sorry you have to go into business. . . . Business is such a bore." And, of course, businessmen were, too. Or worse. As Fortune magazine noted not so long ago, businessmen were typically portrayed as crass, philistine, corrupt, predatory, domineering, reactionary, and amoral.

Now Ernie wanted to fly high, to make his dreams come true through business. It seemed nutty. Could a person really be anything other than a beverage salesman by hawking a super-caffeinated soft drink on weekends? But Ernie was onto something. Indeed, within a few short years his notions of what one might attain through business, in particular through an entrepreneurial business, would be embraced by the New Economy and then by the country at large.

Recently, the New Economy has been judged harshly. Where were the bottom lines? The realistic expectations? The adults? The New Economy is like a sports team that's just lost. People want a trade. Fast. (The media, as a rule, are terrible scolds.) But a larger, and now-obscured, point is this: For a time, a new business culture touched something in people. Business—*business!*—was linked to people's desires, hopes, longings.

And, if all the businesses didn't last, and if some would prove less noble than their lofty mission statements, still something important remained: changed notions of business, its accessibility, its possibilities, and, indeed, its meaning. Business would become a way to fulfill your dreams. Not your dreams of accumulation—or not only. Soon, every businessperson would sound like Ernie. Indeed, the very subject of business no longer seemed to be corporate profit, but personal hopes for a meaningful, satisfying, even happy life. Business culture would become our aspirational culture. Business, I swear, sounded like the seventies, the era of self-fulfillment, when I'd come into adulthood.

In 1999, this rollicking new business culture even made me want to join, and here was the other part: I could. In the late nineties, business unexpectedly, and a bit incredibly, threw wide its doors, beckoning all. And I decided to take this new culture at its word.

This is not a research-heavy tome. I have some arguments to advance about the new business culture, but it's also the tale of a personal adventure in a new place, a peculiar one I came to think of as businessland. Hopefully, there will be some intrigue, some charming people, a chance for some excitement, and some profit, as well as some fun. We've lately been through a dramatic time, but bear in mind that the New Economy, where much of this book occurs, was full of high flyers and young people, which, to my mind, is a formula for comedy.

New York magazine was interested in my adventure and gave me $3,000, which my editor sunnily called seed money. I have no doubt that some businesspeople were encouraged to talk to me because of my connection to the magazine. For my part, my undertaking was as sincere as could be and always presented that way. Indeed, in a terrible and unanticipated development, I caught the bug myself. I'd spend close to a year on this thing. And somewhere along the way, I discovered that I desperately wanted my business to succeed.

There is a chance that much of the activity identified with the New Economy, and in particular the part that centered on the Internet, will be recalled as a fairy tale; as an amateurish period bracketed off from the course of professional business events. Much of what occurred in businessland had the feel of an amateur event, and that's the culture in which I'm particularly interested. And yet this is no put-down, not in my mind. We're a country for the enthusiastic, the venturing, the unabashed. We are, as I like to say, a Karaoke Nation, singing loudly and doing business to our heart's content.

A Business Prologue

Doing Business

"FUCKING THIEVES!" I first heard those two sharp words down a long carpeted hall. They were awfully loud. Someone seemed to be unhappy. And getting closer. Worse, it occurred to me that the someone was Russell Simmons, the godfather of hip-hop and the person on whom I'd lately convinced myself the future of my business venture depended.

It had been almost an hour ago that Russell's assistant had deposited my team in Russell's roomy office with the suggestion that he'd arrive momentarily. A couple of times she'd poked her head in and assured us that Big Dawg, as employees occasionally called Russell, was hurrying back. He, too, was eager to meet, I'd gathered.

"Russell was held up," she'd apologized. (At the time I couldn't appreciate her double meaning.)

"No problem," I'd said. I was sure he'd have a clever excuse. I couldn't wait to hear it. And, really, I didn't mind. This was to be among my first real business meetings, my team's first chance to pitch our venture, make some headway. If anything, the delay added to my excitement. Soon, I told myself, Russell Simmons, who'd launched Public Enemy, the Beastie Boys, LL Cool J, and Slick Rick, would consider the "value proposition," as I'd recently learned to say, of what I'd started to think of as my end of the music business. The thought literally made my skin itch.

From what I could tell, my team shared my enthusiasm. At one point, Clemente had blurted out that he was thinking of cutting his long hair, which I took as a sign of nerves. Luckily, Consigliere was there. *"He's thinking of cutting his hair,"* Consigliere repeated in a dire tone that thankfully snapped Clemente out of it. He settled down. We all did. In fact, about a half-hour ago we'd started to make ourselves at home in Russell's office, which, for a guy who made a point of "having fly shit," was a touch perfunctory: two respectable couches, a low coffee table, a desk, a bookshelf, blinds, and a half-refrigerator that I'd unplugged in order to plug in my computer. Consigliere sampled the reading material. "*Hamptons* magazine?" he read. He seemed perplexed. I think it was Clemente who pointed out the pictures on the walls, all of which featured Russell, though our favorite also showed his wife, the half-black, half-Japanese model Kimora Lee.

"A straight-up ghetto bitch," I think I said.

Consigliere shot me a concerned look.

I shrugged—Russell had described her that way in a magazine— and then flopped on to a couch. We were approaching the hour mark and I was on the point of stretching out. Might as well, I thought, when that booming voice brought us all to attention.

"Fucking thieves!" came a second, louder call.

Then Russell charged through the doorway at such pace that his long feet seemed to trail him. I'd done my research. I knew that Russell was a nut for relaxation. He took long beach weekends, kept a copy of the *Bhagavad-Gita* handy, did yoga, stood on his head *every single day,* ate vegetarian, none of which, I noted, was doing the trick at the moment. Russell appeared on the point of turning things over. His arms moved with frightening, water-treading energy, an energy focused, I found myself hoping, on the aforementioned thieves. Unless this was his greeting for my team, which, it occurred to me, he'd caught tiptoeing around his office.

But Russell—and I guess this was a break—didn't appear to notice us. He shouted into his phone or, actually, into the wire that dangled from his ear. Russell was famous for holding heated phone conversations in public. (I knew someone who'd overheard Russell at a café yelling into his phone, "If the $22 million isn't there tomorrow the deal is *off.*") Russell seemed to direct his anger at the person on the phone's other end. Just then, however, a middle-aged blond woman in prim business attire glided into the office. "But we haven't heard his story," she said. She spoke in a peaceful, sing-songy voice, the tone of someone whose job might be to keep a lid on the boss's blood pressure. Perhaps she was another relaxation strategy. If so, she too was striking out. Russell was uncontainable.

"I don't want that *motherfucker* in the store!" Russell shouted, referring I assumed to the SoHo store of his fashion line, Phat Farm. "Don't let the *motherfucker* in."

The woman placed her hands on the hips of her pleated skirt, kind of teapot-like, as if to indicate, Oh my, what language.

"Get the *motherfucker* out," continued Russell. I still wasn't clear if Russell was addressing her or the person on the phone. Or maybe he was *simultaneously* talking to the oh-my woman *and* the person on the phone, both of whom, in any case, he suddenly dispatched with a single machete-like arm motion.

Then he turned to me. "What's this about?" Russell snapped in that same fearsome tone.

Apparently there were to be no clever excuses.

I suddenly had no idea how to respond. Is this how business is done? I wondered (and not for the last time). How *had* I gotten myself into this? Or, to use Russell's words, What *was* this about?

PART ONE

Chapter One

Throwing Elbows

I HAVE A PRETTY GOOD IDEA *where* business started for me. The why is fuzzier. I was at a Tribeca loft attending a midweek cocktail party, an after-work fund-raiser for a worthy politician without a chance. There were perhaps thirty people at the party, broken into small groups. I stood near a long, gray counter. Really, the entire apartment seemed as gray as a factory floor. "It needs updating," I could imagine my wife, Cristina, saying. The counter was chest-high, which is too high for a counter. As I set my beer down, I almost missed it. Recovering, I poked blue wire-frame glasses up my nose, a not entirely attractive gesture, smiled, paused, considered a story I'd just heard, and then, as if the outcome of my miscue, the slight embarrassment it caused, the story, and no doubt my own bullying past, I found myself thinking, "Today I set out to make a million dollars."

This was an unusual thought for me to have. After all it wasn't like I suddenly knew *how* to make a million dollars. I hadn't gone fumbling for a pad in the middle of the night struck by a "vision" of a new way to do things, which people would later impress upon me as important. Nor did I have a unique "skill set," "a core competency," a dynamic new "business model," all things that I'd eventually hear were helpful in business. Frankly, I didn't know what a business model was. Soon enough, I'd meet a shaggy-headed fellow who shut himself in a closet—he insisted it really was a closet—and emerged six months later with a brainy software package. That wasn't something I was likely to pull off. I spent too much time on the phone with tech support. I could go on. The list of business advantages I *didn't* have was stunning.

Plus, it's probably worth mentioning, I didn't really think of myself as someone motivated to earn a million dollars. Growing up, I'd had my share of after-school work, the kind that I'd later hear indicated an entrepreneurial disposition. I'd delivered newspapers, cut lawns. I'd assembled gaudy costume jewelry in a neighbor's basement. Frankly, I'd tried lots of jobs. That wasn't unusual in my family, which went in for a fair amount of vocational experimentation. At a time when my father held an executive position in New York City, he stacked jewelry catalogs in the foyer of our suburban home. He sold inexpensive peace-and-love medallions through the mail, not unlike those I put together in that neighbor's basement. Later, my parents would look into a laundromat business, then a tutoring center. Briefly, they'd spend time in pay phones, collecting bagfuls of quarters in their Ford Escort. They seemed to audition futures, and long after my lawn-cutting days, I occasionally indulged in the family pastime as well. Once my wife Cristina and I even tried to launch a little business in, as I came to think of it, the pest accessories industry.

Cristina works for a nonprofit. (When asked, she says, "I'm an activist.") One day she mentioned that she hated the look of those black Combat discs—almost as much as she disliked the cockroaches they were meant to kill. She figured you could create an illustrated cardboard facade to hide the ugly gadgets. We mentioned the project to a neighbor, who offered to help. He was an artist and plumber with—him too—an activist streak. Once his toilet was blocked; to fix it, he'd broken into an uncooperative neighbor's apartment and secretly installed a length of pipe, a bit of initiative I'd long admired.

For a few hundred dollars, we commissioned a prototype. A design student came up with a lovely origami model of a cockroach hotel. It folded ingeniously and looked like a New York City townhouse. Sadly, the project soon came to nothing. Despite early enthusiasm—and some wrangling over future profits—there were too many hurdles: design, distribution, production. Strangers had to do things they didn't seem inclined to do. Convincing them was tedious. Once the fun went, so did my commitment.

Moneymaking, I concluded, hadn't really gotten its hooks into me. (I'm not sure it had really latched onto my parents either. My father literally whistled every time he shipped off a peace-and-love medallion.) As a primary focus, I was happy to tell myself, money seemed dull, pushy, limited, obvious. I was after bigger fish, I assured myself.

And anyway, journalism, which I'd done for twenty years, was a fine, useful profession. A person could do it forever. The work was varied, interesting, worthwhile, and I didn't have to get up too early. I wrote long stories about colorful characters. Oddball extremes was how I sometimes thought of them. Johnny, a favorite, had tried to blow up his hometown. "You had to really like Johnny to like Johnny," his best friend told me. I liked Johnny. Just as I liked the hoboes I got arrested with, or the scared volcanologist, or the Harlem kid with a genius for chess, or the hustlers on the outskirts of Hollywood, people with unusual, even uncontrollable urges. I even—and I can't account for this—took to a serial killer I'd first met when he picked me up hitchhiking.

And yet lately, I had to admit that journalism wasn't entirely riveting. Recently, in fact, I'd found myself perseverating on a disturbing encounter from my first newspaper job. Two decades ago I'd worked for the *Miami Herald*. One day a fellow reporter told me of meeting a farmer near Lake Okeechobee. The farmer asked my friend what he did for a living. Actually, his formulation was more pointed.

"You go around and ask people things and then put them in the paper?" the farmer asked.

"Yes," my friend told him, a little surprised himself.

"And they pay you for that?" he pursued.

When I thought of what I did for a living, the patient notetaking, the patient listening, it all seemed absorbing of course, *fascinating*. Still, recently I had to admit that my job lacked a certain intensity, a connection to a larger story. Let's face it, I was pretty much indifferent to work in the categories that made sense these days. Lately, I felt as marginal as my colorful characters, which no longer seemed very original.

I'd probably felt this way for a few years, and in that, it was comforting. Let's say that the tenor of my discomfort was comfortable. Recently though, I'd started to wonder what I'd do if I left journalism.

Then one evening I found myself at that cocktail party for a movement Democrat, a liberal from New York's Upper West Side who sometimes championed the kinds of people I wrote about. He was a short man. Perhaps that encouraged me; a physical squaring-off seemed possible. I poked a finger at him. Wise up, I said, the world has changed. It was leaving his good-natured outlook behind. I raised my voice, rattled on. He grew a smile, the kind you give someone else's misbehaving child.

"Your husband's something else," he told Cristina when I finally let him go.

I turned from him toward that too-high gray counter and started to listen to a handful of nearby people, some of whom I didn't know, not entirely concentrating, the way one does at New York parties. I heard some laughter across the room, a few isolated words, and then a guy next to me in a brown suede coat began to tell a story. He was tall, mid-thirties, with a full head of dark hair, black rectangular glasses, and an inviting style of speech. He called people he'd just met "brother" in a half-familiar, half-ironic way. I thought someone said he was a novelist. Apparently, he'd recently been an entrepreneur. He was describing how you'd go about meeting with venture capitalists in order to raise money.

"You want one of the people on your team to be button-down, your banker, your grown-up," he said. He may have rapped his knuckles on a chair.

"Grown-up?" I asked. In context, the term was intriguing.

"He's got to instill confidence," he said. His head seemed to adjust to an ever more precise angle.

"Oh," I said. "And who else?"

"A flashy guy. In an Armani suit maybe. This guy has to promote the vision," he said. "Then you want someone, maybe a celebrity, somebody who could casually say, 'I was just playing golf with Quincy and he *loves* this idea.'"

My eyes lit up. It was as if this guy let slip that he was a Navy SEAL. The drama of a meeting like that! Anything could happen. Magazines lately wrote about lone entrepreneurs upending entire industries. Perhaps this fellow was one of those. My imagination raced. I pictured stare-downs with investors. Shouting matches. Had he, I found myself wondering, ever been double-crossed? I'd lately thumbed through the business pages. Who hadn't? They read like the sports pages. You could almost hear the cheering. People in business seemed to be having the times of their lives.

"Which guy were you?" I asked him.

"Brother," he said to me, "I used to own a black Armani suit."

Looking back, I believe that it was at just about that moment that I'd experienced, jumbled with self-consciousness and the aftereffect of that story, a vague . . . what was it? What I seemed to experience was an *urge,* though now that I say the word aloud—*urge*—that sounds wrong. It wasn't all that forceful. It was probably just a mood. (Certainly, it was *just* a mood.) As close as I could tell, this one had to do with wanting something, meaning something other than what I had. "I want more than anything . . ." I thought, but there I hesitated.

Everybody wants something else, I assured myself reasonably. You can't get away from it. *I want, I want. I want.* It was a roar. But what did *I* want? My aptitude for wanting hadn't ever been very high, not for focused wanting, the kind you heard so much about these days. With me, desire headed into the cosmos, disappearing like radio waves. It was a little embarrassing. After all, my determined family boasted serious goals. In past generations there'd been choppy crossings in the dead of night. I had a great uncle who swam a river—I forget which—to escape. (Talk about focused wanting!) My energetic father had eventually walked away from an established career. He'd switched futures. Together he and my mother started a small school.

Then at that party in the gray room, I suddenly knew what I wanted, wanted with an intensity I am tempted to describe as ancestral. I wanted *my fill.* I wanted to give as good as I got. To get into arguments. Some tussling. A showdown or two would be fine. Maybe

I could be double-crossed. Yes. I wouldn't mind having a hand in the future. *Not at all.* I wanted something that landed me. *Landed me.* I wanted to be in the thick of things. And I wanted stories to tell.

And that, I believe, was the precise moment when, reaching my beer toward the chest-high counter, the one I almost missed, I smiled, paused, pushed those goofy blue wireframes up my nose, paused again, and then thought triumphantly: "Today I set out to make a million dollars." Though, on reflection, I may have uttered these words aloud, seeing as how nearby partygoers tightened the grip on their drinks. Two women, I noticed, turned to one another and shared a wide-eyed look.

I hardly cared. Look what I'd been missing, I thought suddenly. I gazed at my brown bottle of beer, which made a sweaty *O* on the gray counter. The million-dollar project suddenly struck me as a lot more invigorating than the doughy desk work at the center of my current life. The roughhouse of commerce. *That's* where it was at these days.

I thought about the manly adventure of business, and the entrepreneurs I might tangle with. I imagined that I'd soon go on about the real engine of the economy, and the shape of things to come. Before long, I just knew, I'd cut people off with a look. "What's the bottom line?" I'd say, "It's now or never." I'd start sentences with "I believe" and float a finger in the air to let people know I meant it. They wouldn't walk away, grins fixed in place.

I took up my drink, wiped the ring of condensation from the counter with my sleeve. Perhaps, on reflection, I wanted to impress the guy next to me, the one in the brown suede jacket, whom I now thought of as the Armani guy. I made a motion with my elbows like a washing machine. "I want to throw some elbows," I said sincerely. I did this beer in hand, spilling a drop, as I tried to explain to this person I barely knew how things would go if—where did *this* inspiration come from?—he were willing to pitch in. I believed it would be more *fun*. Yes, fun was the word that came to mind.

"Come on," I said to this guy, the one I now seemed to be addressing. I may have been shouting. Who could blame me? I was suddenly intent, a fine development in and of itself. I saw my future. A bunch of them. "Let's make a million dollars! Why not?" I snapped. "We'll give it a year," I said. "If it takes ten months, then we'll take two off."

I already liked the million-dollar goal. It seemed robust, vital, martial, the way I used to feel playing touch football, breathing quick, steamy bursts into fall air. And it seemed full of possibilities, as if—looking back, I can still hardly believe this—it was something original. I felt springy, full of purpose. Taken together, it was one sharp feeling. I took a sip of beer and grabbed for a chair, at which point the knot of partygoers dispersed, perhaps relieved.

$ $ $

Of course, simply declaring my million-dollar intention—however mismatched it and I at first appeared—put me in a very popular group. I knew this because, at about this time I met a fidgety Ivy League graduate, a good-looking, slightly reedy woman with intense red hair and a sharp, insistent manner. Mary was one of those people, I soon understood, who always seems to have a hand in the air indicating something smart and entertaining to say. "I'm an insecure overachiever," she said. Apparently she knew lots of them.

We were at a café drinking lemonade as Mary explained that she had a future to plan. She seemed optimistic, more or less. (Optimism, I sensed, wasn't Mary's strong suit.) Until recently, she'd been involved in an entrepreneurial venture with two other employees, both friends, both unpaid, and all working out of her apartment. I gathered that the business had something to do with bonds and the Internet. Mary didn't feel I'd get it and so spared me a detailed explanation. In any case, the venture collapsed when an investment banking firm decided to go into bonds in just the way Mary had contemplated.

As a second lemonade arrived, Mary's narrow shoulders pulled taut as a birdcage. I sensed some discontent, though I wasn't immediately sure why. She mentioned she hadn't gotten the *pop* she wanted, a term that apparently meant money. Still, Mary was entertaining job offers. She was the kind of applicant people sought. And tomorrow she was off for vacation.

She signed. Her vertebrae seemed to click into place. Did she have to spell it out?

Perhaps that would be best.

So she did. "Why aren't I a millionaire?" she asked forlornly. She added, "I'm thirty, well, almost."

You didn't have to be approaching thirty to experience the special tug, and accompanying ache, in that question. You didn't even have to be a businessperson, not one of longstanding in any case.

To set out to make a million dollars connected a person to what seemed for a time the country's most popular ambition. According to what I read, *most people* expected to be millionaires. In 1997, a survey of American college students found that a stunning 77 percent believed they would someday earn a million dollars.

Were they wrong?

At one point, the *New York Times* reported this perversely precise statistic: On any given day, said the paper of record, sixty-four new millionaires were minted in California's Silicon Valley alone, which is at a rate of 23,360 a year—about the population of the town in New Jersey where I grew up. By about 1999, someone had counted 84,000 millionaires in the Silicon Valley region. (Another 134,000 were half-millionaires, at least on paper.) These new wealthy weren't just computer programmers, those who suddenly seemed to know everything worth knowing. They were managers and manual writers; they were in PR, in sales. Wealth suddenly seemed a routine assignment and—reversing a decades-long trend—was being completed at a young age.

In New York, too, people I kind of knew appeared to be doing very well. I heard about the person whose son was on a friend's son's soccer team and whose company was going public. (And, still, he worried about his son's playing time.) The new wealthy always seemed to be regular folk, someone with no particular aptitude. As one friend with an unusually compromised attention span exclaimed, "This guy answered an ad in a free newspaper." I think the free part really got to him. "And now," he added, his attention riveted, "he's worth $35 million." The process might be baffling—free newspaper? $35 million?—but the import was clear. These days riches seemed as available as the air, if you just knew where to look.

$ $ $

In a few minutes, the Armani guy wandered over to where I sat.

"You're tic-y," I said from my chair. It was mainly in his foot and occasionally in his head, which could shift with camera-shutter speed.

"I'm a ticker," he concurred.

"Do you ever feel . . ." I pursued, looking for the right word. ". . . pent-up?" Lately, I did. I had it in my legs, shot through like a drug.

"All the time," he said quickly. Then, without a segue, he offered to help. "I have some experience with business plans," he mentioned casually. "I could look at one for you." I thought that was terrific, though I'd never seen a business plan. No matter. I told myself things were falling into place. I had a team forming. (*Team.* I already liked saying the word.) From the start I thought of the Armani guy as my business consigliere. His name was Steve Reynolds. Consigliere was what I liked to call him. Later, when I got to know him better, I'd sometimes call him Consig.

In time, I'd learn a few salient details about him—not that it was ever easy. It was like pulling teeth, as my mother would say. Consigliere, it would turn out, had ample business credentials. Before becoming an entrepreneur, he'd been a leading Internet consultant, often quoted in *Fortune* and *BusinessWeek*. He occasionally referred to that as *my business act,* which led me to think there were others. And indeed not long ago, he'd written an inventively titled novel— *The Impact of the Energy Crisis on Haircuts and Other Matters of Inner Peace.* Consigliere was a business guy who longed for a three-book deal. No wonder he seemed to keep a lot of energy under wraps.

At the party, Consigliere abruptly put his elbows at his sides. He twisted his arms in his brown suede jacket, a gesture that at first confused me. Then I got it. My first company would be called Throwing Elbows, a Limited Liability Corporation.

December 1999
Nasdaq 3353.71

Chapter Two

No Freaking Clue

ONE DAY I phoned my local dry cleaner. I was looking for a delivery of some shirts. James, the owner, was a polite, chipper young Korean man who carried a cell phone and sometimes wore a ring of keys on his belt. He was reliable, his service was good, but lately he'd disappeared. His mother ran the business. "James ver, ver busy," was the only explanation his mother's cryptic English would permit.

When James unexpectedly answered the phone, I had to ask, "Where have you been?"

He had a quick reply. "Mr. Fishman," he said intently. "I'm an Internet entrepreneur now."

From what I gathered James had made some good contacts through his dry-cleaning business. His customers seemed to like his ideas, his Internet ideas. They, he said, talked about funding him. James no longer had time for the dry-cleaning business. His Internet ventures, he suggested, were advancing too swiftly.

Just a couple of weeks later, I ran into James on the street. "How's your business going?" I said casually, not expecting much. "Your Internet business?" I specified.

"Really good," said James. James was usually upbeat.

Still, I was surprised. "*Really* good?" I asked doubtfully.

"Yeah, we've got two deals in the works," he said.

"You're kidding," I said.

"Yeah, we got ahold of some missile assembly software," James said evenly.

"Missiles?" There may have been alarm in my voice. As far as I knew my able young dry cleaner did not have a background in missile technology. "You're in the missile business?" I asked.

"Yeah," he said calmly "You can imagine how many parts are in a missile."

Was it possible? My dry cleaner, now an Internet entrepreneur, was in the missile business, headquartered for the moment, as he quickly told me, in the un-air-conditioned basement of the dry cleaners.

This was a bit surprising. After all, even I had some idea that for much of the past fifty years, business had tightened up qualifications, emphasized credentials and in-depth skills. Management was said to be rigorous, like science—and just as in science, there was research to pore over, journals to read. As recently as half a dozen years ago, anyone flipping through the Sunday want ads couldn't avoid the impression that business courted the professional, the expert, the specialist. In the *New York Times,* I found ads that called for "analytical expertise," "supply-chain knowledge," "data-mining background." Or else they preferred fifteen-plus years of "directly related experience," or, in another ad, experience with "acquisition management in the telecommunications and government industries." Lots of employers wanted MBAs, which, a quick check revealed, went in for math in a big way. At Wharton, core courses included financial accounting, managerial accounting, financial analysis, statistical analysis for management—and the student better *already* know calculus.

Something, clearly, had changed. As my overachieving acquaintance Mary (and in his way, my overeager acquaintance James) had been kind enough to inform me, "Business isn't rocket science." (In James's case, that apparently held true even for the rocket business.)

Intuitively, of course, I concurred. Always had. As far as I was concerned, everyone ought to know calculus. (Late in life, I'd tried to learn it myself.) But no matter how much business boned up on math or science, I didn't think of it as demanding, definitely not intellectual. Certain branches of philosophy, novel-writing, police work, *those* were difficult. In my view, the real trick in business was finding the time and, of course, working up the desire.

Now in a devilish twist, the business world seemed to have come around to my way of thinking. Nearly everyone I met these days appeared to believe that launching a business—*even a missile business*—mainly demanded time and energy. From what I could tell, no one really felt excluded.

"It's a gold rush out there," explained one recent millionaire, stirring a martini with a brisk, confident finger.

"Out there?" I repeated, dipping a finger into my own martini.

The gold-rush metaphor would often be applied to the Internet. And yet, this gold rush wasn't exactly like previous ones. In the eighties, bonds were called a gold rush, and in the seventies real estate had been labeled a gold rush. But to be in bonds you had to land a job at one of a few elite Wall Street firms. And to partake of real estate, it helped to know your way around complex legal entities like the limited partnership. The entrepreneurial gold rush that James and Mary were part of—and that I suddenly itched to join—was more in keeping with that first eponymous gold rush—the one that emphasized rush as much as gold. In that one, as readers of the *New York Daily Tribune* of 1848 learned, not only did great fortune seem to lie "upon the surface of the earth as plentiful as the mud in our streets," but, get this, it was there for the taking. "The only machinery necessary in the new gold mines of California is a stout pair of arms, a shovel and a tin pan," wrote Horace Greeley.

The Internet presented similarly low barriers to entry, as I'd start to hear them called. Suddenly people who did little more than view the World Wide Web as it popped up brightly and, most often, slowly on their computer screens wanted to be part of it. And here was the clincher: They could. You didn't need much more than a stout pair of arms, or a moderately apt brain, to get in on the New Economy.

The Internet might be a sophisticated piece of technology—it came out of the U.S. Defense Department, the top American universities, the European Organization for Nuclear Research—but anyone was pretty much welcome to take a shot at a little Internet business. "For a time," as Casey Hait and Stephen Weiss observed in their book *Digital Hustlers*, "anyone who could register a domain name could start a business," and *anyone* could register a domain name. It took five minutes.

"You can have absolutely no background and succeed," was how Stacy Horn, the founder of the online community Echo and a professor at New York University, put it. People were starting companies without ever having worked at a company. Scott Heiferman founded i-Traffic, an ad agency that would have offices in New York and San Francisco, even though, as he explained, "I'd never seen an ad agency before; I'd never physically been in an ad agency." So? Lots of Internet entrepreneurs boasted that they knew nothing about business—*nothing at all*. That didn't seem to hold anyone back. Kyle Shannon, an out-of-work actor before founding Agency.com, which would become a multinational consulting agency which would grow to $200 million sales in one year, figured he was part of "a community of people who literally *all* said, 'We don't have a freaking clue, but let's go do it anyway.'"

Don't be shy. Stay loose. Ask advice. Do it now. That was state-of-the-art counsel one Ivy League college professor gave aspiring business-people—guidance that might also, it occurred to me, be useful at their first mixer. Background? Expertise? Fifteen years supply-chain experience? Grounding in management science? Experience was nice, sure, but not required. Let's not get hung up on it anyhow. That would just slow you down. Gallup found that something like 70 percent of entrepreneurs had never started a business before. "Experience doesn't have much advantage anymore," the college professor said.

The current crop of entrepreneurs turned out to be more like me than I could have ever expected. Like me, they didn't pay much mind to the credentialist trend that had recently dominated corporate business and, in fact, much of American life. Think of it. You could get credentials in flower arranging (referred to as "floral arts" in credentialing circles), funeral directing, Swedish massage. There were certificates for circus performers and Pilates trainers, plumbers, gemologists. But if you were going into business anytime recently, as two young entrepreneurs explained, "What you don't need is a Harvard education, or any extensive formal education."

At Cornell, the two student entrepreneurs who launched theglobe.com, a friendly online community that allowed people to chat, play games, and e-mail, and that would be worth nearly $1 billion after its IPO, decided to play it safe. A bit contrarian, they thought experienced management might not be such a bad idea. So, reasonably, they placed an ad in the student newspaper seeking management, specifying that applicants had to be *at least* a junior. That was experience New Economy–style. (Hundreds, by the way, applied.)

$ $ $

The business world seemed to have fallen head-over-heels in love with the inexperienced, the untutored, the naive (a category that I couldn't help but think included me). And yet, as stunning as this seemed, you didn't have to go far back in business history to find a precedent. Indeed, the latest batch of entrepreneurs could seem to take their cues, at least their rhetorical cues, from a previous entrepreneur, the self-made man who rose to popularity in the nineteenth century. That American archetype also dismissed the advantages of birth, of training; he scoffed at college, at bookish pursuits in general. The self-made man even refused to credit big brains for success. Genius, as a rule, wasn't played up; on the contrary, it was considered vain and showy and might lead to "dawdling," as one author put it.

Benjamin Franklin was perhaps the forefather of this self-made man. Before he got caught up in founding the country, Franklin had been a runaway teen and the founder of his own printing business. CEO Franklin was as talented, as brainy, as any of his era. Yet on one transatlantic voyage—while intermittently speculating on the origin of crabs and the implications of eclipses—what he decided was this: "Industry and patience are the surest means of plenty." It was in this same tradition that as talented an inventor and entrepreneur as Thomas Edison could quip that he didn't need to know mathematics.

"I can hire mathematicians," he said. What he did need was stick-to-it-iveness, nerve, and an appetite for work. Through the nineteenth century, business seemed a matter of sweaty hand over hand. Thus Edison, who still has more patents than any individual in history, could famously, and a bit incongruously, assert, "Genius is one percent inspiration and ninety-nine percent perspiration."

In the heyday of this self-made figure, no one talked about boning up on business method; self-help manuals didn't deal with accounting, finance, advertising, management. Refined skills, an accumulated knowledge base, even proven aptitude didn't seem to count nearly as much as self-discipline, prudence, persistence—these were the watchwords of success. Steel magnates, like shopkeepers, "attributed their success to faithful observance of those traditional American expressions of thrift, sobriety, and hard work," as steel magnate Andrew Carnegie's biographer explained. Of course, as usual, no one was pithier than Franklin on the subject. In his *Poor Richard's Almanac,* Franklin published a series of aphorisms that summed up this view: "Great talkers little doers," "Industry need not wish," "Diligence is the mother of good luck," "A penny saved is a penny earned."

For Franklin, an experimental scientist of renown, business wasn't like science. In science if a hypothesis didn't work, you discarded it, tried another. But business, of the type Franklin came to symbolize, maintained just the opposite: The reason something didn't work was also the reason it would work in the future. So keep at it. Relentlessness counted, not cleverness. This was the spirit in which as endowed and ruthless a nineteenth-century businessman as John D. Rockefeller Sr., at one time the country's richest man, liked to recount how on his first job hunt he walked the streets six days a week for six weeks, sometimes soliciting the same firm two and three times, before landing a spot as a bookkeeper, not, he emphasized, because of his skill with accounts—that subject was never broached by his future employer—but because of his persistence.

Another self-made man, Cornelius Vanderbilt, once wrote to former associates in a company organized to transport boats overland across Nicaragua, "I won't sue you, for the law is too slow. I'll ruin you." Vanderbilt signed it "Yours truly," then, putting to work his vast financial resources, executed a sophisticated stock maneuver to carry out his promise. And yet at his death in 1877, the *New York Herald,* in keeping with the times, celebrated his integrity and courage as the keys to his success. "He had no advantages in his battle, no political, social, educational aid. It was one honest, sturdy, fearless man against the world, and in the end the man won," said the obituary.

Through the nineteenth century, business seemed a drama internal to each person. Failure was a failure of self-belief, of initiative, of effort, success a matter of, as historian Richard Hofstadter put it, "marshal[ing] the resources of the *will.*" This entrepreneur wasn't slowed by a boggy past—by *any* past. He was a work-in-progress, always fiddling, always advancing, ever chipper in the thought that rising early or knocking on one more door would get him to his goal.

The New Economy entrepreneur inherited a good dose of his predecessor's blunt faith in applied energy. And, also, his scorn for remarkable talents. He disregarded advanced degrees, analytical expertise, management skill, even innate ability. Peer into the recent entrepreneurial world and you could nearly believe that skill-based employment didn't exist, that MBA programs didn't flourish, that an entrepreneur needed nothing but, as the earlier self-made man would have agreed, what was *in your gut,* to use a recent entrepreneurial phrase. The past didn't hold sway; at times, it hardly seemed to exist. "We don't care where you are, we don't care what your past was like, we're not going to look at your résumé," said Clay Shirky, once chief technology officer of SiteSpecific. "If you can look me in the eye and say you can do this job, let's do it." In tenacity, verve, want-to, this latter day entrepreneur seemed to find almost all the elements necessary for business, a message the self-made man would certainly have understood. Then as now, the story of entrepreneurship was to be told as a triumph of spirit or, to use Hofstadter's term, of will.

Certainly, the Internet revolution was built on real skills. A C++ programmer was nothing to sneeze at. But, like Edison a century earlier, these entrepreneurs *talked* about something else. And perhaps like Edison, they figured they could hire programmers as needed or even, in a crunch, do it themselves. I met a painter whose previous job experience consisted of five years driving a truck. He interviewed for a job on a Friday and nodded yes, of course, when asked if he knew how to build a Web page. He didn't, but figured he'd learn over the weekend. (And did.)

Like the earlier version, the self-made aspirant of the nineties simply didn't feel that he had to be a genius or have, as one author put it, "a Bill Gates–sized brain." Indeed, the New Economy entrepreneur had all the earmarks of an entry-level position—the qualifications were often the same—even if he was called CEO. The subtitle of *Upstart Start-Ups!* a book about entrepreneurship in the nineties, said it all: *How 34 Young Entrepreneurs Overcame Youth, Inexperience, and Lack of Money to Create Thriving Businesses.* Of course, another recent instructional book didn't see anything at all to overcome. In fact, *The Young Entrepreneur's Edge* suggested that the edge *might be* inexperience. As its subtitle proclaimed, the key was *Using Your Ambition, Independence, and Youth to Launch a Successful Business.*

Certainly one significance of a new category of business book, the one aimed at kids, was to highlight the *un*importance of qualifications. Talk about falling in love with the naive! Here, by definition, was an audience without business experience or, for that matter, a monthly phone bill. And yet the logic of the era suggested that this group was ready to issue forth self-made boys and girls. *The Totally Awesome Business Book for Kids* came with twenty ideas for new businesses. Another book, *Whiz Teens in Business,* covered not only "choosing the right business" and "obtaining financing," but specialized teen business concerns like "handling parents" and "coping with the school workload." The books found audiences. One twelve-year-old reader of *Whiz Teens* said, apparently with a straight face, "I have always been interested in starting my own business." Another reader said the book "makes you realize even you can do it," as if—and here he was right on target—the real requirement of contemporary entrepreneurship was self-belief.

Will and character—bucked-up confidence, gumption, assertiveness, perseverance, luck—were still of primary importance to the businessman even in the age of the Internet. Give them a chance and the latest batch of entrepreneurs talked a nineteenth-century language to rival Rockefeller's. "Rest assured, that success is a pretty direct function of hard work," was how the *Harvard Entrepreneurs Club Guide to Starting Your Own Business* put it. Apparently, though, there wasn't really any rest, assured or otherwise. "As an entrepreneur you should have at times what feels like the energy of an entire office staff," said the guide.

Then as now, entrepreneurship turned out to be a rebuke of privilege—the privilege of birth, training, connections, brains, or talent. How encouraging this all seemed to me, fitting neatly with my own prejudices. Let the games begin, I thought, everyone on equal footing. And me too. Like Franklin, like Rockefeller, like James, like any of those teen CEOs, I felt full of nerve, pluck, assertiveness. I had a slightly queasy stomach (from the excitement perhaps) and energy to spare—as much, I sincerely hoped, as an entire staff.

Chapter Three

Twenty-five Dollars and an Idea

IT WASN'T YET DARK and so, really, it wasn't the moment to be at a nightclub in the East Village, even if I'd heard that Mick Jagger had recently caused a scene there. Just now—and how embarrassing—no doorman was in sight. People breezed in and out as if the place were a department store. Inside, the overhead lights were up, too bright, in my opinion. The place looked cobwebby. And it smelled—a mix of spilled beer and cigarettes. Needless to say, there was not a whiff of Mick or scandal in the vicinity. Rather, a couple hundred wholesome young businesspeople circled one another like midwestern conventioneers. It was six o'clock. Most had lite beers in hand and gummy rectangular nametags on their shirts. "Hello my name is . . ." the tags cheerily announced, though many people seemed to write in their business's names instead.

Once inside, I was quickly approached. "Let me tell you what I've got here," one prematurely balding young man in a blazer told me. He looked more like the headmaster of a private high school than a businessman, I thought. I was wrong. He pulled me by the elbow in the direction of the dance floor. He had an idea for some kind of holistic health-care service for pets, an idea which he apparently felt would benefit from some discretion. A guy whose forehead sloped like a roof announced, by way of preamble, that he'd introduced the chocolate chip cookie to Sweden. Someone had to, I supposed. Now, he had an Internet business secret to confide. He moved close to my ear. "Porn," he said, explosively enough to blow out a candle. "A moneymaker."

I leaned toward another attendee, a young, pigeon-toed man who wore his shirttails out. I read aloud from his nametag: "Hi clubnyc.com." I said, "How are you?" This apparently was a business to provide info on New York City nightclubs like the one we were in.

What had I put on my own nametag? I didn't yet have an idea. *Don't be shy,* I'd found myself thinking, as that professor had suggested. "Make a million," I'd written hopefully.

"That's great!" someone shouted at me and pointed at my lapel, which made me doublecheck my nametag. "Everybody should try."

As far as I could tell, nearly everyone was. Statistics based on government filings—such as incorporations—suggested that hundreds of thousands of people started businesses each year. But that didn't begin to quantify the business urge. A study by the National Federation of Independent Businesses based on a survey of households— where Gallup asked individuals what they were actually up to—revealed that by the mid-nineties, 6.4 million people started businesses in a single year. To put that in perspective, keep in mind that in the nineties more people launched businesses each year than participated in Little League baseball and Boy Scouts *combined.*

The entrepreneurial impulse seemed to me like an airborne virus. Apparently every single person in this room—and there were a few hundred—had come down with symptoms, beginning with a feverish desire to share a business idea. One entrepreneur—he was *temporarily,* he emphasized, stuck inside a cushy corporate job—had an idea he was sure would shake up the music-publishing business. "In five years, I'll be a major," he confided to me. He meant one of the major music-publishing companies, of which there are five. Another would-be entrepreneur—also momentarily saddled with a high-paying job—suggested that once his idea came to fruition, the record companies would *come to him.* All these ideas, and this optimism, was a little overwhelming until another beleaguered conventioneer, perhaps noticing the look in my eyes, confided. "Too many ideas," which in a room like this was like declaring yourself against a safer automobile. Still, I was happy to follow his lead. Glancing at a nametag, I noticed, he'd poke his beer bottle in the air accompanied by a significant nod, then politely speed on.

The evening, though exhausting, convinced me of one thing. If the self-made man, former as well as current, rallied those iron wills of theirs, the latest version, the one I hoped to become, proposed one further inner resource: the imagination. Franklin's self-made man wore you down with his minor gifts. By contrast, the new self-maker was a bit more "airy-fairy," as one business book put it. The contemporary entrepreneur, it seemed, would talk your ear off with his next winning scheme.

Indeed, days in and around the Internet could seem like an idea-sharing marathon. There were those boozy evening idea fests. Then you could run into the same people the next morning at breakfast meetings where people got up in front of a room and for five minutes explained their business ideas. (Business for a while resembled an open-mike night.)

One morning, a twenty-eight-year-old CEO with wet, combed-back hair and an amphetamine user's tendency to walk in place, explained that he had an idea for changing the world, which he felt was best explained with accompanying rap music. "What are we about?" he shouted, "Commerce and content for Generation X—but with an edge!" Unfortunately, that morning the microphone seemed to get an idea of its own and started a trippy feedback loop that didn't exactly enhance his presentation.

Whether ideas were shared in the evening or morning or in a few grabbed minutes in a coffee shop, early on I noticed that fundamental to what was sometimes billed as an "idea explosion" was the concurrent belief that this was not big-brain stuff. True to the self-made tradition and—how convenient!—consistent with my own intuition, you didn't need a mind that could bend spoons to hatch a worthy business idea. The idea culture was inherently encouraging. Just as the rhetoric of the self-made man embraced anyone who worked hard, the new age of ideas excluded no one *a priori.*

The Young Entrepreneur's Edge suggested that the aspiring businessperson slip into an idea-making groove, which anyone could do (perhaps, it occurred to me, with some deep breathing exercises). In such a groove, idea production apparently became an "uncontrollable subconscious urge." Encouragingly, in the grips of such an urge, any casual observation might lead to a tenable business idea. If this uncontrollable state eluded a person, then, fortunately, according to another helpful book, garden-variety curiosity, the kind every conscious person had, would do the trick. "Often great businesses begin simply with a childlike question about why something is the way it is and why it can't be any different or better," suggested *Upstart Start-Ups!* "So pretend you're a kid, and ask away."

No wonder teenagers seemed to have ideas a go-go. "I am soon going to open Next Level Networks with a budget of only $30," said that twelve-year-old-reader of *Whiz Teens* who apparently was building Web sites. And CEO Joshua Motta of Kansas City, who started his business—his *first* business—when he was thirteen, offered local merchants a storefront on the Internet. "I did not have any previous experience doing business," he said amiably. What he'd needed was "$25 and an idea"—and clients who understood he couldn't take calls during school hours.

Lately, I noticed, people looked at businesspeople of all ages and saw an imagination at work. "Who would quarrel with the idea that ideas themselves are the most powerful currency in the new world of business?" asked one business writer. "Ideas Rule!" trumpeted the cover of one magazine, adding, *if they spread.* (Reasonably, one story in the issue featured the business ideas of an eighteen-year-old cofounder of two businesses who was also, the article informed, intent on using the word "like" less.) In the world of business, the new one, inventiveness was *in.*

There was some evidence that people were, in fact, coming up with more ideas than ever. During the eighties, there'd been a total of 1.2 million patent applications in the United States. By the end of the nineties that figure had reached 2 million. And the annual rate seemed to be racing. In 2001, there were almost twice as many patent applications as in 1991. Edison had suspected that the major inventions had all been proposed during his lifetime. But by 2001, there was a patent application filed, on average, every other minute, twenty-four hours a day, every day of the year. Never had so many believed that a germ of invention resided within *each* person.

The U.S. Patent Office, a good sport, appeared to accommodate those who wanted to get in the ideas game. Not long ago, applicants were required to demonstrate a "flash of genius," which proved an unfortunate brake on inventiveness. More recently, "useful" and "nonobvious" had become the standards of patentability. (Though perhaps, really, the most meaningful standard was persistence, since, according to one study, more than 90 percent of all applications eventually become patents.) The new standards opened up the field. Indeed it could seem as if people whose creative outlet was once, say, detailing their minivans, now rushed to the Patent Office with homegrown innovations like: "landing lights on a toilet seat" for those inconvenient middle-of-the night put-downs, helium-filled furniture that could be stored out of the way, i.e., floating near the ceiling, and, a personal favorite, a prosthetic arm that allowed the lonely sports fan to give himself a "high-five." Kids, too, got in the act. One five-year-old received a patent for inventing a new "method of swinging on a swing." The side-to-side method earned patent number 6,368,227.

More important to business, and in particular to business on the Internet, was the creation of a new category of patents, one that seemed to conveniently expand the idea of invention itself or, as some claimed, to redefine the ordinary as novel. This was the business process patent. As recently as 1994, a federal circuit court had thrown out an attempt to patent a method of competitive bidding, because— you can almost see the judges scratching their heads—there was no gizmo or gadget, no clever appliance to create a "physical transformation," which they felt important. By the late nineties, that had changed. You didn't need a machine or, in fact, *any* physical thing. Now your method or model or process for doing something could be new and novel—especially, perhaps, if it involved the new and novel Internet.

The turning point for the business process patent probably occurred in 1999 when the Patent Office issued Amazon.com a patent for one-click purchasing for return customers. Click with your mouse on the "purchase" button at the Amazon Web site and you effected a purchase. You can patent *that?* people asked. It seemed as if Amazon had wrangled a patent for an ordinary business practice, the kind business routinely did. After all, you were already able to make purchases on the Internet with three or four clicks.

Process patents were eventually issued for the *concept* of paying consumers to view ads on the Internet, for the *idea* of giving frequent-flyer miles in exchange for online purchases, and for a *method* of forecasting business performance based on weather trends (perhaps—though here I'm guessing—involving helium).

In Franklin's era, the self-made man hadn't always believed that ideas held such charm, or such commercial force. Franklin, as clever as they came, hadn't emphasized imagination. Nor had the inventor of the popular Franklin stove patented it, saying "we should be glad of an opportunity to serve others by any invention of ours." Even Edison, a virtual idea factory, thought the importance of ideas was overstated in creating products. He emphasized assiduous effort, not fleeting inspiration.

In the business culture that sprang up around the Internet all that seemed to change. By the late nineties, the Internet was like an old-fashioned California, every inch of it—or every noun of it—waiting to be claimed by a business idea. Soon there'd be businesses called furniture.com, liquor.com, meals.com, music.com, drugstore.com. (Idea formation could seem a Mad Lib.) Even toiletpaper.com was claimed. And how about weddings? I read that six businesses would help plan your wedding—wedding.com *and* weddings.com, as well as weddingchannel.com, theweddinglady.com, weddingnet.com, and theknot.com. (Apparently, like an old LP, it was possible to get stuck in a particular idea-making groove.)

Philip Kaplan, a programmer who'd later found a Web site called fuckedcompany.com, pointed out that a bunch of Internet business ideas were "solutions without problems." Perhaps it was difficult to know what pressing need the Internet business called Joke-of-the-

Day was meant to respond to. Or the one selling vegetarian meals to pets. (Did legions of dogs really refuse to eat meat?) And someone came up with a clever business designed to solve "the most frustrating part of hearing a song on the radio," which apparently was not knowing its name.

And yet an article of faith in the idea-driven economy was that the true utility, like the real commercial potential, of an idea couldn't be judged in advance. Down the road, everyone knew that some ideas might turn out to be more powerful moneymakers than others. But for the moment, contemporary business culture took the sound approach that premature emphasis on revenues might dampen creativity, which was paramount.

For a beginning entrepreneur, the important point, as Greg, until recently a freelance journalist, suggested to me, was to get with it, to get going. Greg had thick, sandy brown hair, a winning smile, and, by way of business qualifications, a couple of years in a graduate English program. He'd started in business by building Web sites for publishers. Soon, he'd gotten ahold of another idea. He was CEO of a company that built games for the Internet, his first full-time job. "Anyone who doesn't get in this now is going to get left behind," he alerted me from his office above a pizza shop. Way behind, Greg suggested. "We intend to take thirty years off at thirty" was how he put it. He was twenty-six at the time.

And so, among my first entrepreneurial lessons was this: Pay no mind to talent, skill, aptitude, training, experience, credentials, degrees, or background. Just grab hold of an idea—any idea—and hurry up. And here was the new version of that old self-maker's promise: Like force of character, my idea just might prevail.

Chapter Four

Balls Out

BY NOW, I'd realized that business on the Internet resembled nature on the Discovery channel; strange larval things yielded butterflies by the first commercial. For my business to take flight, what I needed most was an idea. Luckily, it was possible to believe; truly, it was impossible *not* to believe that I too might have a spark of ingenuity—*business* ingenuity—like everyone else. Consigliere had intimated as much. "Ideas come from everywhere," he reassured me. (He would always be reassuring.) And Consigliere—I'd managed to get this much out of him—was something of an expert. Recently, he'd divulged that he'd appeared as a business authority on the *McNeill-Lehrer NewsHour*, paired with the president of Microsoft, though, of course, he told the story for a laugh . . . on himself. (Apparently, he'd chummily addressed his interviewer as Charlene. Her name was Charlayne. After that she declined to ask him any further questions.) Plus, he'd been the number-two guy at an entrepreneurial venture, RealTime Syndication Network, and in that capacity had helped raise a couple of million dollars. His company had syndicated sports news, actually, given it away to Web sites hoping to sell ads against it.

If I didn't immediately hunt for a business idea of my own there was just one reason. I wasn't sure *how* to hunt. I had the $3,000 from *New York* magazine, a princely sum it seemed to me, though others re- acted less optimistically. I mentioned it, along with my million-dollar goal, to the owner of an Italian restaurant where, one night, I ate with friends. The owner wore a thin gold chain at his belt, connected, for some reason, to his beeper. "I'll tell you how to make a million," he said. He seemed confident. "You take the editor who gave you the three thousand to dinner and you put a gun right here"—he pointed two fingers to his own chin, it seemed a professional gesture—"and you tell him to give you a freaking million dollars."

Instead, I found myself thinking of the professor's counsel. *Ask advice*, he'd suggested. I turned to my wife. She was good with ideas. The cockroach hotel had been hers. Okay, that hadn't worked out. The past, I knew by now, had no claim on the future. I'd lately heard that failure might even be an entrepreneurial credential, one of the few. So, during a trip with Cristina, I proposed a kind of parlor game, though this one occurred in a car. We spent a five-hour trip hatching business ideas.

"How about . . ." Cristina said, pausing to stare down a motorist, "an alarm clock with a message you can record." Cristina, I knew, was reasoning from personal experience. Though a go-getter, she had trouble waking up in the morning.

"Like, 'Get out of bed, sleepyhead'?" I said.

She hardly paused. She had another idea. She reeled them off. "A device so that if you're on the phone and want to get off, you can trigger a fake call-waiting click." Once under way, she didn't like to waste time.

I got in the spirit. "What about," I said, speaking now from my own needs, "a program that allows you to cheat at computer solitaire?"

"That's stupid," Cristina assured me in the tone of someone choosing between detergents.

I didn't see why. You'd like to peek under a card once in a while.

Cristina refocused. "What else?" she said.

"Maybe something to eat," I said.

But I wasn't over my idea hunt. Not hardly. For a time, every-where I noticed business ideas, mostly other people's. We're Nuts About Nuts was a shop on the corner of my street, and, no doubt, a shrewd hunch about a health food trend. "A. Fleisig and Sons, Boxmakers" was an intriguing sign I passed on Broadway. "Boxes!"

I could just hear the sons say when they'd heard Dad's latest plan. "Dad, we want *in.*" The world, I suddenly noticed, teemed with commercial energy.

I tried to look at common objects differently. My refrigerator, for instance. Why not, I wondered, a business that took its random contents—beer, rosemary, blue cheese—and shot back an easy-to-make recipe? Or, looking at a nephew's snapshot, how about posting baby pictures online and, at the same time, allowing me to buy the newborn a little gift? Or, maybe there should be advertising on ordinary cars—actually, why not on people's eyelids? Had I come down with an "uncontrollable subconscious urge," the entrepreneurial one? I certainly hoped so.

Still, I couldn't immediately see a reason to pursue one idea instead of another. I resolved to stay alert to opportunities. And to maintain a positive outlook, which I'd read was important to entrepreneurs. I thought of my father as he'd searched for opportunities. How had *he* come up with peace-and-love medallions? (And why hadn't I had the good sense to say, "Dad, I want *in*"?) My mother often said he was an accomplished optimist. He could watch one of his sons toss a ball in the air, swing with a bat, miss the ball by a mile, and think, Wow, what a pitcher. Recently, I'd started to hope I'd inherited some of that.

Looking back, I think I must have been in this heightened state when a friend just back from two years in Japan led a group of us to Japas, a karaoke bar near what was once a thriving drug rehab center in the East Village. At his departure Ilan, who was from Queens, had been fit, trim, and quiet, even shy. If he went to a bar, likely as not, he'd fall into considered discussion. He had a penchant for the big questions—Nietzsche or Kant, Mozart or Beethoven—often prevailing, in part, because Ilan didn't drink alcohol. That also made him the designated driver, a not altogether happy occurrence, since Ilan was, by nature, a terrible driver.

After a couple of years in Japan's karaoke bars, Ilan had apparently been transformed. He was now a sake drinker, forty pounds heavier, and, from what I gathered, the life of the party. In Japan, he'd made a name for himself as a drummer, dancer, karaoke singer, and, inevitably, driver. (He'd had four car accidents in two years, a few notable enough to make the local newspaper.)

As we entered Japas, Ilan told our group of half a dozen that he'd selected this place because, with its long dark wood bar, narrow stools, and pass-around microphone, he found it "*very* Japanese." Perhaps I didn't seem suitably convinced. "It *is*," he insisted. I had no cause to dispute the authenticity of Japas. Karaoke, a national pastime in Japan and most of Asia, had lately become quite popular in New York; nonetheless, I'd never been to a karaoke bar. And for good reason. In karaoke you choose a song. Music plays while lyrics scroll across a TV screen. You hold a mike and sing along.

Innocent recreation? Not for me.

I am devoid of the most rudimentary musical talent, a fact revealed in painful stages. The first came when as a twelve-year-old my parents asked me to please *stop* practicing the clarinet. Another more compelling indication occurred a few years later when my mother pounded on the door of the bathroom where I showered— showered and sang. "Are you all right? Are you all right?" she shouted. Apparently my singing suggested distress.

Since then I'd ducked nearly every invitation to sing, which required more vigilance than you might think. Opportunities for song were endless—you have *no* idea. Birthdays were treacherous, that went without saying. In classrooms, at any public gathering, really, people could break into song with little warning. People sang *everywhere*. And they made a fuss. "Oh, come on, your voice can't be *that* bad." Occasionally, I'd been coaxed into providing a small sample. People thought I wasn't trying. *I was*. Then one inviter smiled frostily and put a finger to her lips. Since then I have made no further exceptions.

And so despite Ilan-san's ruthless encouragement, I avoided singing that night at Japas. It didn't matter. Everyone else sang, led by Ilan, who ordered hot and cold sake then strutted the length of the very Japanese bar, microphone in hand. There was no genre he wouldn't try: Sinatra, Jewish folk music, Motown. He sang in Japanese to the waitress. He sang everything except hip-hop, since there was virtually no karaoke hip-hop.

"Why not," my wife suggested when our group left at four in the morning, "open a hip-hop karaoke bar?" Yes, why not? (She was good with ideas, I recalled.) Perhaps karaoke was the thing I was supposed to look at and ask, Why can't it be any different or better? Through Ilan, I'd been made aware of karaoke's transformational power. I noticed that MTV had a daily karaoke show. Plus, karaoke seemed to be popping up all over New York. Perhaps not in classic Asian-style, but still, in Manhattan alone there was punk karaoke, Asian-Italian karaoke, transvestite karaoke, and celebrity karaoke hosted by a Jewish woman who called herself the Queen of Karaoke.

I'd open the first karaoke bar in Harlem. It would be called hiphopkaraoke—H2K, for short, again my wife's idea. (This was during the Y2K scare.) Karaoke had spread across New York but none of the venues featured much hip-hop. That seemed an oversight. After all, hip-hop had become mainstream youth music. Plus, as anyone who'd walked a city street knew, hip-hop fans naturally sang along with the music. Hip-hop lovers would take to karaoke, you just had that feeling. So would Harlem.

Of course I was ill-suited. I had little knowledge of hip-hop, no affinity for karaoke. Yet I remember thinking at the time, if *I* recognized the appeal of hip-hop karaoke, then just imagine the enthusiasm of people who could carry a tune. Or people who loved hip-hop.

Plus, H2K might be fun—*that* word again.

I felt unusually invigorated, focused, which was all so sudden. Could I be the white guy who introduced hip-hoppers to karaoke? I wondered with an unanticipated thrill.

I scheduled an exploratory meeting for the Odeon, a restaurant where I like to go in part because you can write on the tablecloths. (They're paper.) I invited Kasaun, an African American friend. He was a chess whiz and a musician, and, I reminded myself, he also spoke Japanese, which might come in handy. Lately, Kasaun had himself become a CEO. He'd formed his own music producing company.

Kasaun brought a friend and business associate, who sat with an earplug in one ear—his phone. He didn't get any calls; still, it lent a mood of expectation. Of course, I'd invited Ilan. Lately, he'd gone on a self-designed diet that included thrice-a-week lunches at Virgil's all-you-can-eat barbecue. In the meantime, he'd taken to wearing trench coats.

Ilan immediately broke into excited Japanese, speaking to Kasaun about, I hoped, a karaoke collaboration. (Later, I'd learn they shared a thought about an Asian woman across the restaurant.)

Still, everybody liked H2K. "It's a beautiful idea," said Kasaun, who not only lived in Harlem but occasionally wrote hip-hop songs.

I agreed, and started to think about liquor licenses and rent and the transformation of 125th Street—a Starbucks was there now, soon Bill Clinton would be. I took notes on the tablecloth. Ilan, looking over my shoulder, pointed out that I'd misspelled karaoke.

Over the next days, I sat at my desk, considered the prospects, and decided that H2K might be feasible. Rents apparently were reasonable. And so I began to worry. Generally, I didn't mind worrying. It was work that needed to be done. It wasn't unpleasant. I was fairly good at it, and it came with benefits. Anxiety generally energized me. And if it was a bit reiterative—you did tend to tread the same thought path—well, still, it often led to something productive. I waited for that something to come.

It did not come. Just the opposite. I got stuck considering a certain genre of security issue. I'm skinny. I have long arms, thinning brown hair, and, as mentioned, blue wire-frame glasses. I pictured myself in a bar, pushing those daffy glasses up my nose, and explaining to one broad-shouldered customer after another: "I don't think he meant it *that way,* sir. I think those really *are* the lyrics." Hip-hop, as even I knew, had some explosive lyrics. The scene depressed me.

Then my editor, the one whose head I was supposed to put a gun to, asked a practical question: "How are you going to make a million dollars from a bar?"

I had no answer. I knew people tried to rouse their sleepy spirits any number of ways. Business had lately seemed just the thing. Didn't it vibrate with life? With excitement? Now, I felt my own enthusiasm dissipate. H2K was on the verge of fizzling, before ever really coming to life. Where was my itch to do, to improve? And my bellyful of industry?

For me, sustained enthusiasm, the oldest ingredient, was a hard nut to crack. I gazed at the cockroach hotel. The potbellied prototype was still pinned to the bulletin board next to my desk. I held it in my hands—it was a delightful little thing, clever and handsome—and suddenly felt a stern resolve. (I'm pretty sure that's what it was.) I wouldn't let go so easily.

"Not yet," I said, and realized I'd said the words out loud, which was a little spooky.

Stay loose, I told myself, thinking of that professor's advice. Let the matter percolate. Perhaps I had some self-making in me yet.

Then, a few days later at a party—I seemed particularly susceptible at parties—an idea hit. A little refinement, really. I could have smacked myself. What had I been thinking? The Internet is a perfect karaoke delivery device. The idea was obvious, which struck me as a good quality in an idea.

Any entrepreneur could readily understand the promise of the Internet. With my roach hotel, production had seemed such a hurdle, relying on cardboard construction and plastic packaging. Distribution seemed even more challenging. The Internet, as even I grasped, minimized those challenges. "Some bozo investing two thousand dollars can compete with Time Warner," was how one person explained it to me. Maybe, maybe not. But I'd heard that building something online was straightforward. And the Internet simplified distribution; any Internet user could be a customer.

My business experience was limited, limited-to-none. And, as far as the Internet went, I was hardly an early adopter. Not long ago, I'd spent some time arguing *against* e-mail. (The phone was enough of a bother, wasn't it?) I had a slow connection to the Internet. Nor, for a would-be karaoke entrepreneur—*karaoke entrepreneur!*—did I have the most basic computer equipment. My laptop didn't, for instance, have speakers. When I'd purchased the computer six months earlier I couldn't imagine why I'd need them. None of this seemed much of a drawback at the time, an attitude that, I was prepared to affirm, put me in the mainstream.

I e-mailed Consigliere. "If you don't do it someone else will," he responded cheerfully, which I remember taking as encouragement.

There was just one further aspect that concerned me, even then. "Doesn't karaoke seem a bit, well, goofy?" I asked Consigliere.

By now I'd managed to extract a few more biographical details from Consigliere. Later in life Consigliere would sometimes seem eager for something a little more provocative than a dependable emotional life, which helped, perhaps, explain his entry into business, with its promise of reliable income. But at some age—it was impossible to pin down the year—he'd had an episode, what sometimes got called a heart attack. For a time after that, he'd pushed back on business life and decided to write plays, to produce others. He'd signed up for grad school where he finished a novel and where, how cagey, Consigliere insisted that classmates call him Harold, his middle name.

People say you ask advice of those who'll give the counsel you most want to hear. As I waited for Consigliere's reply to my business question, I found myself thinking of his life as Harold, the one of novelist and playwright. Then I pondered another non-business story, one I'd wheedled out of him, one from an even earlier period of his life. Consigliere had grown up in a working-class neighborhood, one without ready possibilities for a young person of talent. Fortunately he'd been a gifted quarterback and had won a scholarship to a prep school. He'd been ecstatic when he'd heard that news, thinking he'd found a ticket out of limiting circumstances. I thought of his freshman year at his new school, the one that represented such possibility, fragile though it must have seemed. One day, the football coach gave the new prospect a chance to get in the mix, show what he could do. Consigliere substituted for the starting quarterback for a few minutes. I imagined there was something at stake. Football must have seemed a chance to secure his future. On the first play from scrimmage, Consigliere considered a running play. Get his timing down with a clean hand-off. Or maybe throw a short pass. Instead, Consigliere called for a bomb. He threw the football downfield as far as he could. I loved that story.

"Would business people take karaoke seriously?" I pressed him after a day or so.

He shot back a response. "Oh, let's just go balls out," he counseled. Yes, let's.

Chapter Five

A Karaoke Nation

A FEW DAYS LATER, I invited James the dry cleaner over to talk.

"James, what are you doing now?" I'd baited him by phone.

"I'm an Internet entrepreneur," he reminded me.

"Me, too!" I nearly shouted.

He marched the short distance, bringing along several of my shirts. (He balanced the hangers on a single finger, a neat trick.) As he pulled a stool up to my kitchen counter, I noticed that James had begun to lose his hair. He struck me as older, more serious. He lit a cigarette. Recently, he said, a dry cleaning customer had approached him to work on an entrepreneurial venture. He had agreed to consider it. Really, though, he was more interested in his own ideas, which he seemed to hatch one after another. Lately, he explained, he'd come up with a plan to install free Internet access in department stores.

"We've already had an offer to buy that business," he mentioned.

"Really?" I said. With James, it seemed my fate to be constantly surprised.

Meantime he and a partner continued to work in the basement of the dry cleaning store on the enterprise involving missile assembly software. Though two recent deals had apparently fallen through, the plan evolved. The software served equally well as an inventory system. Instead of assembling missile parts, James had decided to track car parts. He thought the auto market would be easier to crack than the munitions industry.

Yet, when James wondered what I was doing, I hesitated. James was Korean. He'd know all about karaoke, I reasoned. All Asians do. And so I was guarded. Lately I'd begun to worry that someone would whisk off *my* wonderful idea. "Be careful," I'd been warned by one businessman with an impressive aluminum briefcase. "Someone could take karaoke from you." I was momentarily sorry I'd mentioned it *to him*. What a powerful attachment I'd developed.

"I'd better wait to nail down a few more details," I said to James, and bent to make a note, as if I'd just thought of something.

"Okay, Mr. Fishman," he said agreeably.

When I informed Consigliere of my precautions—a flawless business instinct, it seemed to me—I was sure he'd endorse my approach. After all I still couldn't get his age out of him.

"Thirty," he'd said implausibly. That could hardly be true. I'd lately calculated that he'd been thirty when he'd had his heart attack.

"Thirty-seven?" I pursued.

"Yes," he said unconvincingly.

"Great," I said and then told him I feared someone would walk off with my million-dollar idea.

Consigliere shook his head. He had thick dark hair parted in the middle, and his headshake was an impressive thing.

Perhaps he sensed I was getting a bit wrapped up. "Think positive," he advised. He thought I'd do better getting input, sharing concerns. He wanted me in the mix. So he sent me a form, a nondisclosure agreement or NDA, to adapt to my purposes. It, he said, would protect me.

Internet businesspeople pushed NDAs back and forth like poker chips. Mine was longer than most.

"Three pages?" said one exasperated twenty-six-year-old CEO. This young exec had been at a Thanksgiving dinner when looking around the table he noticed all the elements necessary to start a business, and did. Clearly, he was used to a rapid pace.

"Take your time," I smiled. In elaborate legal language my NDA claimed the concept of Internet karaoke for me. Helpfully, it set out with whom the signer could share my secrets. Plus, of course, it served as notice that an important moment was at hand.

In short order, I collected a folder of signed NDAs. Once I had them, I slipped back into character. I told everyone my plans. It was a delightful turn of events. Not only did this approach suit my nature; it permitted me to partake of the era's peculiarly gabby ambiance.

$ $ $

At some point, I realized that, like nearly everyone I met, I embraced contradictory views of business. (Once, I mentioned this to Consigliere, who wearily agreed that, of course it was true, then jauntily added, "Wonderful, isn't it?") If pressed, I'd admit that power was no doubt still concentrated in a few reliable hands. I even hoped to stumble into a hardheaded business insider who'd take me under his wing and say, *This is how the thing is done.* Most of the time, though, I relied on a more magical idea of business, one I believed proper to the Internet. I subscribed to what I thought of as the rule of propinquity. To start, this rule held that just talking about something could help it come true. You might casually strike up a conversation and discover you'd stumbled onto an early-stage investor or a strategic partner. New businesses seemed to partner promiscuously in the Internet—something I longed to do.

Indeed, in the Internet, people behaved as if opportunity abounded. Perhaps this would not have been the case if they'd wandered into mixed nuts or cardboard boxes or, of course, cockroach hotels. But in the Internet, people seemed to feel that even before they started actively looking for a thing, it would pop up. Moreover, many—and this was the heart of the rule of propinquity—considered that nearly everyone *represented* an opportunity.

In heeding this rule, I assumed, and others did too, an almost mathematical relationship between a person and an opportunity. The closer a person, the greater his or her potential to provide aid. It was this rule, for instance, that helped explain some unorthodox Internet hiring practices. For instance, Clay Shirky, former CTO at SiteSpecific, recruited during visits to the Barnes & Noble on Sixth Avenue and Twenty-first. "If I saw someone reading an advanced PhotoShop book, I'd say, 'Excuse me, are you looking for a job?'" he said.

I quickly adopted this congenial rule as my *modus operandi*. In a bar, I met a programmer and tried to interest him in a little business I was contemplating. ("Recruiting developers" was how Consigliere suggested I refer to this activity.) On the back stairs of my apartment, I ran into a banker who lived in the building, and asked if he wouldn't mind lending a hand. We all exchanged numbers. I had follow-up conversations. Things, I told myself, were coming along. I'd become convinced they always would. And so, when a friend called, it hardly surprised me that he suggested a drink with an Internet lawyer. After all, I'd been hoping for legal counsel, something I'd recently learned businesses needed.

I'd met Pat Shields, an aspiring filmmaker, because when not making movies he washed the windows in our apartment building. Pat had braces, a big heart, and a quirky genius for publicity. (One day, I'd picked up *New York* magazine to find a full-page photo of Pat washing windows.) Like the dry-cleaning business, the window-washing business brought Pat into contact with many useful people. (Pat understood this. He often tried to raise movie funds from his window-washing clients.)

Fortunately for me, Pat had become interested in the Internet. He intended to show his movies online; though first, he'd decided to cyber squat. He'd purchased the name Digeo.com for a hundred dollars, betting this made-up term would become the digital age's "video." Amazingly, someone thought he was right and Pat bartered the name for a digital movie camera.

Once Pat heard I was going into business, he periodically called with useful contacts. One day he invited me to meet his attorney friend, though, at first, I admit, I'd been confused. The phone connection was terrible. "Attorney friend" sounded like "hernia end." There was a roar of noise in the background. I thought I heard waves crashing. Was Pat near the ocean? Did he need an operation?

"Where are you calling from?" I shouted.

"From work," he said, his voice goosed with energy.

"From work?" I asked.

"I'm out on a ledge," Pat clarified. Pat was standing on a wide window ledge over Park Avenue. The crashing wave sound was traffic, which Pat was almost literally hanging on top of. Apparently, Pat couldn't really tolerate doing just one thing at a time. So he sometimes made phone calls while washing windows.

"Don't worry," Pat reassured me.

"Why not?" I said. *"You're on a window ledge."*

"I'm not using a cell phone," he said. It seemed a non sequitur. But as Pat explained, the real danger of phone calls on window ledges was the chance the phone would fall which, Pat later told me, had once happened. Since then he always borrowed the client's corded phone.

Usefully, Pat's attorney friend specialized in Internet start-ups. Howard was short, portly, and, in my memory, snaggletoothed. We met at a bar, chitchatted for a few minutes about Walt Disney World, which Howard seemed sure used to have an S&M-themed bar. Then, as drinks and appetizers arrived, Howard invited me to explain my idea. If he liked it, there was a chance he'd help.

Unfortunately, I began with my night at the karaoke bar, which seemed to give Howard the impression that I'd started this whole thing as a drunken caper. Howard speared shrimp from his plate—he seemed to use the fork as a weapon—and shifted uncomfortably. As a result, I spoke more rapidly.

Soon Howard interrupted. "I feel like I'm in *The Player*," he said, an apparent reference to the Robert Altman film in which fast-talking producers have thirty seconds to pitch movie ideas.

Perhaps, though, nothing would have helped me. Howard was apparently unfamiliar with the broad appeal of karaoke. The only person he could remember singing karaoke was Imelda Marcos.

When I finished talking, Howard looked me in the eye. I waited hopefully for his reaction.

"Are you going to eat those?" he said.

When I shook my head no, he stabbed two shrimp off my plate.

I made a mental note to work on my presentation.

A few weeks later I ran into the director of a start-up company's design department, his second start-up. This was at a party for an art magazine. The host, an artist, mended broken spider webs with red thread.

When he asked about my venture, I leaned in, touched him on the wrist. I'd boiled down my explanation. My eyes may have opened wide. He was one of a select few, I wanted to communicate.

"KaraokeNation.com," I whispered not far from his ear, pronouncing the domain name I'd purchased for $119.

He didn't respond at first, but just looked off in the direction of that red spider web. Then he said slowly, "Terrific," adding, "I'm already getting some ideas." I named him to my advisory board, which lately I noticed other businesses had.

Sometimes Consigliere called with contacts. In matters pertaining to his own life, he could be gloomy. "I have heavy shoes," he once said, a poetic phrase alluding to an unspecified burden. Yet, on my behalf, he was hopelessly upbeat. When I told him all the people I'd been talking to, he said, "Next year I can see us trying to figure out whether to buy the Super Bowl."

One day he called to say, "I think I may have just the person for us." (Consigliere often said encouraging things like that, as if I merely lacked an element or two.) Consigliere knew someone who'd recently retired from television with millions of dollars. He was wealthy enough to buy motorcycles from catalogs sight unseen, and apparently he was looking to get involved in an Internet venture. Consigliere offered to set up a conference call. I was very excited since it would be my first.

Mr. Big, as I thought of the retired TV exec, would participate and so would a mutual friend of theirs. Peter Clemente lived in Palm Springs, California, where he worked as an analyst following entertainment trends on the Internet. In the early nineties Clemente had worked with Consigliere. Clemente, Consigliere said, was genuine, trustworthy. "That's not a feeling I always get, even with people I like," he explained. Clemente was now a vice president at Cyber Dialogue, a consulting firm.

By now I realized that there was a theater to the go-getter culture; it had costumes, props, set pieces. I knew of one company that recruited friends to occupy its offices before client visits, just like extras. They helped give the impression of a bustling enterprise. Of course, the conference call was a core dramatic element. As far as I could tell, not many people held one-on-one conversations any longer. Rather, everyone participated in conference calls, often involving cell phones, another essential prop. Every businessperson owned one, often more than one.

"Man, you've *got* to get a cell phone," I was told by one CEO. So I did. It was a loaner—from my wife. Still, I quickly got the hang of it. Now, I occasionally shouted into the phone while walking my dog, my leash hand rotating like a snowblower blade. I even came to believe, as I'm sure others did, that the waterlogged quality of the connection emphasized the importance of a communication.

And so when Consigliere suggested the conference call, I thought that though I'd be in my office, I'd do it on the cell.

Consigliere's plan was that I introduce the idea, "take ownership of it," as he explained, a straightforward approach that induced panic in me. After all, what could I possibly say? That I went drinking one night and, d-u-u-u-de, you better get out your checkbook because, lucky for you, I wandered into a karaoke bar, which was the regrettable approach taken with Howard. Nor, I realized, could I be as succinct and mysterious on the phone as I'd been at that art party.

"No, no," counseled Consigliere in a soothing voice. Consigliere wasn't intimidated by business. Once I'd asked him, "What's a businessman?" "Someone in business," he replied nimbly, suggesting, I thought, that the category included me. Consigliere advised me to be flexible with Mr. Big, and not to worry. "Say you're a technology writer," he said.

"Okay," I agreed, which, in effect, left me with no story at all. Adding to my discomfort was the insight that, as even I occasionally recalled, KaraokeNation might not strike everyone as an obvious business proposition. (The word *karaoke* sometimes still struck *me* as funny.)

And yet as the call got under way and I launched into my talk, neither Clemente nor Mr. Big laughed. Perhaps it was really true, as people said, that no one knew where the next moneymaking idea would come from, and so every proposition required attention. Or perhaps it was that I sounded serious, couldn't have sounded more serious, employing, as I recall, words like *potentiality* and *preconfigured* and *development stage,* and seriousness is catchy. Unfortunately, the longer I spoke, the less I focused on what I said, and the more my attention was drawn to the echo-y quality of my voice on the cell phone.

A moment later, my concentration shot, I turned the conversation over to Consigliere who, it seemed to me, had developed a radio announcer's silky voice. He spoke in a slow, friendly manner I associated with country-and-western music. While not actually saying all that much, he used the right words. He mentioned *branding strategies,* a *private labeling* approach, terms I heard constantly. "Someone will do this," I heard him say. Then he said, "The franchise in this is up for grabs." Finally, he added, "Time for the nice guys to make some money." Had he delivered this in person, I felt sure Consigliere would have clapped Mr. Big on the back and called him brother.

Mr. Big hesitated. He wanted to think about it—a way of saying he wasn't interested—but, this was important, Clemente seemed enthusiastic. Clemente in fact had arguments of his own to add. He said that to judge by what people liked to do on the Internet, it was primarily an entertainment medium. Clemente said that 70 percent of adults went online to do something entertainment-related. He appeared to have a head full of numbers. Or else he was reading from a book. Of those entertainment enthusiasts, 37 percent did some music-related thing. Clemente asserted," Music is the Internet's first true killer app."

App—I looked it up—was short for application, a software program that allowed people to do something on the Internet. E-mail was an application, so was online chat. Killer simply meant great. Lately I'd entertained the notion that karaoke, which I still sometimes recalled I'd never actually done, could be the air guitar of the

Internet generation. Now Clemente seemed to agree. Clemente spoke with conviction. And if you thought seriousness contagious, just try conviction. Karaoke wasn't goofy, not an activity only a Filipino dictator's wife would like. "Anything to do with music could be big," Clemente said.

Since Clemente seemed so excited, Consigliere prodded him for a favor. Every quarter, Clemente's company conducted a survey to probe the entertainment preferences of Internet users. Normally, businesses paid to have questions posted on the survey, the oldest and, by some estimates, most reliable to deal with the Internet. As a favor to Consigliere, Clemente agreed to sneak in two questions designed to ferret out the hidden karaoke practices of adult Internet users.

"That's about a ten-thousand-dollar favor," Consigliere told me later.

"Great," I said with real excitement. Recently, I'd read, "Part of entrepreneurial success is maintaining passion and commitment." I certainly felt it now. And how wonderful it was, like the surprising return of energy after a bout of flu. I just felt full of oomph; I felt *there*. This business thing felt so genuine. So I hadn't mastered all the details yet. (And didn't own a cell phone.) Things would work out.

A few days later, Pat-the-window-washer called from his window ledge to say, "You have to meet Alex. He's CEO of a company called RadicalZoo. It's an entertainment network and he really likes karaoke."

Of course he does, I thought.

RadicalZoo's office was next to a gun shop. A plastic pistol as big as a couch hung outside. Alex had a pale spade-shaped face and tarry black hair. He was coughing. "I'm sick as a dog," he said. It was nearly noon. We appeared to be alone in his small office. (Perhaps other employees worked later shifts.) We took seats in a small waiting area near a fish tank. There were a few old directors chairs; on one, I saw what appeared to be an old black-and-white TV.

CEO Alex quickly signed an NDA then explained that he got excited every time he described his vision. "I get goose bumps." For some reason, he sat on his hands. To contain his excitement perhaps.

Who wouldn't be excited? One day, he'd been a middling employee at Disney—some kind of production designer. The next day, he'd decided he wanted *to be* Disney, more or less. He quit his job there and then and started RadicalZoo. I gathered that there'd been an initial investment, perhaps by some family. He guarded the details closely. His vision, though, he shared. He intended to launch Internet TV shows, movies, music publishing, a record label. He mentioned interactive comic books. I lost track. His site hadn't launched yet. There was nothing to see. It did, though, sound very exciting.

In a moment, his CFO arrived. He was a Brit with pink socks and a remarkable Austin Powers accent. He smoked constantly, using water in a plastic container as an ashtray. Alex kept running off. I wondered if it was the cigarette smoke, but he said, no, he was checking the fax. He was expecting a contract, he reported nervously.

The CFO explained they'd just partnered with a roller-coaster site called Thrill Ride, which he pronounced Frill Ride. He talked about a partnership with KaraokeNation. The CFO had some ideas for "a win-win scenario," a scenario I'd soon hear many people propose. The immediate benefits to me seemed to include office space and, perhaps, legal representation. They handed me their law firm's brochure. In short order, I'd receive a letter. RadicalZoo wanted to use KaraokeNation.com "as a source of content." It would furnish me with a set of "digital tools." There were several other notions about joint marketing. And then the CEO, identifying himself as chief zoologist, concluded, "This is the start of an amazing adventure, and RadicalZoo is proud to have KaraokeNation.com as a strategic partner."

A strategic partner! Wasn't that terrific?

Chapter Six

Falling Through Floorboards

I DIDN'T KNOW if I could ever be Daniel Ratner, but I had to admire his enthusiasm. Everything I know about Dan came from his dashed-off paragraph (96 words) to Brown University's alumni magazine, which I happened to look at because, in the mid-seventies, I'd attended Brown. Usually, I'd turn right to the Class Notes section—that's where I'd come across Dan's news—which prints brief updates from grads and, as a result, is a pretty good sampler of the lives of the school's new alums.

In 1999 Dan, class of '97, wrote that he was "involved in his second high-tech start-up venture since graduation." Dan reported that his first start-up—he mentioned something about "systems integration"—was "thriving." At the time he wrote, Dan couldn't have been more than twenty-three or twenty-four. He couldn't have had any particular training in business. Dan, it occurred to me, was winging it and, from the sound of things, having the time of his life. No need to slow down, though. Dan said he was on to another start-up. He cycled through businesses the way twenty-year-olds used to go through girlfriends. His second company was a provider of "high-speed Internet technology," which, in case you didn't know, Dan allowed was "the latest and greatest."

At first Dan's tone almost made me want to snicker—or blush. Was everything with this kid high-tech and high-speed, latest and greatest? But he was so caught up, so enthusiastic, I couldn't hold it against him. Plus, he seemed to be on to something. And the subtext was clear: It just might be big. His second business already had three offices, and "we are now going national," he wrote, which, even I knew, was a pretty good place to go. Dan's future—his near future—sounded very exciting. He signed off not just with an address, as most entries did, but with a slogan. "Watch out, world," he said, "here we come."

We?

Brown is an Ivy League school and a very competitive place, but when I'd attended, the lords of liberal arts prevailed, as they did through much of the college world. And they ran a tight ship. Nowhere tighter than at Brown. Students, as one university president explained, were supposed to lead an examined life, a reference to that patron of the liberal arts, Socrates. When I'd been there, the school couldn't have cared less about preparing students for business. Brown didn't have a business school. I wasn't aware that it offered any business classes.

Not that any of this mattered to me. No one I knew at Brown even *talked* about business. Well, just one person. (And, to put that in perspective, I knew *two* people who'd suffered breakdowns.) The one business type had a head of curly hair like hundreds of brown buttons and had been a liberal arts major like the rest of us. Then one day I spotted him on campus carrying a *Wall Street Journal* folded in sixths under his arm. (It wouldn't have been the *New York Times*—*that* paper didn't have a separate business section when I was in college.) Soon we learned he was applying to Harvard Business School. It was as if he'd said he didn't like jazz or Dylan. I briefly thought he'd gone nuts—a third one. In the seventies hardly anyone went directly from Brown to business school; barely over 3 percent one typical year, according to career office surveys.

There was good reason. To me, and to most everyone I knew, the very word *business* suggested a vast, frosty landscape where nothing of interest occurred. Come on, I mean, an accountant! In high school, I'd known a guy who spent study halls counting to a million in a special notebook—*he* wanted to be an accountant. That an adult would choose to labor over buggy columns of numbers was beyond me. Or that a young person, one with high hopes and positive self-regard, would aspire to be, say, a VP for administration, someone who'd spend his day fiddling with boxy management charts, I couldn't imagine. Business just wasn't where it was at in the seventies. It surprised me not at all when a Harvard friend reported that her 1980 graduating class actually booed business-school grads as they marched up to receive diplomas with, I imagined, my curly-haired acquaintance among them. The reason? Good old-fashioned disdain.

And why not? To my mind business played a limited role in a person's imaginative and emotional lives, which were the important ones. Among people I knew, you'd have had trouble getting a date if business was close to your heart—or a large part of your conversation. The corporation was soulless. That was an article of faith. Capitalism, in general, was not a celebrated idea on campus. If some graduate strayed into business, well, little could be done. Still, as one Brown administrator told me, "The institution seems uncomfortable with people who went into business."

And yet, not only was Dan Ratner giddy with business enthusiasm, but the more I paged through recent Brown alumni magazines, the clearer this became: Business seemed a craze at good old liberal arts Brown. It was difficult to overstate. In fact, if I poked into the student newspaper or clicked on Brown Web sites, I couldn't avoid the impression that the entire campus was hoarse with business excitement, an astonishing turn of events. There were on-campus business clubs. The university was on its way to endowing—with $4 million—an entrepreneurship chair. I even read that Brown University was recently celebrated by a national business magazine as "Start-up U." Apparently Brown had "turned out some of the top young entrepreneurs in the United States," according to the publication.

And so I wondered this: How had I missed the boat? How come I'd never considered business? Why hadn't people I'd known, people my age, my generation, been onto a second start-up by twenty-four? Why could I name more students who had gone crazy than had gone into business? Had I been so out-of-step? Or, I wondered, had business?

$ $ $

Not long before I'd arrived at Brown, academic requirements were overhauled to make the examined life a bit easier to pursue. The "New Curriculum," ushered in by mass demonstrations, allowed students to opt out of pesky obligations—like grades and distribution requirements—that might stand in the way of true learning. (One year just 3.1 percent of students took all letter grades; I didn't take many myself.) Standard majors weren't required; students could concoct their own. ("Death" was one, I recall. "Saintliness," the focus of another. Both, obviously, required lots of reading.) Independent study was big, sometimes in groups. Six students got credit for studying the Colorado River in preparation for a summer of . . . paddling down it.

One semester, I took advantage of this freedom to sign up for Buddhism, astronomy, and Russian literature, thinking that, well, they sounded interesting. Lots of people planned their academic lives according to their interests. (I ran into another person who chose almost the same courses as me. She would become a professional astrologer.)

No doubt lax requirements appeared flaky to some, but they were what Brown liked most about itself. According to a survey by the Daniel Yankelovich Group of alumni from 1973 through 1985, three in four continued to think the New Curriculum "excellent." Daniel Yankelovich, head of the company at the time as well as father of a Brown student, said that in thirty years of studying schools, he hadn't come across one so well regarded by its alumni.

One seventies grad described what many felt about the New Curriculum in the alumni magazine. He went on and on. Frankly, he sounded as if describing a first drug experience: "A wonderful new world unfold[ed]," "we ranged broadly," "our whims took us," "we dabbled beyond our reach." The prose was a muddle, but the sentiment pure. College was a time for each student to pursue his own grand adventure, the adventure of learning (even if it took you down the Colorado).

If the adventure of learning was one reason to avoid business, I knew another. Just peek at the lives of my classmates who went into business. Again, my information comes from Brown's alumni magazine.

A year after graduation Susan J. Pilch, class of '77, wrote to the alumni magazine that she "is a loan specialist with Industrial National Bank, Providence." That's the entire entry—nine words summed up her young professional life. Or Timothy E. Driscoll, also '77, wrote, in eleven words, that he "is an account executive for Merrill Lynch in its Providence office." "Elizabeth Munves is employed in the stock research department at Salomon Brothers." "Cynthia Ruotolo is a buyer of men's and women's fragrances for Abraham & Strauss." One lucky grad landed a spot as "investment and financial counselor, an associate with Karbo, Karel, Nevin & Smith." There was an "assistant account executive at the Marshchalk Advertising Agency," a "sales representative with Proctor & Gamble Distributor Co.," a "market sales representative for Market Central Air Conditioning in Englewood Cliffs, NJ," an "actuarial analyst with Allstate Insurance Co.," and an "account executive with Travelers in Hartford, Conn., specializing in group pension sales."

These terse announcements really wring the heart with their imploring titles. I could just picture their respectable wide-shouldered suits and navy skirts, cadged from the era's classic business manual, *Dress for Success.* The race to become a professional was on.

Okay, the seventies wasn't a prosperous decade—it featured inflation, unemployment, recession, you name it. Entrepreneurial opportunities were said to have shut down. Still, as these entries intimated, if you pitched in for the corporation security might be had. (Pension sales *does* have a solid ring.) And who, my business-oriented peers seemed to ask, could want more?

Yet to me, these bulletins from the corporate world suggested dull, restrained steps, as restrained, I thought, as my classmates' hopes. Which were what? An annual bump in pay and a week at the shore? Might as well count to a million. No wonder I'd stayed away. The everyday life of my business-oriented peers sounded like a perfect bore.

No doubt many of my parents' generation, which entered adulthood in the fifties, would have encouraged their kids in these positions. Following your whims was fine for undergrads. But as loan specialist or sales rep, a young person could get a leg-up, a first mortgage maybe, and a new car, an economy model of the kind President Jimmy Carter advocated.

Still, I thought I knew another reason no fifties parent would take issue with these first jobs. It was because my seventies business peers had followed in their parents' footsteps—in their *exact* footsteps. All I had to do was thumb through the Brown alumni magazine of the fifties. If the companies weren't identical, they appeared interchangeable.

Special agent at Mutual of Hartford in the fifties instead of group pensions sales at Travelers in the seventies; Cardner Advertising in the fifties instead of Marshchalk Advertising in the seventies; assistant buyer for JC Penney in the fifties instead of perfume buyer at Abraham & Strauss in the seventies. In both eras, people had gone off to be sales reps at P&G. If seventies business culture seemed to call for toiling diligently in the prescribed way, it was a way prescribed in the fifties.

And, in case you missed the popular rendition, the fifties businessman—he was nearly always a man—was a mild-mannered soul who didn't care to rebel or experiment, who didn't desire to be a millionaire or president of the company. The ambition of these men, above all, was to belong. "Belongingness," William Whyte awkwardly called it in his classic study of the era, *The Organization Man*, a figure I was acquainted with. My father had, for a time, been one.

Whyte looked at young managers of my father's robust corporate age and discovered that they were in a hurry for little more daring than adulthood—which by their mid-twenties they'd achieved. My parents were typical to this extent; they married as seniors in college. By twenty-five, they'd started a family. If Whyte's execs didn't want to outshine one another, still, they worked hard and intended to rise on the tide that lifted all boats. Within a few years, my father was a department head at Foote, Cone & Belding, a large New York City ad agency. Whyte would have recognized my father's success, and praised it. He took pains to declare himself an Organization Man. And yet, perhaps because of that, his criticism was all the more stinging. "[They] dream so moderately," he said.

Would Whyte have said anything different about my Brown peers who'd landed the plum spot of account exec at Merrill Lynch or fragrance buyer at A&S, even if it was for men *and* women? I didn't think so.

And, frankly, moderate dreaming wasn't what I was after when I entered college in 1973. As far as I could see, I wasn't the one out of step. After all, for most people the notion of being young as we now mean the term came into its own in the seventies. (Most of the sixties happened in the seventies.) In the seventies campus life, and most of youth culture generally, was remade top to bottom. Music, sex, politics, as well as relationships to authority, to family, to education, to success, to gender roles, to living situations—for students of my generation all these areas were dramatically different than, say, for our fifties parents.

By the seventies, dissent was quite popular. President Nixon was chased from office, and so, our poli sci instructor speculated, his party was doomed. When asked, just 33 percent of people said they trusted government, which, nonetheless, was more than twice as many as trusted business. At Brown, protesting students took over administration offices. Early one foggy morning we circled that red brick building like Minutemen. (The FBI put us in its files!)

If I wasn't interested in business, then what did I and, as far as I could tell, most people, hope to do with our lives? Toward the end of the seventies, Bill Trogdon, a little-known academic, broke up with his wife, concocted an Indian name for himself, and set off through the back roads of America. "Chuck routine," he wrote under the name William Least Heat Moon. Moon's book *Blue Highways,* which spent almost a year on the *New York Times* best-seller list, added this advice: "Live the jeopardy of circumstance." Who knew what those words actually meant? Still, I was sure of this much: There was no jeopardy to be found in the circumstance of loan specialist or air-conditioner salesman or, for that matter, in *any* career. I was hardly unusual. In 1978, only 13 percent of people said work was at the center of their lives.

I wanted to be challenged *existentially,* and to wear bell-bottomed jeans while doing so. And, also, I wanted to have *fun,* which was very big back then.

And so, I took time off.

Time off? The term was quite popular. One woman from Brown went on a European "freak out," living on a boat in the Seine. One guy, after dropping out of law school, did nothing at all. "Everyone I knew was doing nothing," he explained with a shrug. It's strange to contemplate how resonant this was in the culture. Goofing off, bumming around, those weren't fringe activities, and not looked down upon, not by peers anyhow.

Bear in mind that for much of the seventies the *number one goal* of students—as many as 70 percent—was "to develop a meaningful philosophy of life," which isn't exactly a strategy for getting ahead.

In fact, when I dropped out of Brown after my sophomore year—Brown, I swear, encouraged students to drop out even if, like me, they never returned—my goal, my quite self-conscious goal, was to lead "an interesting life." That was a thoroughly banal concept—I couldn't have told you what it meant—and yet, at the time, it staked out a profound divide, the one between interest-seekers and career-strivers. As Brown student Rufus Griscom later said, "There used to be a paradigm where you could either make money or do something interesting, and that made not making money appear very attractive."

My parents had experienced little confusion about what they ought to do with their lives, none that I knew of anyhow. They weren't preoccupied with leading an interesting life. Their language ran more to responsibility and sacrifice. Plus, my guess is they found everyday adult life plenty interesting. They moved us to a leafy dead-end in a middle-class suburb, and poured their energies into their kids and their few-tenths of an acre.

They were like pioneers in this regard. Alone or with neighbors, they poured cement for a patio, terraced the backyard like it was the Tuscan countryside. In one delightful urge, my father decided to dig for water, just behind our rear screen door. (This was a period when he walked around tunelessly singing—him too—a favorite song, "The Impossible Dream," from the musical *Man of LaMancha.*) As I

recall, he rented a dense, squat drill. Then he finished it off by climbing to the roof and, each day after work, pounding a pipe home with
a sledgehammer. (Oh, and he struck water.)

Yet, inevitably, this suburbia, such a proving ground for my parents' generation, seemed settled and bland to me. The roiling lives we
all felt inside seemed out of place on its well-tended streets.

I hardly had the details worked out, but I knew this much: I
wanted to be part of the whole world, of *its* story, and get away from
my own. I hungered for experience, the wide-ranging sort. My parents' generation remembered the Depression and World War II,
events that suggested to them an unwelcoming world. I, on the other
hand, was impressed by Costa-Gavras's 1982 movie *Missing.* "We are
just two normal, slightly confused people trying to be connected to
[the] whole damn rotten enchilada," was how Sissy Spacek explained
why she and her husband had visited Chile at a dangerous time. I
knew exactly what she meant. The world might be dangerous; Chile
certainly was at the time. Yet somehow the other—the unknown
other—seemed so much more interesting, so much more *real* to me
than the safe, suburban neighborhood I'd grown up in or the steady
career I might ladder-up through.

And *real-ness,* deeply felt, was awfully important. Deep feeling, in
general, struck a chord. "People nowadays complain of an inability to
feel," said one writer in 1979. "They cultivate more vivid experiences." This was intended disparagingly, but I didn't see it that way. I
wanted intensity, engagement, some euphoria and, of course, I
wanted stories to tell—nothing I'd accumulate, as far as I could see, as
associate financial counselor at Karbo and Karel.

Like everyone else I knew, I was sensitive to needs and feelings,
my needs and *my* feelings, which, I soon learned, led lives independent of me. (Lives I was meant to get to know.) Still, I was less fascinated with myself in isolation. My generation, a slice of it anyhow,
also popularized the world—repositioned it, I'm tempted to say, since
the seventies invented positioning—as an object of interest, a source
of instruction, a privileged setting for adventure. I took "ranging
broadly" literally. Different people, different cultures, were meaning-

ful. *Difference* in and of itself was a deeply held value—the seventies was the decade that made diversity an American ideal.

I read Orwell on London, Hemingway on Paris, Kazantzakis on Greece. I can't tell you the longing I felt for places I'd never seen; the nostalgia I experienced for times I hadn't known! "The world is *out there,*" I wrote in a journal I still have. *Out there,* an empty phrase that seemed magical to me long before I'd heard of the gold rush *out there.* I wasn't alone. The *Let's Go* guides, those student-written travel books that reported intimately on exotic destinations, began in the sixties, but flourished in the seventies.

Events would work in favor of travelers. The airlines were deregulated in 1978, airfares dropped. In short order, I'd have friends who took off with nothing but a continent as a destination; two, I recall, ended up in a Mexican jail for a few days. "Wow, what was it like?" I said and was properly jealous.

For my part, I investigated purchasing a used mail truck. I intended to tool around the country, my own Blue Highways adventure. When that plan fell through, I'd take off in the middle of the night to hop trains; I'd buy a motorcycle and drive it to the beach; I'd hitchhike through California. You could hitchhike back then. You almost had to. After all, we all read Tom Robbins, the self-consciously wiggy writer whose 1976 best-seller, *Even Cowgirls Get the Blues,* featured a heroine with a special deformity: oversized thumbs, the better to hitchhike with. Hitching wasn't always predictable. Robbers relieved me of thirty pounds of lovingly amassed camping gear. (I had a snakebite kit, a collapsible chain saw. Who knew what to expect *out there?*) I only asked that they leave my journal. My robbers were accommodating, and with little but journal in hand, I set off to hitchhike again. Through the early eighties, I'd hitchhike—and also live—in Europe and Africa and Central America.

What work ought I to do? The question preoccupied me, not that I had many focused ambitions. Compared to the precise paths of my business-oriented peers, it might be said that I had none at all. "We made choices," I recall my mother saying. I cultivated mine like tiny oysters. Money wasn't the top draw for me, which, by the way, put me in the majority. As I entered college, less than 45 percent of freshmen said a top goal in life was to be "very well-off financially." Indeed, anyone who went to college in the seventies was free to believe that striving, especially if it targeted money, was a bit déclassé. (We even looked down on premed students, and one reason was the field's tendency to produce a dispiritingly steady income.) No wonder in 1981, Yankelovich asked, "Why this ambivalence about getting ahead? Why does it trouble so many?"

As far as work went, I responded to themes that the social critic Christopher Lasch articulated. "What is missing is the kind of work that might evoke a sense of calling," said Lasch, who, a bit of a pill, sounded pretty well fed-up. He added, in case you missed the point, "A calling, as opposed to a career, implies a belief in the intrinsic value of a given line of work." Business yielded money, status, security. Intrinsic rewards were something else. Just what wasn't clear, but as Robert Bellah reported in *Habits of the Heart,* meaningful work was on just about everyone's mind coming out of the seventies.

My father once remarked that it was comforting to him—and should be to me—to learn that his feelings weren't unique, but shared by many others. He'd been upbeat about this. I'd never heard anything more baffling. To be like everyone else was to be forlorn. "I had stopped feeling unique," was the way Kirstie Alley described her unhappiness in the film *Sibling Rivalry.* It was a generational shorthand that anyone brought up since the seventies immediately understood. After all, we were continually informed we had unique potential, most of it inborn, all of it waiting to pop out as poem, story, painting, or movie. Past generations had gone on about their souls; self-expression was our racket. Everyone I knew wanted to do something creative.

One of my roommates, son of a Seventh Avenue clothing manufacturer, was determined to be a poet and a drummer. An acquaintance graduated to hand paint ceramic tiles. The friend who'd helped boo the Harvard Business School went off to try painting; later, she'd write a novel. I knew a guy who became a marijuana smuggler because, as an aspiring writer, he said he needed material.

I vaguely thought I'd like to be a writer, too, which seemed not only interesting but related, vaguely again, to a desire to figure things out, a goal I thought meaningful. One semester at Brown, I'd taken creative writing. You had to apply for the course. So eager was I to learn if I'd been accepted that, like a burglar, I boosted myself through a window of the locked English department. The department, it turned out, had added creative writing classes—we were all accepted.

Creativity—Yankelovich called it "the creativity life-style"—was a generational victory, of course. It was the one attribute that the dependable Organization Man, representative of the Age of Conformity, spectacularly lacked. Authors Paul Leinberger and Bruce Tucker interviewed over a hundred children of Organization Men, members of my generation. Guess what? They reported that virtually everyone "harbors artistic aspirations." The artist, they concluded, was our occupational ideal.

Impressively, people stuck to this ideal no matter what they actually did. Take Robert G. Berger Jr., who wrote to the Brown alumni magazine in 1979. He might have been attending Harvard Law; still, he wanted to assure fellow alums he "has been doing some creative writing in his spare time." (*In his spare time!*) Twenty years later, the era's ideal persisted. In 1999, a member of the Brown class of '78 put it nicely. "I'm busy as a stomach doctor," he wrote to the alumni magazine. "Like everyone . . . who can type, my hobby is writing."

Journalism, when I fell into it, seemed just about perfect. It was far-flung, meaningful, somewhat creative, and not threateningly remunerative. (And interest there was: I'd go to war, to Hollywood, to jail.) Plus, though journalists' approval rating has slipped recently, a few years ago they seemed nearly heroic. They told the truth—*there's a calling!*—and were portrayed in movies. Robert Redford and Dustin Hoffman played the *Washington Post* reporters who helped reveal the Watergate scandal—it was a movie I sat through three times. I wasn't alone. In the Brown alumni magazine, classmates reported driving furiously around the country to compete for entry-level jobs at small newspapers, just like the one I landed for $100 a week in 1975. (That's what I'd done when I'd taken time off.)

Through my twenties, I had a bunch of good journalism jobs, and yet they didn't exactly add up to a career. Every so often, I'd quit on little notice and without much pain. My parents had initially, and generously, seconded my instincts, and even visited me in Europe and Africa. Yet in 1982, when I announced my intention to leave another good job, the best one yet, at the moment of the deepest recession since the Great Depression, my father groaned. I was considering a trip to Nicaragua, a country in the midst of revolution. "Enough's enough," he said. Perhaps it was a reference to the danger. For me, his succinct phrase suggested that I was dawdling, not only on my way to marriage and family—people I knew would be famously late to such undertakings—but to the seriousness of purpose that signaled adulthood.

No doubt this was true. My sense of making good, of getting ahead, indeed, of getting on with the concerns of mature life was so different from that of my parents' generation or, for that matter, of the more sensible business-oriented members of my own. By now, they were, as I could read in the alumni magazine, "promoted to assistant underwriter at Connecticut Mutual Life" or to "Midwest regional sales manager of Easco Aluminum in Girard, Ohio," and thus, this young fellow must have been delirious to report, "responsible for all sales and customer-service personnel at the company's facilities in Illinois, Indiana, and Ohio."

I was hardly concerned. As far as I could see, dropping out, journalism, traveling, writing, pursuing interest, put me in the thick of things, an exciting place to be. No doubt assistant underwriter promised a split-level in the suburbs. (I lived in a fifth-floor walk-up in Greenwich Village.) But where in wholesaling air-conditioners or in pushing soap and related products for P&G was the excitement, the fun, the confusion, the adventure of being in your twenties?

So, when I wasn't much older than Dan Ratner, I headed to Nicaragua. "What a twist of emotions," I'd note in my journal shortly before taking off. "Just this morning, unable to sleep, I thought: Better go, better go." What was the feeling? Very vivid indeed. "Like falling through floorboards," I wrote. "A new place. The end of places. I'm off to buy malaria pills."

There was *my* watch-out-world.

$ $ $

So let me get this straight. Twenty-some years after I'd helped take over that administration building, dropped out, headed to Nicaragua, conscientiously done all the things a dutiful Brown student was supposed to do, the university had gone and gotten itself named "Start-Up U."

Officially, I learned, the school still claimed that Socrates ran the show. And publicly Brown continued to turn its nose up at a business school. "We must remember that our society is more than a vast market," the university president told Dan Ratner's graduating class. Students, from what I gathered, still hurried to Brown with vague intellectual yearnings. "I just wanted to do interesting and intellectually challenging things . . . ," said Nicholas Butterworth, who graduated about half a dozen years before Dan. That, as far as I was concerned, was pitch-perfect Brown-speak, the good old tradition, the one that precluded a job in business. As far as I could tell lots of Brown students still followed that tradition, assiduously pursuing their whims. A peek at the alumni magazine revealed that recent grads enjoyed spending time as priest, rapper, circus performer.

And yet, by the turn of the century, Dan Ratners seemed about to overrun antibusiness Brown. In alumni postings, a number of recent grads listed themselves as founders. "I'm working to start my second Internet-related company in three years," wrote one the same year Dan's entry appeared. I noticed the word "launch" a lot—not a very seventies word. But then start-up wasn't a noun I would have recognized. People apparently flocked to business careers now. Not that Dan Ratner's path sounded much like a career, mind you; not, in any case, like those moderate seventies versions. Was *anyone* an associate financial counselor any longer?

Brown still might not have a business department; it did, though, have a few business courses tucked away in the engineering school.

Apparently, they'd always been there. And in fall 1999, *nearly one tenth of Brown's entire undergraduate student body* signed up for one of them, the one taught by Barrett Hazeltine, an old (in fact, a retired) engineering professor. Hazeltine had to split the class in two—what was the alternative with 539 enrollees? For a time, he held office hours seven days a week, and lectured four times a week, a particularly rugged schedule for the sixty-nine-year-old since each time a student correctly answered a question he'd leap from the stage, run the aisle, and shake the respondent's hand.

Apparently, most of his students wanted to be entrepreneurs. Recently, several of them had launched—that verb again—an entrepreneurship program. It appealed to the many undergrads who apparently couldn't delay their business gratification until graduation. I noticed that, at one point, the club's Web site ran what seemed like personals ads, matching hopeful entrepreneurs to attractive business projects. Two candidates recommended themselves as "good with people." One added, "I can think of ideas." (*Great! We're going to need those!* I could imagine a young CEO snapping.) And aspiring CEOs were apparently everywhere. Aspiring was the key word, since the businesses seemed kind of notional. "My ideas are vague," noted one founder-to-be, "but if you want to make cool clothes, please join the team." Another founder-in-the-making didn't have his business worked out, but he did have an extensive "to do" list, which he published. Another, also fuzzy on details, was nonetheless considering something that "would create a new industry." (Apparently, moderate dreaming was out.)

College, in my view, was a time to get right with your prejudices, the ones that would take you comfortably through life. Mine had coalesced around creativity, self-expression, adventure, interest, experience, difference, fun. By taking time off, living in Africa, doing journalism, and, of course, by disdaining business as a dreary, provincial, life-depleting exercise, I felt sure I'd landed on solid ground.

Now it seemed that if a young person could only be involved in any sort of business start-up, all would be fine. The occupational ideal was no longer the artist, I was pretty sure of that. Now, no doubt, it was the businessperson, the aspiring CEO. Across the country, college grads now rushed into business. Twenty years ago, an equal number had sought MBAs, MDs, and JDs. Two decades later, there were more than twice as many MBAs as doctor and law degrees *combined*. No one, it occurred to me, would boo MBA candidates nowadays. They wouldn't dare.

The times appeared to have left me, and my generation, behind. And yet the more I poked around, the more it seemed that this wasn't the entire story. The occupational ideal might have switched. But here was the strange thing: The terms of the new ideal were strikingly familiar. Weird as it seemed, those earnest young businesspeople of the nineties and those artistically inclined people of the seventies described themselves in remarkably similar ways.

Students hadn't changed. Business had. It was entrepreneurial now. And—was it possible?—the entrepreneurial spirit seemed to have adopted the very values so precious to the artistic one.

$ $ $

I, of course, had suspected that we were all painfully unique beings endowed with creative natures—a generational insight. The business world I'd glimpsed in the seventies seemed to indicate that creativity was, like fingerpainting, for kids. But even the most cursory peek into the campus business culture suggested that individual creativity was *in* once again. Apparently, though, creativity was no longer best expressed in novel, screenplay, or painting, but in, guess what, a little business of one's own. Sam Blackman, Brown '98—who'd taken over a campus dating business—said it explicitly. "Students have some of the best creative minds out there," he began. And business, to his way of thinking, offered the best way to "to take advantage of them." Set out in business and, I soon recognized—and what a shock of recognition it was—here was the underlying promise: You could become the creative person you had always wanted to be.

Certainly, dozens of recent grads agreed that business was a creative outlet—perhaps *the* creative outlet. Just as Brown grads—be they law student or stomach doctor—had once seemed unable to give up the dream of writing fiction, lots of alumni now suspected they had a little business to birth. One alum, on reaching that ticklish age, "almost thirty," quit a good job to start his own company. Why? His wife told the alumni magazine he needed "to set that entrepreneurial spirit free." No other explanation was necessary. Apparently everyone now understood that the entrepreneurial spirit was there innately, like a true creative self, itching to get out.

Not everyone was ready to quit job—or school—to start a business. But many were tempted by a related urge: to try their hand at a little business plan, which seemed the era's response to the creative writing impulse so many of my generation had felt. "A long time ago it was all about the great American novel, then the great American screenplay," explained a "content editor" for Kozmo.com, one of the era's splashier new businesses. "These days it's the great American business plan." Undergrads agreed and participated in contests sponsored by the Brown entrepreneurship program. Apparently sensitive Brown students still liked to stay up nights and pour their hearts out in prose. Now, though, they preferred to compete for $30,000 in seed money. One year, they wrote nearly a hundred business plans.

This outpouring led the alumni magazine to conclude: "Brown may not have a business school, but that doesn't keep students from pretending."

Once, I'd sought an interesting life, which had led me to Paris, Dakar, Managua. Interest still seemed the focus. "You want to . . . get as close as possible to the things with which you're truly obsessed," said Tom Gardner, Brown alum and founder of the Motley Fool, an offbeat investment advisor. But now you were supposed to let your interests guide your life, your *business* life. (And not in the direction, I'm guessing, of air-conditioner sales.)

No one apparently considered slotting into preestablished jobs anymore. Business now seemed an empty vessel into which you could fit—indeed, *had* to fit—whatever stirred you. Now someone could apparently say, Well, I *love* music, and so start a music-retailing business, which appeared to be what happened with the music-loving founder of CDNow, Brown '94. Or how about if you loved a specific slice of music, real counter-cultural stuff? Why not sell weird indie music online, the kind you just knew people would find irresistible if only it were more available? In that case, you might set off to create a "gateway to the underground community," which is what a founder of insound.com, Brown '96, did. Ranging broadly, following your whims, those weren't passé. It was just that the best way to get on with such highfalutin goals was, incredible as it seemed, to cook up a little business.

That was true even if you were a person with a conscience—Brown still produced them by the scores—the type who might be tempted to teach deaf Nicaraguan kids sign language, as one seventies couple featured in the alumni magazine had done. In the nineties, business seemed a way to express, get this, your idealism. Andrew Yang's stargiving.com was, as he told the alumni magazine, "going to make philanthropy engaging, accessible, and fun for everyone." If he seemed to be quoting his business plan, well, I got the impression that was lately a very Brown thing to do—just like, no doubt, carrying an expertly folded *Wall Street Journal*. (Though it might also be the *New York Times,* which now had two separate business sections daily.)

Clearly, self-expression was still the going racket. Lately, though, the unsurpassed expression of who you really were was a little entrepreneurial venture. Business sounded like bildungsroman these days. Brown alum Jeff Smith had worked for a global information solutions company. He'd also been an analyst with Prudential. But Jeff's real interest, it turned out, was to snowboard, surf, ski, climb. To maintain, in his words, an "active and thrilling lifestyle" was what he was really about. So he founded Soulgear.com. Of course it was "a marketing solutions" company for the action sports world. But Jeff called Soulgear "our movement." "Our movement is my top priority," Jeff explained on Soulgear's Web site, "because it is in line with the pursuit of adventure, personal growth and discovery, relationship building, environmental awareness and soulful living." Jeez. Sure didn't sound like those junior management spots my seventies comrades had duckwalked off to. Even crunchy Brown wouldn't be uncomfortable with business types like these.

I'd only been acquainted with one business student, that curly-headed guy. But then to me business was drab, straight, corporate, stodgy, and hardly individualistic. No doubt these days everyone at Brown knew business students galore—quirky, cool, idiosyncratic ones. In story after story the alumni magazine highlighted some adorable aspect, some lovable detail, *something* that suggested how very personal, how very touching business now seemed to be. Jessica Nam, who'd apparently started her baking company out of her dorm kitchen, named her creations for friends. JJ's Most Moist Mocha and Kelli Belli Jelli Banana Bread. The cofounders of Nantucket Nectars—friends from the class of '89—printed private sayings under their bottle caps, one of which referred to a favorite Brown professor, Hazeltine, of course.

The lords of liberal arts once believed that if you opened students' minds to education's "higher tastes and aims," you'd lead them away from business's narrow goals. Tantalize them with Shakespeare, and you couldn't very well expect them to spend their days in front of a column of numbers. Business, though, had been remade. Now you could come to it from any walk of life, any interest, any major, no matter how dreamy or impractical, and still thrive in this new entrepreneurial world. You could major in semiotics, and still, like Rufus Griscom, end up CEO of a publishing venture, Nerve.com. You could concentrate in linguistic anthropology like Jessica Nam and head into a baked goods business. You could, like the founder of the Motley Fool, major in English and start an investment advisory company.

Even the New Curriculum, Brown's grand experiment in learning, had been reoriented. Perhaps dabbling beyond your reach, which the New Curriculum encouraged, was once thought to conflict with the serious adult concerns of corporate business. The recent generation squinted at the New Curriculum and perceived a gateway to the business world, the entrepreneurial one. "People who go to Brown set their own pace and define their own academic search," explained Randy Haykin, class of '85, founding manager of Yahoo! and more recently a partner in iMinds. "And that's the same kind of person who's likely to start a business." And so the academic freedom that had led me to Buddhism, astronomy, and few marketable skills (since I didn't want to be an astrologer) now seemed a forcing bed for business initiative.

By the late nineties the adventure had somewhat gone out of adventure, at least as I'd once conceived it. These days entrepreneurship seemed the adventure of the era. Indeed, from the way people talked, entrepreneurship seemed a way to organize your life *as adventure*. Hitchhiking might no longer be possible—the world had been repositioned again, again it was threatening. But how about a start-up? That was the wildest adventure of all. "Like your first roller-coaster ride or high-school romance," said one participant. (Perhaps *fun* was still in fashion.) In the nineties, one entrepreneur explained, "It's difficult to understand the rush until you've been along for the ride [on a start-up]." The *rush?* Talk about intensity, engagement with life! In the nineties, the jeopardy of circumstance might, it seemed, be found in business. Not that the jeopardy was really all that great— had it ever been? As Hazeltine suggested, if you flopped, well, "go to the beach for a few days, and it's all better." For the experience-hungry, business, even a failed one, seemed pretty cool—so what was it *really* like?—perhaps like a few days in a Mexican jail.

All this was fairly remarkable. Business, once soul-deadening routine, now seemed a thoroughgoing expression of an impassioned and idiosyncratic youth—the youth the seventies had popularized. And, of course, now it was doable. Just as adventure travel had become feasible once airfares dropped, business now seemed the possible adventure. Adults didn't even have to be involved. "Imagine," said one youthful participant, ". . . all of a sudden being able to start a company . . . and not having to ask anybody's permission."

By now, this much was clear to me. All those really seventies, liberal arts values that I held, that people once held, hadn't disappeared. Just the opposite. They'd resurged, oddly vibrant. Business, at least its current entrepreneurial version, was the great synthesis.

No doubt, it was still possible to distinguish the career-ambivalent seventies from the profit-friendly nineties. Fewer freshmen these days were intent on coming up with "a meaningful philosophy of life"—

40 percent down from 70 percent in my day. Nonetheless, an important, unrecognized point was this. The nineties took the bell-bottomed
seventies, with its self-serious, arch, hippie-ish, really Brown values—
creativity, self-expression, individuality, desire for adventure, ambivalence about career—and re-outfitted them for a sleeker future. Once
business had been grown-up, mature, responsible—*There's a job to be
done,* that was a business slogan—and businesspeople seemed that way
too. Now, you could be as green and rebellious, as oddball as you
wanted. You could be *anti*business—most young businesspeople *seemed*
to be—and still hatch a little enterprise. You could call yourself creative, you almost had to; you could indulge eclectic, eggheady hobbies
or a taste for the exotic; you could pursue the most marginal, most alternative interest and still, at some point say, Hey, wouldn't this be a
neat little entrepreneurial venture? People who wanted something,
anything, now turned expectantly to business.

And so a strange thing occurred. I'd begun this project as an out-
sider. I'd wanted to angle my way in toward the center of the new
business culture, and hadn't anticipated a warm reception. Now, it
seemed, this business world would welcome someone like me—with
my background, my interests, my antibusiness prejudices—with open
arms. This world I'd once avoided, once dismissed, sounded familiar
and oddly stirring. Had I been holding out for the wrong reasons?
And me a joiner! If I'd been in college any time recently I wouldn't
have the missed the boat. I wouldn't have gone off to Nicaragua. I'd
have spoken an entrepreneurial language, dismissed credentials, gotten on with a hush-hush creative venture. Like Dan Ratner, I'd have
a couple of businesses under my belt, at least one of them the latest
and greatest. Perhaps I'd even have tried to be like Nicholas Butterworth, the Brown grad who wanted to do "interesting and intellectually challenging things," which he was sure excluded business, and
who ended up CEO of the Internet music start-up, SonicNet. Let's
face it, it was *totally cool* to be an entrepreneur now—and cool in a
way I understood.

February 2000
Nasdaq 4051.98

Chapter Seven

The Hugeness of the Opportunity

I FIRST HEARD what I'd later think of as *the news* by telephone. I was in the extra bedroom of my apartment, a small room that had for years served me as journalism office and that, lately, I thought of as world headquarters of KaraokeNation. The room had several standard office features, bookshelves, filing cabinet, and corkboard (to which I'd pinned that forlorn old cockroach hotel), as well as an assortment of photos and knickknacks from over the years. There was an aerial photo of a Colombian volcano I'd visited, a collection of carved betel nut containers that I'd collected in Indonesia (and which now held paper clips), a carved African mask, a drawing of Josephine Baker from a Paris flea market, and some family photos, including one of Cristina with a large monkey on her back and one of me in a state of fear. A photographer had snapped that shot of me as I prepared to leap from a plane three miles high, something I once thought would be fun to try. I stood hunched over in the plane's open door where I made the mistake of casting a glance at the earth below. Just seeing that photo brought the fear back—every time.

When the phone rang, I was seated at my large old wooden desk that, as usual, was littered with papers and telephones. There were five phones, three of which for a variety of reasons had stopped working. (I tended to switch wires around.) When I heard the ring, I cheerfully grabbed the nearest phone, "KaraokeNation," I answered, an upnote on the last syllable.

Unfortunately, I'd selected the wrong phone. I reached for another and repeated my greeting.

"Peter Clemente," said Clemente, quiet as a small-town librarian. For some reason, he often introduced himself by his full name. Clemente said the survey of Internet users' hidden karaoke habits—a phrase that tickled me no end—was in. "I have the results," he said. "You won't believe it."

At Consigliere's request Clemente had asked Internet users a couple of basic market research questions. The answers could prove invaluable or, of course, they might crush my venture here and now. "Well?" I said and gazed at the brick wall just outside my office window. "What do the survey numbers *say?*"

Silence.

"Clemente!" I shouted, trying to get him going.

He wouldn't budge. Not for me, in any case. I'd lately hatched a little theory about Clemente. He treated people as if they came from one of two places: the *informed* place or the *uninformed* place. Consigliere, in Clemente's mind, was from the informed place. "He's very strong in business," Clemente had confided, a real compliment. Clemente also resided in the informed place and, I knew, was trying to extend his holdings. As part of this effort, he'd written a book, *State of the Net,* with 103 charts and graphs. (Consigliere had penned the foreword.) I, on the other hand, was a passport holder of the uninformed place. Not only was I inexpert but I combined that with an eagerness to express my opinion. "So many opinions," Clemente would say dismissively. Sometimes, if I directly questioned his point, he'd say, *"Where have you been?"* He didn't pay my opinion much mind.

And so, though I hoped he'd quickly divulge the few salient numbers, that was not in the cards. Clemente felt business required discipline and restraint. He had a bunch of methodological concerns to wade through, in part perhaps to suggest the weightiness of the technique involved. The results, he noted, were preliminary. If the survey were done again he might get different numbers. "They didn't come back clean," he said. "They haven't been weighted yet. So don't get over- or under-enthusiastic." I felt like a patient unable to get the fateful diagnosis from his doctor.

"Are you sitting down?" Clemente said finally.

"For God's sake," I responded, a rubbery bubble of anticipation on my lips.

The next words seemed taken out of context, as if I'd missed something. ". . . the hugeness of the opportunity . . ." I heard and at first had no idea what he could be talking about.

$ $ $

Generally big-shot consultants like Clemente were a bland-looking bunch: short hair, navy blazer, white shirt, and a voice as toneless as an NPR host's. They might be Jews or Italians, you'd never know; they all looked midwestern. They'd pop out of a rental car, pump your hand in their doughy grip. They were making money by the fist-fuls—they, arguably, were the real winners in the Internet economy—and one reason was that they fit in anywhere.

That, however, was not Clemente's style. The first few times I met him, I thought: *He's in recovery, right?*

At forty, Clemente had unruly brown hair to his shoulders and the deepest facial creases I'd ever seen—I occasionally wondered if they were scars. He dressed impeccably—he owned thirty-four beautiful designer suits—and might have been a fashion plate except for the inner biker he couldn't quite subdue. He sometimes wore three or four gold hoop earrings. Of course, he rode motorcycles, unmuffled Harleys that his wife claimed she could hear ten city blocks away. Plus, his internal systems showed considerable wear and tear. There was insomnia—Clemente slept as little as three hours some nights. And gastrointestinally, he seemed totally cooked. As a result, he'd sworn off alcohol and, from what I could tell, several food groups. Needless to say, he was skinny as a bone.

Clemente wasn't in recovery, though. Unless perhaps it was from the eighties when, from what I could tell, he'd been one of the most energetic rock 'n' roll drummers *ever*. At Fordham University, Clemente would put in a full day of classes, then play three gigs a night. Later, he toured with David Bowie and members of the Cars. ("He played Wembley Stadium!" Consigliere told me, and we'd both looked off, imagining a field of screaming teens.) Eventually he formed his own group, Diving for Pearls, which recorded a well-reviewed CD for Epic Records. On the album cover, Clemente wore a black Italian lace shirt, gold bracelets, a gold ring given him by the Hells Angels, his father's silver dog tags, black jeans so snug they appeared to be tights, cowboy boots *and* spurs.

He looked like a goth Liberace, and I'd once asked him for an explanation.

"The eighties," he shrugged.

These days, he didn't like to talk about his music past, except to say what a hassle it had been always chasing a paycheck. Then about ten years ago, Clemente started a career as analyst and consultant; for the past three he'd been with Cyber Dialogue. He gathered interesting, unique data in that quarterly survey. But more important, as *Ad-Week* pointed out in a profile, Clemente had a talent for seeing what was coming down the pike. The magazine suggested Clemente was a leading Internet visionary. To my mind, Clemente was *the vision king*.

Business would claim that it had long counted on vision, but in most instances, vision had been little more than an idealized version of the present. Mainly it had been useful in explaining to the kids what dad did all day. Vision was Merck, the pharmaceutical company, saying something inspiring like "We are in the business of preserving and improving human life" rather than, you know, "We sell as many drugs as humanly possible."

The Internet helped shift vision forward. As the authors of the *Visionary's Handbook* put it, "The closer your vision gets to a provable 'truth,' the more you are simply describing the present." Visions were the terms of competition in the Internet but when it came to Internet visions, the present and, conveniently, the provable, weren't very useful. These days, visions had to respond to the question, What will people want to do on the Internet in the future?

Clemente's vision focused on the future of entertainment and, like many visions, started with a problem. Clemente believed the $15-billion-a-year music industry, as currently configured, was doomed.

Half a century of commercial history had forged a mass market that music companies contentedly exploited to their ends. Industry giants pushed a handful of bands through TV, radio, and magazines. Market Britney Spears to everyone fifteen or younger; some percentage would buy her music. (Other bands, as Clemente knew only too well, had to fend for themselves; Clemente had walked away from music after his debut album got lost in the shuffle.)

Clemente, though, felt the mass market was about to go kaput. "Control is being wrested right out of their hands"—the hands of some of the country's largest corporations—"thanks to the Internet," said Clemente. Songs, Clemente pointed out, were nothing more than digital files that could be copied on any computer and, using the Internet, distributed across the world.

Internet idealism was usually rooted in technical possibilities. Still, I couldn't help but notice that technology took sides. The new business world presented itself as a kind of morality play. In it the Internet seemed to wear the colorful, tight-fitting uniform of superhero.

In a mass market, so the story went, technology had served the corporation, bending the hapless consumer to its dark will. The Internet showed up as avenger. "The internet is about choice," said Clemente boldly. Specifically, the Internet was going to restore choice, the one stolen from artist and consumer alike. Using the Internet, artists could cut out record companies, which usually cheated them anyhow, and go right to fans. Fans could download songs from dozens of sites, no longer limited by a few industry marketers. Technology allowed the individual to assert his tastes, which Clemente contended was what the individual would really want to do on the Internet in the future. Especially when it came to entertainment.

Consigliere, who could be a little cynical, once cracked, "When there's no history, it's a great time to be a fortune-teller," his way of saying visionary. And, of course, everyone knew vision was a bit of a shell game. After all, if you were right, as the *Visionary's Handbook* informed, your vision would change the future and, conveniently, prove your vision wrong. But, as far as I could tell, not many were troubled by such concerns. So many people jammed conferences where Clemente spoke that his image sometimes had to be projected on a giant screen. With all that hair, skinny Clemente looked top-heavy and, I thought, in danger of tipping over. No one seemed to worry. The crowds listened raptly as Clemente delivered his music-industry eulogy, solemnly, earnestly. It was the tone he used for all business matters. Still the words, well, they sounded like Lenin. "The Internet has shaken the foundation of the traditional music-making business," he'd tell the crowd. Even a staunch capitalist like Clemente seemed exuberant at this prospect.

If a mass market survived, Clemente asserted, it would be "a mass market of niches." Like a niche for eighties hair bands or, I couldn't help but think, a niche for hip-hop karaoke. Fortunately, as Clemente told CEOs in follow-up meetings, the Internet could service a mass market of niches, the one it helped create. (Many CEOs were from the *uninformed place,* it turned out.)

"Don't fear," Clemente told *AdWeek.* He wasn't really going to leave the business world hanging. (Clemente had been a conservative Republican even before he'd been a rock 'n' roll drummer.) The Internet could find customers cheaply, and the right ones. If the music industry would wake up, then the Internet offered it a one-to-one marketing tool without parallel.

If karaoke was, as I delightedly told myself, a potential niche, more good news was on the way. When Clemente studied his survey data—I pictured him poring over numbers late into sleepless nights—he found evidence that people didn't like being couch potatoes, which the mass market had made them. His research suggested that the newly liberated consumer—liberated from the mass market—had all along wanted to be an activist, a participant, an individual. Clemente discovered that people on the Internet hoped to interact with their music, even create their own, which, again, I counted a positive sign for karaoke. What could be more interactive than karaoke?

This brought me back to Clemente's survey results, those I was still trying to wrest right out of his hands. As far as I could see, all signs were positive. But what were the numbers? By telephone, Clemente's company had asked one thousand Internet users two questions.

Do you own a karaoke player or have you participated in karaoke in the past three months? Clemente finally told me that a number representing 11 million adult Internet users responded yes.

Would you be interested in an online karaoke service that allows you to sing along with the music? A number representing 14 million adult Internet users said yes.

Those were pretty healthy niches. But as if that weren't enough, when Cyber Dialogue tossed the duplicates, it turned out that 21 million people either owned a karaoke player, had recently participated in karaoke, or would like to participate in online karaoke.

Incredible as it seemed, one thing that newly empowered individuals apparently wanted to do on the Internet of the future was create karaoke songs. I was bowled over. This guy Clemente might look like an escapee from rehab, but, I reminded myself, he had the future nailed. He was the *vision king*. Now he was prepared to fold karaoke into his vision of the digital future.

"The hugeness of the opportunity" were the first few disjointed words I'd heard. Now, I understood, they referred to the business opportunity for KaraokeNation. We didn't know if these future online karaokers would pay anything. Still—was it possible?— karaoke seemed awfully promising. I made Clemente say it again.

"Huge opportunity," he repeated in his sandpapery voice.

Could Internet karaoke truly be a good idea, in tune with some of the Internet's central propositions, and thus, and not incidentally, a solid moneymaking proposition?

I didn't have music capabilities on my laptop. I couldn't play a CD on my computer. Clemente didn't see barriers. Never had. The future, as he saw it, was a realm of possibility and, what's more, constantly banging on the door would get you in. Not that it seemed much effort was necessary. He made it sound like all you really needed was to get going.

"This is incredible," I said. "Actually, it seems ridiculous."

"Where have you been?" Clemente snapped. I forgot about his touchy side.

What had I gotten myself into? I suddenly wondered. In my little office, I peeked at the photo of me set to jump from a plane. There it was, quick as a pin, the familiar surge of fear. I'm going to have to clean my desk, I thought. And get those phones working. *The hugeness of the opportunity.* The phrase turned over in my mind, a feather in the wind.

PART TWO

Chapter Eight

Russell Digs Karaoke

WHEN I'D IMAGINED my meeting with Russell Simmons, one of hip-hop's founding fathers, I'd felt sure of one thing: We'd get along. We were bound to. Russell had been described to me as a people person. "He can make you feel like you're the only person in the room," I'd been told. Plus, the early indications had been so positive. Russell's staff had seemed eager to set up a meeting. "It's an Internet entertainment idea," I'd said cagily. His assistant hadn't pressed me for details. Perhaps she sensed the potential. No doubt good assistants had a nose for such things. "How much time will you need?" she asked amiably. She'd had to reschedule a couple times. Russell had some last-minute panel to sit on, some fashion show to attend. But in each instance, she'd assured me with the same unflappable good spirits, in fact, with the same encouraging phrase *word for word,* "Russell could go for it."

So I'd planned things out. This was to be one of my first high-stakes meetings, and I wanted everything to go just right. I intended to start with a simple handshake—I was thinking of *everything*—not the three-step hip-hop contrivance that I had a tendency to bungle. A firm, businesslike up-and-down. A reliable lead-in to the business at hand, which, I assumed, would be attended by serious-minded staffers who, for some reason, I pictured in billowy white shirts. Russell might have grown up snorting angel dust; still, I felt sure, Big Dawg, as he was sometimes called, would want to hear details. He was a numbers person, a talent he'd apparently honed through memorizing models' phone numbers. Perhaps he'd summon an accountant or two. We were ready. Clemente had a presentation loaded onto his tiny laptop. I had a short animated film on mine. (I'd wanted something special for Russell and had, initially, hired an intricately tattooed young illustrator whom I compensated, in part, in tattoos. Sadly, his drawings proved a bit too scary.) Consigliere was ready to hint at future possibilities, blue-sky kinds of things—we'd kicked around a hip-hop-karaoke TV channel. (*"That's* your million-dollar idea right there," one entrepreneur had told me.)

If all went well, I felt that Russell would turn his warm, friendly gaze upon us, and say, *"HiphopKaraoke? For goodness sake, I've been waiting for something like this!"* Consigliere thought Russell might even want to invest. "Russell could go for it," Consigliere had said. Curiously, he'd used the same phrase as Russell's assistant. (Perhaps it was a business phrase.) I had prepared terms just in case. I was determined not to give the thing away no matter how hard Russell bargained.

In retrospect, perhaps I'd failed to take into account a few details. Russell's alarming energy, for one. Nor had I imagined he'd use the word "motherfucker" quite so much.

Russell had let my team wait for nearly an hour. Then he rushed into his office like a fireman. He shouted about not letting "the *motherfucker* in," and getting "the *motherfucker* out." Russell spoke so fast that, for a moment, I could only distinguish the words "shit," "fuck," and "motherfucker." I comforted myself in the thought that those sharp words were directed at associates, those whom Russell referred to as "fucking thieves." Still, Russell's energy—not quite what I'd expected in a CEO—brought to mind a caveat. "Russell can turn it on like Bill Clinton," I'd been told, "unless he's distracted." I had to admit the possibility that Russell might, for a few minutes, be distracted.

"What's this about?" Russell snapped at me, though he didn't wait for an answer. He settled into his desk chair near a mechanical, chest-high waterfall, another of his relaxation strategies. (Apparently, there was to be no handshake.)

Russell had been carrying a brown paper bag of Chinese food. At his desk, he tore open the bag, spread it flat, creating a kind of rustic placemat.

"I hope you don't find it too insulting," he said. The insult, I noted, was only a matter of degree.

"No-no-no," we chorused. Made to wait like children, now, nonetheless, we were eager to please.

Consigliere patted his tie into place, hurried over. Clemente and I grabbed seats behind our computers, which sat on the edge of Russell's desk. (I'd unplugged Russell's half-refrigerator in order to plug mine in.)

In photos taken in his twenties Russell was the tall fellow with receding hairline and advancing belly. Now in his forties, Russell was leaner and shaved his tawny head. He had wide, sad eyes that made him look a bit Asian. Three distinguished ridges creased his brow.

"My whole day is meetings," Russell announced a propos of nothing. "I just got off a plane," he said, "I came back from Virginia [where AOL is headquartered]. I'm at Yahoo! [based in California]. I'm sitting with Edgar Bronfman [Jr., former head of Seagrams and now vice-chair of Vivendi Universal] trying to sell him. I'm trying to sell someone else. I'm trying to get my round of financing. I have this whole Internet staff that grows every single day. I'm trying to manage a budget." Where Russell was headed with this, I didn't know. Perhaps he didn't either.

Russell had been powerful for a while; wealthy since his record business sold for $130 million. Yet Russell's fate, it seemed, was to appear beleaguered. Grabbing meals on the run and constantly pitching his next bright idea, trying to get into the building, the one where, he was convinced, "the *real* money" was to be made. And so, as if he couldn't pass up any chance, no matter how small, after appealing to AOL, to Yahoo!, to Vivendi Universal, Russell began to entertain *us,* to sell *us.* "We're doing a very, very elaborate kind of special focused hip-hop effort online," he wanted us to know. "We're going to be brand builders. We're going to be clothing and other kind of commerce people. And we're going to be very heavy in music marketing."

Russell's speech was sometimes lewd and always fast—I occasionally had to replay his words in my mind to catch the meaning—and
also because he had a gentle lisp, a bit comic. I found him wildly
entertaining and just wanted to listen, a contrary urge I knew, since I
should be selling him. "It's expansive," Russell said, and started using
words like "leverage" and "synergistic opportunities," plugging in
dizzying business talk the way, in other circumstances, he would slot
in dizzying street talk.

"The point I'm trying to make is . . . ," he said, pausing to pluck a
bone from his mouth. Russell formed a neat pile of small bones on
his desk. Oddly, vegetarian Russell appeared to eat chicken.

"Be careful of the bones," said Clemente helpfully. He was, I
knew, trying to clear a little verbal space, something we might sneak
into.

No chance. "I mean it's mind-boggling to people who've seen
the presentation. And I mean that," said Russell, which I'd later
understand as an indication that Russell was making it up. "There's
something called I-Zone," Russell said. "It's interactive. The entire
site is interactive and fun like a roller coaster." Russell paused, perhaps, it occurred to me, imagining a roller coaster. "I-Zone has all
kinds of battles," he picked up. "Has all kinds of meters to use technology to make battles better and more engaging and all kinds of
creative stuff."

I momentarily wondered if Russell had seen his site lately, since
his I-Zone had little more than a rudimentary crossword puzzle and
a phone-in rhyming game.

Clemente leaned in. He had a coiled energy. Even in an expensive suit, he seemed about to leap onto Russell's desk. I was ready too.
Consigliere, of course, could speak business with the best of them.
Now, maybe, was the moment to lay karaoke on Russell. This was
going to take some daring. (How could I have ever imagined business a collegial affair?) *The future of hip-hop is karaoke,* I thought to say,
but hesitated. I'd never pull that off.

$ $ $

From reading Russell's autobiography, which he'd published at age forty-four, I knew several important facts about him. Generally CEO memoirs opened with a personal crisis—Michael Eisner, who runs Disney, had chest pains; Lee Iaccocca, former head of Chrysler, was fired—and Russell's was no exception. Russell's was the result of almost "bust[ing] a cap" in a kid who was ripping off neighborhood drug dealers, an occupational category that included Russell at the time. Russell aimed a pistol, fired, and missed, a lucky break of the kind CEOs tend to get, and then learn from. Russell's lesson was to "take the entrepreneurial energy I was putting into drugs and create a business . . ."

As a rule, CEOs were supposed to be plain speakers with humble beginnings. Russell spoke plainly—though his plain-speaking tended to rely on words like shit, fuck, and motherfucker. And his background wasn't flashy, though his neighborhood in Queens was probably more middle class and suburban than the gritty urban settings often portrayed by hip-hop music. His parents both graduated from Howard University and had good jobs—his father, who sometimes quoted *Hamlet,* was a teacher, his mother a director for the Parks Department.

In the seventies, though, Russell would break with the CEO genre. While chief executives often tended to win by staying true to the clean-living lessons learned early—see, for instance, Jack Welch, the ex-GE CEO who talked at length of his mother's importance—Russell's life took inspiration from a slightly less wholesome experience. Unlike his CEO confreres, Russell spent considerable time, as he put it, "high," "tripping," "twisted," "dusty," "stoned," "wasted." He also sold drugs, though Russell sometimes sold fake drugs, an early entrepreneurial strategy that produced income while avoiding arrest.

Later, Russell would say he was lucky to have escaped jail or death. Yet, for the most part, he exulted in his past. And in particular, the encompassing new music that was part of it. Hip-hop lent coherence to every aspect of his young life, even, in his view, the busting-a-cap incident. "Sounds like a lyric from a rap by Slick Rick or

Chuck D, right?" explained Russell. "Nah . . . it was my life." (Actually, it was Russell's life just once—the single time he fired a gun in anger.) Still, as Russell saw it, hip-hop not only provided narratives to explain a young person's life, it matched the emotional pitch of that life. Hip-hop was exciting, and everything it touched felt a little more exciting, too.

Which was pretty much the defining insight of Russell's business life. He may have been among the first to understand that hip-hop would prove more than a passing musical style. Like rock 'n' roll, it would be a force in youth culture, black *and* white.

Russell had started in the music business as party promoter, then became music promoter and band manager. Later, he'd help start the first big hip-hop record label, Def Jam, which would become the Motown of its time. He followed with a fashion company, a magazine, an ad agency, TV shows, and films. He constantly spouted new ideas. "We're gonna do suits! Sharkskin," Russell would say. Or else he was gonna do a modeling agency, a café, a twenty-four-hour rap radio network. Some worked, others didn't. But as the influence of hip-hop spread from Harlem to Beverly Hills—informing everything from kids' clothing choices to their hand movements—Russell, with his stable middle-class upbringing, was well-positioned to bring this angry urban culture to the suburban mainstream.

Recently, he'd expanded to the Internet, launching 360hiphop.com, a site he sometimes said would be home for all things hip-hop. It wasn't entirely clear what Russell planned to offer at that online hip-hop home—or what he didn't plan to offer—but this much was certain: The Internet had become an imperative for every entertainment company. All the music companies, all the TV stations, practically every radio station, they were all doing *something* on the Internet. If Russell were to continue as an organizing force behind hip-hop, he'd better get with the Net.

Russell's friend Donald Trump once explained, "Russell sees the future." Russell, though, had been a little late to the Internet future. He wasn't what you'd call an early adopter. He didn't go in for e-mail. (An assistant read his.) There wasn't even a computer on his desk. Not long ago he'd gotten a sky pager. He was pecking at it inefficiently when a message came across.

"Welcome to the twentieth century, you asshole," it said.

"I almost waited too long," Russell muttered.

By the time Russell got around to launching 360hiphop in 2000, others had already been alerted to the promise of the urban space as it was called. Soon a dozen companies would compete to marshal the hip-hop demographic—the one Russell had helped create. Competitors would collect close to a $100 million in investments, and attract hundreds of thousands of regular visitors. And several of them—Hookt (which was affiliated with Puff Daddy and Eminem) and Urban Box Office (which raised close to $50 million)—would soon figure *they* were the destination for all things hip-hop.

Personally, Russell might be popular—some kids apparently recognized him more readily than the vice president of the United States—still, when I thought of his online project, I didn't see why people would stay at his site once his name induced them to visit. Russell threw out lots of reasons, sometimes, it seemed, whatever came to his mind. The Internet would be another "distribution channel" for content, he said. Russell once suggested that he had a specialized strategy for Internet content. He'd work with actors and rappers he knew—they, not bankers, had invested in his site—to develop characters, songs, sketches that could be distributed over the Internet. "Content incubation" was the term that someone came up with for this, as if Russell might be running an online workshop. Other times, he said he'd sell things: clothes, music, even ads. He'd do branding. He had a political bent, and saw the attraction of building a community of like-minded people. Russell had always been an opportunist. (I thought of him pushing fake drugs.) And the Internet was the next opportunity. But just what the nature of that opportunity might be Russell clearly didn't know.

Small wonder the Internet lately seemed one pounding headache to him. "I didn't realize I'd be coming into work every single day," he said not long ago. "That they'd be driving me fucking crazy, that [the Internet] would be my core focus."

Of course, when I looked at Russell's situation, I knew what he needed. Something to make visitors to 360hiphop hang around. Then, he could do anything else he wanted, sell stuff or advertise, build community, or incubate content. Karaoke, I figured, was just what he needed. Microphone in hand—and many computers came with one these days—hip-hoppers could record versions of their favorite songs, e-mail them to friends. They'd stay forever.

And so, as I gathered my wits in Russell's office, I told myself not to be intimidated. So business was a high-wire act. Still, I wasn't peddling a party trick. I had an important application, one which I still occasionally recalled hadn't yet been built; one which I wasn't entirely sure *could* be built. No matter. As I looked across the desk at the growing pile of chicken bones, I sensed that soon we'd get back on track. Personal chemistry failing and, admittedly, it hadn't gotten off to a roaring start, I counted on the force of my idea. With renewed resolve—and how revitalizing it was—I straightened myself in my chair and thought, *Russell* needs *me*.

$ $ $

So far, of course, Russell had managed to conceal his enthusiasm. He continued to eat and to talk. Perhaps I should say something, just to get us going. I fished around for the right thought. I suppose a few sounds might have escaped my mouth. "Let the man talk," Clemente said to me, referring to Russell. Which was the right advice. Russell had shown little interest in hearing what we had to say.

Russell began to lecture us on the attraction of the hip-hop demo. They're trendsetters, Russell wanted us to know, though as far as I could tell the trends they set were primarily in what the fashion industry calls accessories. "Hip-hop decided that the diamond and platinum Frank Muller watch was hot," said Russell. "They had it before the Syrian Jewish community of Ocean Parkway. That new Rolex that's not out yet? They wanted it. Jay-Z's had it way before anyone had it. That rubber Cartier that came out last week? These guys have had it for a long time. The platinum pager. The platinum mobile phone."

As he spoke, Russell carefully set pale chicken bones in a pile. It was like watching sand accumulate in the bottom of an hourglass. Our time, I sensed, was drawing to a close. I *had* to say something.

"Do you think," I interjected, "the hip-hop community would go for hip-hop karaoke?"

Russell leaned forward. His shaved head looked as glossy as a piece of wax. "What did you say?" he said. He seemed angry.

"Hip-hop karaoke," I repeated tentatively, three words I was certain Russell had never heard in one unbroken string.

Clemente shoved his $10,000 marketing favor at Russell, according to which, 14 million people said they'd be interested in an online site where they could sing along with the music.

"That's huge," Russell said. (Russell *was* a numbers person.)

"I think we've come up with an exciting, compelling, community-related application utilizing karaoke," said Clemente, speaking as fast as Russell, though as always, in a tone as steady and comforting as a therapist's. "We want to clearly communicate that we see a major opportunity here," he concluded. The word "major" might have been a bit much, but you couldn't blame him.

Russell wasn't moved. He'd finished lunch, folded the brown wrapper, packed it away in the trash. Our time was up. "You got to tell me what I can do for you," said Russell pointedly and, to my mind, confusingly. On one hand, he wanted to do something. On the other, he was about to bolt.

I caught Consigliere's eye. Maybe this wasn't the moment to introduce hip-hop karaoke TV. I'd reviewed with Consigliere what specific commitment we might ask for, though, truthfully, I'd imagined less pressured circumstances.

"Money," Consigliere had said. "Ask for money."

"But what are we selling him?" Clemente had wanted to know. He could be a stickler.

"How much?" I'd asked Consigliere.

"A hundred thousand." Consigliere said this like it was birdseed, though to me it sounded like quite a lot at a first meeting. Wouldn't that offend him? Any less, Consigliere had suggested, and he wouldn't take us seriously.

I wanted to be taken seriously. I thought of Russell's autobiography. "Nothing happens the way it's supposed to" was a piece of advice he passed along. (CEO memoirs almost always contained advice.)

"We'd like you to invest a hundred thousand," I told Russell, in what I hoped was an inoffensive tone.

Russell didn't bat an eye. His arms lay on his desk, describing a trapezoid. "Can't do it," he said.

"Okay," I said, and moved to the backup plan. "We'd like to build a hip-hop karaoke lounge on your site," which was the next idea Consigliere and I had discussed.

Russell pushed back then. He wore a bulky sweater. His bald head looked as large as a dinosaur egg. "*That's* what I wanted to get to," Russell said as if, remarkably, he'd all along been herding conversation this way. As if the hawking, the petulance, the put-uponness— as if the drama of the fucking thieves—were all an act. "I think it might be a great idea," he said, succinct for once.

"You do?" I said.

Russell smiled, his first. It was an ear-to-ear kind of thing, and made you want to smile too. "This sounds like a great traffic driver, sounds like a lot of fun. It sounds like there's a bunch of ways to leverage it," said Russell. I felt his charm.

"Who else is competing with you?" he asked.

"Nobody," we said in unison. "We're alone," an assertion we were happy to make, though it couldn't possibly be true. Having said that, though, it was easy to say more.

"We can put people in a virtual room and have them sing," I said.

"To one another," Consigliere added.

"You can do that?" said Russell.

"Yes." By which I meant I'd seen it done and, well, why not aim high?

"What a great community device," Russell said, just as Clemente had suggested. "I want to set up a meeting with you guys."

Russell went for his phone, which like anything technological was not on his desk.

"Where the *fuck's* my phone?" he said. He located it on the floor against a wall. He asked for the executive editor of 360hiphop. Russell put her on speakerphone. Now that we were all on the same side, he invited us to participate in a little joke.

"That karaoke part of the site is very good," Russell told her.

There was a pause. "Russell, I have no idea what you're talking about," she said.

"Good," Russell said. We all smiled. It felt great to be on Russell's side. "I just want to make sure before I send these guys down there," Russell explained, "They seem like they're pretty smart. If you meet with these guys I think something good could come of it. They have a whole elaborate karaoke plan."

A whole elaborate karaoke plan. I loved the phrase.

"It sounds great," said the editor.

"I'm going to put my friend on," Russell said, then turned to me. "What's your name?" he asked.

I reminded him. Russell passed me the phone and disappeared. As we let ourselves out of his office—I was careful to plug his refrigerator back in—we spotted him in heated conversation, apparently trying to sort out the theft from his store.

Chapter Nine

Majestically Skyward

LATELY I'D BEEN LOOKING at business plans, most of which read like zany cookbooks. They were heavy on the ingredients, with a single direction: combine. There was one important differentiating factor, however. They didn't have a cookbook tone. Business plans were generally couched in deep purpose and, in case you missed the point, "confidential" was marked all over the place.

More and more people asked for my business plan and so I decided to take a stab at one. In writing a plan, help was widely available. The Internet was full of business plan kits, do-it-yourself kinds of things that marched you through the steps. At one point, I tested the consultant waters. How about, suggested one consultant, something along these lines: "Karaoke commercializes a basic urge, the urge to sing," which I thought pretty strong.

In the end though, I opted not to model myself too closely on other plans, or get bogged down in lots of advice. I was after originality, I told myself. And, lately I'd begun to think I had a knack, an idea encouraged by a short dream. One morning I'd awakened with a curious phrase in my mind: "Monetizing eyeballs." The phrase was doubly curious since its meaning completely escaped me. Only after some research (and a call to Clemente) did I learn that my subconscious was turning over how to make money from the people who viewed a site—people, I learned, were referred to as eyeballs. I was enthralled. Not so much by the moneymaking challenge as with its appearance in my dream, which I took to indicate some aptitude for its solution.

And so, filled with an unexpected sense of suitability, I set out to write a business plan *my way*. I'd make it a narrative. The story of my business would communicate the excitement of the karaoke experience—the "look-feel," as I heard everyone call it. "Imagine yourself in a room with friends . . . ," I began. I worked up quite a head of steam. There'd be a host who'd guide you through the site and be your karaoke friend. And you could go to different rooms for different genres. We'd offer back-up dancers. I did, it turned out, have *a whole elaborate karaoke plan*.

Of course, "monetizing eyeballs" made an appearance. So did "sticky application." These days, Clemente had let me know that everyone in the Internet hunted for a sticky application, one that would make a user stick on a site.

In karaoke, it seemed, I had one.

"Very sticky," Clemente had agreed, which had made me quite proud.

Karaoke, I figured, might just be what the Internet really needed. "Listening to you gives me the queasy feeling you might be right," one doubting friend had conceded.

I'd taken a look at my competitor. Despite assuring Russell that no one else was doing karaoke, of course someone else was. For 99 cents, eatsleepmusic.com sold a karaoke song that could be played on a computer, an approach that immediately struck me as crazy. I figured most karaokers already owned the songs they liked to sing. Eatsleepmusic bet it could entice people to buy the same song twice, this time for a computer.

A business model, I'd lately learned, was how you'd make money. "How you *said* you'd make money," corrected a cagey entrepreneur. It gave me great pleasure to dismiss eatsleepmusic's business model, now that I knew what one was. I called Consigliere at work where he generally had to be quiet. "I live in cubicle land," he'd once whispered.

"We'll give it away for free!" I shouted at Consigliere by phone. I hadn't figured out how *I'd* make money. Still, I thought giving it away a brilliant strategy for gaining market share. "We'll kill them!" I continued, thinking of the competition. "Destroy them!" I might have added.

"You said you wanted to throw elbows," Consigliere replied quietly, though just then it occurred to me that, perhaps, what I really wanted to throw was tantrums.

Consigliere promised to take a look at my business plan. A few days later he showed up at the Chelsea Coffee Shop where we liked to meet at a tall round table. He wore high-top sneakers and an untucked shirt. Sometimes I thought how he'd been into the Internet early, and known many of the early players. He'd had a chance to join Jupiter Communications at the start, a company that went public. He declined, thinking it would never survive. His Internet company, RealTime, had been a portfolio company of idealab!, which had backed some high-profile Internet businesses. The first time I'd heard these stories I'd looked at him and said, "Wow, you *really* should be a millionaire."

Consigliere rolled my plan up into a trumpet of paper. "This isn't bad," he began and then listed the faults that as usual Consigliere managed to suggest weren't really mine, but due to the knuckle-headed nature of business. "Businesspeople don't really like to read," he said. "They prefer bullet points and charts. Get the narrative out of your system."

I knew that Consigliere was lately busy at his job. (After Real-Time folded, he'd gone to work for a consulting firm, and seemed to be in charge of getting the company's Web site built.) I knew this because he was sometimes curt on the phone, though he'd later apologize profusely. "Can't even keep my calendar up-to-date," he'd write in a follow-up e-mail. "Sorry for my haste." Then he'd add, "I've been having a blast." He said he was still willing to shoulder some key tasks. "I look forward to peeling into a spreadsheet over the weekend," he wrote. I was delighted. I'd never seen a spreadsheet.

At our next meeting at the Chelsea Coffee Shop, he flattened his spreadsheet on our usual high round table. His hyperactive leg bounced out a beat. "I think I discovered some ways to make money," he said. I felt as if he'd just pulled a quarter from behind my ear. Consigliere explained that we'd establish an Internet address— a destination site—where people could come to sing along with hip-hop, or whatever music they liked. Consigliere suggested they'd pay for this privilege, say ten cents a song. (He apparently dismissed without a thought my clever idea to give it away for free. He also dismissed, for the moment, the idea that we'd build karaoke for another site, which was what we'd told Russell.) It would sit on our site like a karaoke jukebox, which seemed straightforward enough. And yet this simple scheme—yes, there it was on paper—would generate millions of dollars. Consigliere's revenue charts curved majestically skyward. Eyeballs, I noted, were really getting mone- tized. Proudly, I transferred these charts into my business plan.

Chapter Ten

Work Rules!

TRAIPSING THROUGH the office culture recently, I found myself in unusual terrain—and I'm not just talking about Russell's place of business. The last time I'd regularly gone to an office was in the eighties when I'd worked at *Success!* magazine, and then I hadn't quite gotten the hang of it. I'd removed the tiles from the drop ceiling over my desk. That's better, I thought, I can breathe. I brought in an exercise mat on which I liked to take an afternoon nap. I didn't last long.

For someone like me, the office of the Internet seemed a most paradoxical place. On one hand, everywhere I went fun was in the air. People brought pets to work and played games and even, according to Nicholas Butterworth, that Brown grad who'd become CEO of SonicNet, then of MTVi group, snuck up to the roof for a quick hit of inspiration, that is, marijuana. Employees referred to this as "doing research." Apparently, the term stuck. One employee would say to another, "Wanna do some research?" Or "Got some research?" Work, it sometimes seemed, had been remade in the image of a college dorm.

On the other hand, I couldn't help but notice that work had gotten longer and more intense. *Much more.* One new CEO scheduled forty meetings a day—one every fifteen minutes over ten hours. He held meetings in cabs and in hotel corridors. He had meetings on the way to meetings. "And he made them all," a partner told me, which many people took as an indication he would succeed. At conferences, he'd set up a separate table for meetings and bang out twenty in a row. This CEO, Gerd Leonhard, of Licensemusic.com, slept as little as three hours a night, always carried a laptop and, since he traveled so much, five cell phones for different regions. This seemed a fairly typical regimen. Jobs, in fact, seemed endless. If it was dorm life, it had the hours of boot camp.

I found this perplexing. Was it really possible that work was so darned fun and, *at the same time,* crushingly demanding?

Work is no mystery. Almost everyone is introduced to it sooner or later. My mother once wished for me a certain amount of debt— she may have said *any* debt—which she figured would instill responsibility. Inevitably, I found a mortgage bill arriving in the mail, and phone and electric bills, and though I did not initially experience this monthly surfeit as responsibility, she was right. It connected me to the responsible world of work, which, I quickly learned, was a place to sit up and behave, act the grown-up, do what you were told, if you wanted to pay the bills. Work—and this was an early lesson— required a different set of behaviors than home. For instance, work had meetings and a dress code. My father had worn pressed white shirts to his office. When I landed an office job, I fiddled with the ceiling tiles, but I too bought dress shirts and borrowed one of his ties. The business world imposed *its* style on you. The office remade you in its image, in its uniform, in its conventions of seriousness.

Now, though, *everyone* in the business world seemed idiosyncratic. You almost had to be. I read about employees who brought to work their smelly pugs or their squawking mynah birds that sat adorably on their shoulders and shat on their keyboards. "Who are we to argue?" said the Web site of one company that seemed to believe that good employees—like good kids—needed to let off a little steam. These days, work embraced youth; not just its energy and talent, but its style. Obviously, the business uniform had been banished. Netscape's Web site suggested that a dress code—*any* dress code—was just a bit too parental. "Wear a neoprene suit," riffed the company, an adult determined to play along. Seriousness—in appearance, at least—was clearly the new faux pas. Unless you wore casual, funky clothes, unless your grooming habits shouted "college," who would take you for creative? For serious?

Even if you weren't all that youthful, work now seemed a place—actually *the* place—to bring out your youthful spirit. Go ahead, decorate your "work area with soda cans," suggested one company, getting the joke. The boss, it now seemed, facilitated youthfulness, even its irresponsible side. Several companies hired concierge services, a kind of *in loco parentis*. Employees could drop off cleaning at work or arrange to have a Mother's Day present bought and delivered.

Of course, recreational pursuits were everywhere in case you needed to get out the kinks in the middle of the day. One office had a rock climbing wall. Another a boxing ring. Another a movie room. There'd sometimes be keggers after work—or occasionally during. Usually, there was a game room. One company I visited had a jukebox and another a basketball court with a regulation-height basket *inside* the offices. Apparently, the CEO just *loved* the game. (Actually a couple of New York offices had regulation basketball hoops in the office.) At Netscape, you could get "a nice massage." At Patagonia, makers of expensive outdoor gear that the company now sold online, new employee orientation included a surfing lesson, surfboards provided. All the new symbols of work now linked it to play. A connection some made explicitly. As the head of Microsoft's Expedia, a Web site that let you book your travel online, said, "Work is not work. It's a hobby that you happen to get paid for."

And yet, while most everything about the technology, and the New Economy generally, was whip-smart, fun, you had to admit, often seemed dumbed-down. It was broad, frat-house fun and, frankly, a bit diligent, as if someone had read the manual, followed the instructions, but didn't necessarily get the spirit. Soda cans? Neoprene suits? It had the feel of a consolation. It was the fun that overachieving programmers had always been permitted. Programmers, of course, were the bright, socially awkward guys lately celebrated for their way with a computer. A few years ago, when I'd spent time with a bunch of them, most, it seemed, were intent on one thing: finding a girlfriend. Meantime, they were having a great time at the office.

At Microsoft, programmers used to enjoy blowing up traffic cones and getting the explosive-sniffing dogs to show up. As a practical joke, one programmer helped plaster up a colleague's door. Programmers were the group who first combined lunatic smarts with persistent horseplay, a combination that the entire free-for-all new business culture now delighted in, as far as I could tell.

And yet while the new style suggested that work was a casual place to kick back, to yuck it up, it was pretty clear that everyone worked longer. *A lot longer.* Maybe no one really seemed *into* a job, not the way they used to be, but they were there, like, all the time. (As programmers famously were. I remember one who limited his sleep to three hours a night until his program was written.) Maybe supervisors didn't "breathe down your neck," as one company said, and that was cool, but there were constant deadlines. In fundamental ways, work was a lot less like play than ever.

For one thing, you couldn't knock off at five. Every new businessperson I talked to seemed to have gotten the message. The new business style was supposed to be bright, positive, committed, *and* busy. "Do you take Saturday *or* Sunday off?" I heard one young CEO ask another. Busyness—along with fun, jeans, and recycling—had become an essential good in the contemporary workplace.

As a journalist, a busy journalist, I continually met deadlines, but my day hardly had the look-and-feel of busy—not contemporary busy. I talked on the phone to a single person. I read. I went off to the library to look up things. I typed, alone in a quiet room. Forty meetings a day? The thought made me woozy. Sometimes, I knocked off early. I talked of the need to procrastinate, to have, as one acquaintance called it, more gypsy time, by which she meant time to wander around without purpose.

How things changed as the New Economy revved up! Everything was geared to squeeze more in—more work. Calls were bundled; meetings stacked up. Was it any wonder that the boom beverage was hyper-caffeinated coffee? (Had anyone really ever had three-martini lunches?) Whenever I talked to Clemente—which was often these days—he seemed to have just stepped out of one meeting and be on his way to the next. In the Internet, as in college, I constantly heard about people pulling all-nighters. Not long ago, a book on "power sleeping"—otherwise known as napping—appeared. "A revolutionary and powerful approach to success in the workplace," crowed one reviewer.

Work no longer fit into a neat nine-to-five container. Already as the nineties got underway Boston University's Juliet B. Schor made a splash with her claim that life was coming to center more on work. People, she said, annually worked 162 hours more than twenty years earlier—which amounts to an additional month of forty-hour weeks per year.

The New Economy put an exponent to long hours.

I'd heard about Scott Kurnit, CEO of About.com, who liked to meet with every new employee during orientation. He could be a likeable, appealing fellow. He had one of those high-school-principal bald heads, and a chipmunk's smile. Plus, he gave each new employee a laptop, and along with it an encouraging talk. He liked to start by telling them—with, I imagined, a self-deprecating chuckle—not to believe everything they'd heard. "It's not that we mean to kill our people," he assured them, which no doubt brought a few titters from nervous new employees. "We're not a sweatshop."

Then, having set them up, Kurnit brought down the hammer, introducing the About.com formula, which was also the going formula in the Internet. "We mean to actually free you up while having you work all the time," he said.

All the time. That had to register with a new employee. No more laughter now. Now, as employees grew increasingly nervous, Kurnit explained the thinking behind the largesse of a laptop per employee. "The reason we give you a laptop is that if you take Monday off that's okay," he began, lapsing again into the understanding boss. Until, he added, "Because you can work also." As far as he was concerned, you could hang out it in the Hamptons. "You can do it"—work—"from a beach house, and you can be productive on your own schedule," Kurnit let them know.

Kurnit had actually codified this work-everywhere, work-always idea in a special language that he shared with the new employee, no doubt with a straight face. "We have nomenclature around here. WAH is 'work at home.' You just see it in the subject line [of an e-mail] and that means you're really working," Kurnit let them know. WOV is working on vacation. "I'm on vacation," Kurnit explained, "but I'm such a freak that of course I'm going to check my e-mail a couple of times a day and you can reach me on my cell phone." There was one designation that, though I got the impression it rarely appeared, did offer some hope of respite. ROV, he said, meant "really on vacation."

If anyone had chuckled as Kurnit began his rousing little talk, they weren't laughing any longer, I was sure of that. The self-made man's emphasis on hard work had, in the Internet, gone a little haywire.

It's worth remembering that as recently as the fifties, when my father caught a bus to the office at the same few minutes past the hour, America seemed on the verge of solving the busyness problem. One result of a booming 1950s economy was going to be a steady gain in free time. The four-day workweek was said to "loom on the horizon," once leisure—*not work*—was extending its reach. Some even worried of an impending crisis. *A crisis of leisure.* Soon, some feared, boredom could become epidemic. After all, it was predicted that by 2000, "we could have either a twenty-two hour work week, a six-month work year, or retirement age of thirty-eight." What a world it might have been! Senior citizen at thirty-eight! Waiting till retirement to have children!

Instead, work became a stalker. It tracked you down on vacation; it located you in the can. By now, it was a commonplace that work-any-where tools—cell phone, e-mail, pager, fax, all those clever devices once promoted as "freeing and empowering individuals," as the ads used to say—had led to Kurnit's work-everywhere culture. Previous generations struggled with overwork. They labeled it a disease, worka-holism. In the Internet, rising Internet public relations exec Michael Prichinello proudly told me he could be reached four different ways when he was on the road. One Saturday night, he joined a group of us at a restaurant. As appetizers arrived, I noticed Prichinello peering under the table, as if staring at his fly. On closer inspection, I saw that he was busily typing with two thumbs on a tiny keyboard.

"What are you doing?" I said with dismay.

"I'm talking to my boss," he answered. He held up his pager, showed me the keyboard. While we'd ordered, he'd received a dozen messages, answered a dozen times. Prichinello explained that his coworkers constantly shot e-mails back and forth on their pagers. Apparently they did this even when they were in meetings—even when they were in the *same* meeting. (Intrameeting communication could be important, Prichinello explained, though there were risks. During one client meeting someone sent an e-mail suggesting that the client was wasting their time and, mistakenly (the keyboard *is* very small), delivered it to the client's pager).

I wondered whether Prichinello's boss understood that he was out with friends. "Does he know where you are?" I asked, suggesting by my tone that an employee ought to have a night out.

"Of course he does," said Prichinello, who showed me his pager.

"Stop talking to those other people," said his boss's latest e-mail, meaning to his fellow diners.

It's difficult to recall all the enforced *non*work time there used to be. My father rarely got called at home or in a restaurant by his boss; work didn't seem to be on his mind unless he was there. My father read doorstop-thick Thomas Wolfe novels on his commute. Now, Long Island Rail Road passengers made urgent pleas into their cell phones, following up on sales calls. They sounded like boozy fans at a ballgame. It got so noisy that at one point the railroad considered quarantining these constant workers.

Clearly, vacations weren't valued as they once were. By the nineties, American vacations had shortened by 14 percent—a trend that bucked that in the rest of the world. Nothing suggested this as forcefully as a visit one summer from a European friend, an attorney. He had six weeks vacation. *Six weeks.* One day he took his family to a lake. The next day I suggested he might like to visit another nearby lake. "Oh, no," he complained. "Today we're just going to take it easy." No one in the Internet wanted to be caught taking it easy.

In the Internet, vacations, if they came at all, were hectic fare to be gobbled down like energy bars. I knew one young CEO who took a seven-hour car ride with a friend, starting one Friday night at 9 P.M. Once in the car, he announced, "I have to leave Saturday night. I have to be at the office Sunday." During part of the ride he worked away on his laptop, specing out a project for his programmers. During another part he slept. As if collapsing, he placed his head on the passenger seat and his torso and legs in the crawl space under the glove compartment. All told, he spent eighteen waking hours on vacation. Then turned around to drive seven more hours home.

He never complained. Just the opposite. "It was heaven," he'd say of the vacation. In fact, he'd call it the best vacation he'd had in six months.

I couldn't help but think that workaholism, once a disease category, had become a welcome new lifestyle. Indeed, one day I visited an Internet entrepreneur—he was on his second start-up—at his small office. Christian, forty-one and married, had curly hair, a *u*-shaped smile, and an appetite for the biographies of successful people. When I mentioned to him that I hoped to hire a sales and marketing team, he said "*You* will be the sales and marketing." Christian said he personally worked a hundred hours a week. If he slept eight hours a night, that left only twelve nonworking hours a week, including reading time.

When I pointed out to him that he worked a lot, he said, "What else is there to do?"

I felt obligated to suggest that there were many other enjoyable things to do.

"I enjoy working all the time," he said agreeably. It didn't really seem he could imagine any other kind of leisure.

$ $ $

Had it really come to this? For so long work and leisure had distinct, equally valued characters. They'd seemed a zero-sum game; the less you worked, the more time you had for leisure, and vice versa. My parents' generation didn't dislike work. Just the opposite. They rose early and worked hard. It was a point of pride for them. They'd inherited this tradition from Ben Franklin, himself an inheritor of this aspect of the Puritan tradition. Hard work was good for you; not just for your wallet, but for your character. (No wonder an excess of leisure seemed such a crisis.)

And yet, for this generation, work wasn't the "end-all be-all," as my mother would have put it. As Peter Drucker, the management thinker, explained, "In the past for people to admit that they enjoyed their work was simply—I wouldn't say it wasn't done—it wasn't expected." Work had a specific, circumscribed purpose. You worked to support your family. Will I be able to make a good living? Will I raise happy, healthy, successful kids? Those, according to Yankelovich, were the concerns of the fifties. Men of my parents' dogged generation were breadwinners. Even as a child, that much was clear to me. "Your father brings home the bacon," I can remember my mother, changing food groups, report. People weren't all the same—even in the conformist fifties. Still, through the sixties, 85 to 90 percent of people defined *a real man* as someone who was a "good provider." Work was instrumental for people of my father's generation, a means to an end. The end was to provide each of the kids a bedroom and a college education.

No doubt my father enjoyed the field of advertising. I had the impression he worked with some sharp cookies who had a pretty good time hoodwinking the rest of us. And yet I can hardly ever remember him *talking* about work. I knew more about my father's fiery socialist uncle than about his colleagues at Foote, Cone & Belding.

My father wouldn't have said that there was pressure to work all the time. And he didn't. *The Man in the Gray Flannel Suit* was one of the most influential books of the fifties. Tom Rath, the hero, explained the attitude toward work this way, "Maybe I could find a good honest job . . . which would pay me a decent living, but not require me to work day and night, pretending I want to be some kind of tycoon. . . . I want to get ahead as far as I possibly can without sacrificing my entire personal life."

For my father, and for Tom Rath, the office was not where they expected to enjoy themselves. In fact, my father didn't expect to be himself, not his *best* self, at the office. A premise of the old world of work was that a business guy could only really let his hair down at his split-level in Long Island or New Jersey. Business people experienced one set of pleasures at work; another at home. Life's most intense emotions took place in the family. That was where this businessperson got his dose of loyalty, devotion, commitment, passion, his "intensity of common purpose," as a writer of my parent's generation explained.

At the end of the workday, my father took a bus home to an armload of kids whose future he was saving for. Family was a "haven," as one writer his age put it. (Specifically, a haven from business.) He nearly always arrived in time for dinner—the theater of his life—where he presided over a solemn roundtable of the day's small events, one kid after the other. Except on the days of a high school soccer game, when he would magically appear at field side at 4 P.M., his suit jacket tossed over a shoulder.

My parents didn't do many of the activities that today pass for leisure. They didn't ski; they weren't beachgoers or exercise enthusiasts. They took vacations, but my father didn't really hang out with buddies, not many that I saw anyhow. He didn't work out at a gym; my mother returned to get her teaching degree as an adult, part of a lifelong interest in learning, but, still, they didn't attend enriching courses at the local college. My parent's hobbies, to the extent they had them, were home-centered. For a time, they improved the backyard. My father coached Little League. My mother led Cub Scouts. Occasionally, my father just liked to relax, which sometimes meant snoozing on the couch, his hands stuffed in his pockets.

He was typical of men of his generation. Doubters should take a glimpse at the business section of the Sunday *New York Times,* which ran large display ads for jobs—it's one place my father would have looked. Ad after ad made clear that good jobs mainly offered one thing: lifestyle. Tellingly, lifestyle occurred *outside* the office. In fact, in the fifties, advertisements suggested that the true advantage of a good job was its location. In 1957 one ad showed a man in jacket and tie. "I work at Delco Radio," he said, the advantage of which seemed to be that his workplace was "ten minutes or less from this homey spot"—the one sketched in the background. "Want to live in a pleasant suburban area convenient to NYC, Philadelphia, and seashore and mountain resorts?" asked an ad for a corporation based in West Trenton, New Jersey. If you worked for Sperry, an early computer company, you should know it was "situated for your maximum enjoyment of living."

The principal appeal of work was life in the suburbs, which was, quite explicitly, a good place to raise a family. "Your home on beautiful Long Island . . . will be convenient to shops and schools," said one ad. "It will be adjacent to the network of parkways which bring beaches, country, and New York City all within easy driving range." A man sought opportunity, of course, but really he wanted a reasonable commute.

Eventually, my parents would start a small school that helped many disadvantaged kids get on a college track. It was worthwhile, rewarding work. My mother directed the school, putting to use her teaching background; my father administered it. In ways, they anticipated themes of succeeding generations, including a willingness to go their own way in the pursuit of fulfillment at work. (My father may have been too much of a maverick for the corporate world. Also, he didn't like wearing ties.)

They worked long hours and were happy at the school. Still, their goal was to get out as early as they could—which they accomplished at age fifty-five. They weren't rich, but they had enough. Though they retired earlier than others, they fit in with their generation in this regard: They put great stock in the joys of not working. (And by the way, they fit in with Franklin, too, who, though he'd forever praise the benefits of constant effort, walked away from his printing business at forty to pursue politics, letters, science.) My parents didn't have big plans for retirement. They looked forward to putting their feet up. They wanted to relax, to enjoy themselves. They had travel plans. Perhaps they'd volunteer. My mother would sign up for courses, and teach others. My father at one point said he looked forward "to doing nothing," another goal resonant with the times.

The writer Frances FitzGerald interviewed retired men who came of age in the 1950s and 1960s. Few regretted leaving their jobs. They were proud of their careers—they'd been successful executives, civil servants, small businessmen, schoolteachers. Yet they retired as early as they could. Why? Work didn't appear to them a lifelong interest. It just hadn't been the most compelling subject of their lives. They'd worked in order to raise families, which they did, and then retired because they were "sick of working," hated "the pressure," had "paid their dues," wanted "to get out of the rat race," as they told FitzGerald. Their work seemed "a means of achieving a satisfactory private life—a 'life style'," as some put it." They'd worked hard all their lives and were happy to retire to that other domain, the one of leisure.

$ $ $

By now, of course, it wasn't always easy to tell the difference between the realms of work and leisure. In part, this was because who could really recall what leisure was like? If work incorporated some aspects of play, it served only as a reminder that work had won. It had overrun leisure like a victorious army. Of course there was foosball at work, and Dad didn't have that, did he now? But that seemed a pale reminder of family- or home-centered leisure, the kind where you could do things for the hell of it, which is the definition of leisure. "The Web has made the line between work and play extremely blurry," said Kyle Shannon, cofounder of Agency.com. "Even the line between taking a break and working is blurry."

Mainly the leisure spirit seemed a piece of nostalgia, sometimes a set piece. Patagonia employees were busy with meetings and a bustling ecommerce business, though of course they still liked to recount the old days when they'd climbed Yosemite or surfed Baja, or pursued "the wild dirtbag spirit," which referred to a time, now long gone, when everyone enjoyed temp jobs and endless summers.

In fact, leisure time, reported one poll, was down 40 percent.

Clearly, the crisis in leisure had been averted. Twenty-one percent of people said they had "no time for fun anymore." People reported stealing time from sleep to get things done. To read, for instance. Or to exercise, which is what play had become, even if it was spent on a treadmill, the one every fifties guy was trying to get off of.

"Leisure is dead," pronounced one writer. And yet, here was the stunning part—few people I met in the Internet complained. Just the opposite. The Internet culture, and indeed, many elements of the larger business culture, said good riddance. "Is there anyone left in this whole country over eight and under eighty who collects stamps?" this writer asked mockingly. Long hours—like sleeping in the car— weren't just a punishing new macho. People said they were happier at work. Home life seemed something to manage, to squeeze in, to worry about, completely reversing the trend of an earlier generation. Here was the real modern dilemma. Work was great. Home life was empty, lonely, without the companions, without the fun of work. After all, the intimacies, the friendships, the emotional life that once took place outside work—all those had shifted to the office. The idiom of family life—of community, of shared purpose, of respite— could now be found at work. "We confide in [our coworkers]," said one magazine. "We party with them and they become friends as well as colleagues."

The new business culture conflated personal and work lives, wrapped them into one pleasurable, dramatic package. Indeed, in Internet culture they weren't conceived of separately. My parents' generation said they worked in order to live, which they did outside of work. Those in the Internet no longer worked so that they could enjoy themselves away from the office or, God forbid, during retirement. As the Internet Age gathered speed, 48 percent of working women and 61 percent of working men claimed they would *still* want to work even if they had enough money "to live as comfortably" as they would like. In other words, the majority of working people could no longer imagine anything better to do with their lives than work. In the Internet Age, work *was* living. As one pundit explained, work, and in particular working long hours, was "more morally edifying" than the "leisure diversions that many imagine to be the end and meaning of life."

Finally, leisure, as one writer proposed, should now be considered "neo-leisure," leisure that took place at work. "Fact is," as this business writer put it, "no one who's living the life of the New Economy even wants a seven-hour day or a four-day workweek. Overwork is the goal. To go home at a decent hour is to be thought a shirker, a weenie, a wuss." The goal, as he put it, was work and leisure rolled into one. He offered the example of a friend. "On most days he knocks off at the humane hour of 6 P.M., makes the rounds of his favorite strip clubs with other members of his creative team, then returns to the office to play video games and "concept" way past the midnight hour," he said. So much for "maximum enjoyment of living" in the suburbs. No reading to the kids, no family dinners, no soccer games, nothing that once connoted leisure in this neo-leisure.

By now, I saw the shift. And no sooner had I become acquainted with the hectic new business world, than I, too, longed to be busy. I dreamed of having meetings stacked up like jets at JFK. To be busy, to *feel* busy. To have business meetings every half hour. To pull on some jeans, work till all hours, and have some fun. Fun the new way. I'd grab a health food bar and a Mountain Dew. I'd do some research, shoot some hoops, reel in the future. *Call out the bomb-sniffing dogs!* I thought. Let's get to work.

Chapter Eleven

Amateurs All

IN THE PAST, I hadn't by nature been an early riser. Now that I was an entrepreneur, I found that I rose earlier and marched directly to my desk, the one crowded with phones. I quickly planned my day, marking it out in efficient blocks. And though my new sense of purpose occasionally brought to mind Wilbur the determined pig from *Charlotte's Web*—breakfast at six-thirty, conference with rat until eight, etc.—I generally noticed a delightful increase in focus. I spoke faster and with added concentration and, on the whole, with the positive self-regard of a go-getter.

"You're really into it," a friend said with surprise.

"Yes, I am," I said, as if delivering a reprimand.

As a journalist, I'd spent a lot of time alone. Though I often interviewed people, frankly, a good deal of my social interaction occurred in my head. I daydreamed arguments with friends, acquaintances, customer service reps. I heard voices—doesn't everyone?—that took the other half of conversations. Now into my fourth month of KaraokeNation, I had meetings, which were intensely social things. In front of a crowd, even a small one, I was resolute, enlivened. Okay, I wasn't doing forty meetings a day, but, at times, I did three a day. Enough so that the same friend said, "All you do is go to meetings. When are you going to actually *do* something?"

He didn't understand anything. Business was mostly meetings. And, occasionally, something happened as a result. Or seemed to.

For instance, Russell's executive editor, the woman he'd put on speakerphone, really seemed interested the day Clemente and I visited her. We'd gone to her office, a large open room in a furniture warehouse. Russell had walked by apparently talking to the voices in *his* head. (Later I'd realize that, of course, he'd been on his cell phone.) Clemente and I pulled up chairs and double-teamed her. Clemente mentioned he'd been on the Internet for dozens of years, long before I knew it existed. He talked about the power of music as a marketing tool. I told her how I'd put people in a room to sing to one another. She said she couldn't wait to see the prototype, the one Clemente and I assured her was under development.

"It's being fast-tracked," I said and as I did, magically, I believed it.

Recently, I'd hired John Pelosi, a smart music-rights lawyer and former musician with a remnant ponytail. Soon I'd hire John Mancini, a button-down corporate lawyer with the most beautiful Rockefeller Center offices. Sometimes, I raised my voice to them. They didn't seem to mind. Apparently this was one benefit of having an attorney: a person you could mouth off to.

Soon, I'd tell people I was negotiating a deal for karaoke music rights. I couldn't actually put karaoke songs online unless I secured some kind of licensing agreement. Pelosi had made an offer on my behalf to one of the music publishers. I awaited a deal, which Pelosi assured me wouldn't be long in coming. Actually, I used the word "deal" a lot. I *loved* the word "deal"—and also the terms "revenue stream" and "market share" and "competitive advantage." These days I employed the vocabulary of business whenever I could.

"When's he getting married?" I was asked about a friend.

"It's a Q4 event," I said, referring to the fourth financial quarter.

I routinely carried a cell phone, and sometimes talked into it as I walked my dog or, occasionally, in a store, gesturing with my free hand. Now and then I'd get an urgent call from a fellow business leader. It happened one day at the deli where I'd gone for a tuna sandwich, a daily high point. (The counterman had, in fact, nicknamed me "Tuna time," until I'd asked him to change it. Recently, at my request, he'd started calling me El Duque.)

"No kidding," I said into the phone and moved to the canned-goods aisle. It was Thom Kidrin, CEO of Worlds.com. Kidrin was red-headed, hard-boiled, and my idea of a real businessman. He wore a coat and tie and carried a fancy pen. Kidrin knew the score. He wasn't taken in by win-win scenarios. "He's going to want something," he'd say of another businessman. Worlds.com created 3D environments on a computer. You controlled animated characters, moved them around, saw what they saw. It was incredible, with one drawback. There just wasn't that much obvious need for a 3D environment yet. Of course, though, Kidrin and I could both see this: It would be great to have a 3D-karaoke lounge. Kidrin had called me on my cell phone in the canned-goods aisle to talk about a deal.

"A deal?" I said feigning indifference. I caught the eye of a fellow deli shopper. He was comparing two brands of vegetarian baked beans. The term deal seemed to delight him, too. He gave me a neighborly thumbs-up. Kidrin and I set up a meeting.

Of course I knew that somewhere out there a class of professional Internet businesspeople existed. Jeff Bezos, founder of Amazon.com, was named *Time* magazine's Person of the Year in 1999, and so I imagined he probably was one of them. He might laugh like a goose—it was some kind of honk apparently—but he no doubt had financial and management skills. He wasn't sentimental. He knew business had one purpose: return on investment.

And yet, the Internet was hardly dominated by professional businesspeople or their parochial concerns. Mostly, business on the Internet seemed a glorious amateur event. All entrants were welcome. Thankfully, the Internet set most measures of success forward some time in the future which, considerately, helped blur the distinction between amateur and professional. At the moment of his glamorous award even Bezos was, as *Time* magazine indelicately noted, "losing his pants."

To be taken seriously in business you really only needed to conform to the new style of business. You'd better spout ideas, work like the dickens, demonstrate a youthful sense of fun (an infectious laugh wouldn't hurt either), and crucially, you ought to be passionate. These days, you heard a lot about "the business case for passion," as one CEO put it, a case previous generations hadn't felt a need to make.

It was worth remembering that for most of the twentieth century, business proposed the opposite style. *Get down to business. Be businesslike. Act professional.* Even those everyday phrases evoked not passion but calm, reasonableness, reliability. From the fifties onward businesspeople "learned to think of themselves as rational problem solvers," reported authors Leinberger and Tucker. And problem-solving "was a dispassionate discipline," as they pointed out. "It was emotionally neutral, detached, and above all, professional." Logic, objectivity, analysis, evaluation—these were the watchwords of business through the sixties and seventies. In his study of American emotional style, Peter Stearns found similar currents. He reported that for most of the twentieth century heated feelings were thought to swamp clear-headed thought, the kind you needed in business. "Emotions," he said pointedly, "interfered with economic objectives." No wonder managers, as Leinberger and Tucker explained, put "faith in their ability to rationalize and measure everything." Indeed, if you couldn't measure it, why talk about it? Financial techniques, inventory control, cost analysis, and all the rest were more than a set of tools. "They became the vehicle through which the manager understood . . . reality," reported Leinberger and Tucker.

Even in the early nineties, an MBA candidate wouldn't have heard much about passion. Charlie Yi, a management consultant who'd later work in the Internet, entered the University of Chicago Business School in 1993. "I don't remember ever hearing the word 'passion,'" he told me. In fact, as Stearns said, business mostly aimed "to replace intensity with a blander emotional regime." Businesspeople of a previous era were supposed to be cheerful, and not reveal their cards; their work style should be "impersonal, but friendly," something like the courteous but unengaged customer service associate.

That was hardly the personality the new businessperson aimed for. Suddenly business was like jazz: hot, improvisational, passionate. Indeed, for a time, passion seemed about the most popular word in business, and not just Internet businesses. Viacom CEO Sumner

Redstone called his autobiography *A Passion to Win*. Jack Welch, former CEO of GE, called passion the trait he most valued in an employee.

In the Internet, passion was the price of admission. Indeed, large parts of the business culture seemed to believe that a key to success was the right buoyant attitude. "You have a far greater opportunity to be successful with something you're passionate about," argued shaved-headed Randy Komisar, a Brown alum who helped launch WebTV and TiVo. Passion was important in promoting an idea, and apparently essential in securing investment. Nobody, it seemed, would fund rational or methodical entrepreneurs any longer. "We sought to prove the thesis that passion for the work and success in the business were inextricably linked," explained Jerry Colonna, CEO of one of the era's best-known venture capital firms, Flatiron Partners. "If you think the Internet is a story about money you're missing the story. It's all about the passion." One passionate entrepreneur, the CEO of StarMedia, a kind of Spanish-language AOL, told Colonna he intended to reunite South America, remaking its national borders, undoing its colonial history, which, though it suggested a thought disorder of significant proportions, was just the right note to strike. "That kind of passion is infectious," said Colonna, who invested.

And so, though I occasionally felt a fake, a rank amateur pushing a cockamamie scheme or worse, a nut exchanging deranged looks with deli customers, to my delight few people treated me that way. I had no background, no particular aptitude or expertise, no compelling story. Yet I did have this: great intent. As long as I was out there trying, talking, pushing, "living and breathing it," as Kidrin put it, as long as I was passionate, I seemed pretty much indistinguishable from almost every other entrepreneur hustling to make his dream come true.

Still, a few niggling doubts persisted. Could my smidgen of an idea, and my passion, really turn into a multimillion-dollar business? One member of my board of advisors thought I should sit down with a seasoned Internet entrepreneur and solicit some feedback. He suggested Joseph Park, CEO and cofounder of Kozmo.com, who, though only twenty-seven, had quickly raised $300 million from investors—including $60 million from Amazon and millions more from Flatiron. Park was perhaps the most celebrated new entrepreneur in New York. Particularly intriguing was that, though now widely respected, Park had very recently been an amateur, just like the rest of us.

"Joe was a hero to the amateur," said one of his top executives. In fact, for all his success, Park struck lots of people as a business kid, antic, stirred-up, a little surprised to be taken seriously. "I'm talking to so many people I used to read about in *The Wall Street Journal,*" I'd heard him gush. "Now these people are talking to me." (Bezos among them.) Park couldn't get over the whole thing.

$ $ $

Only a few short years ago Joseph Park had worked at Goldman Sachs in Los Angeles—not a hotshot dealmaker, but an analyst. Still, he was a banker, a prestigious position in the minds of his immigrant Korean parents. And yet to Park, it had seemed a little dull. I'd heard Park explain this by alluding to Kevin Spacey's character in the film *American Beauty.* "Spacey was living a very boring life," Park said, referring to Spacey's job selling advertising over the phone. "This is exactly what I was afraid would happen to me. I didn't want to be that guy in the movie, someone just very average."

In his forties, Spacey escaped his bland life to lift weights, smoke marijuana, chase a teenage girl, and work at a fast food restaurant. Soon, Park told his parents—who owned a couple of dry cleaners—he'd quit one of the more impressive jobs anyone in the family had ever landed to launch Kozmo, a bicycle delivery service named, in part, for his favorite cocktail, a pink Cosmopolitan.

Kozmo wasn't a particularly complicated or technology-dependent idea. *Why didn't I come up with that?* most people thought, which was part of its allure. (Actually, I had to check, but I thought I *had* come up with it during those brainstorming sessions with my wife and neighbor.) One day Park had ordered John Grisham's *The Rainmaker* from Amazon.com, which promised him the book within a couple days. Park, though, wanted his Grisham instantly, and he figured others wanted their purchases instantly as well. Park decided to cater to impulse shoppers. He would take orders over the Internet, then dispatch messengers to deliver the goods. And he wouldn't just deliver books; he'd deliver lots of things, from aspirin to CD players. (Kozmo would become the largest seller of Ben & Jerry's ice cream in New York. "I bet we feed half the potheads in New York," Park once said.)

Park had a vision, which he'd sometimes invite a listener to experience as a vision. "Close your eyes," he'd begin, "and imagine a time when no one will go to a physical store."

Soon thousands of Park's messengers bicycled to thousands of doors with videos and a snack. I'd seen Kozmo's business plan. It was actually quite forceful—I understood why one investor was alleged to have jumped on the idea. (Urban Fetch, a competing business, was launched by a venture firm who'd seen Park's business plan.) It wasn't clear to me how Kozmo would make money. Still, you had to admire Park. At a time when he was living on a couch, he told people, "We'd like to eliminate the word 'errand' from the language." Later, he'd add, "We want to be eFedEx." Though in an instant, Park changed his mind. "We'll buy FedEx," he shouted.

I knew Park's parents had been shaken by his job decision. Dull respectability hadn't seemed such a burden to them. They recalled that their son hadn't always appeared a shoe-in for success. As a teen, he'd crashed the family car, been kicked out of school. No wonder, Park had hesitated to let them in on his latest career move. In Park's telling, the family was at dinner when, while asking for the *kimchi,* he snuck in the information that he'd quit Goldman. The news pushed his father into a long brooding silence. Get yourself to church, counseled his mother.

Instead, irrepressible Park moved to New York to set up what seemed like a business clubhouse. He and several employees—his college roommate was a cofounder—lived in the Kozmo warehouse. Park showered at the gym. (Then lent his ID to someone else who, as Joe Park, also showered at the gym.) By day, he tried to raise money in his only blue button-down shirt; at night, he and the rest of his company played video games. Or else they made deliveries, promising to get orders to a customer in under an hour. Once CEO Park, racing downtown on a banana-seated bike, got sideswiped by a car. (He headed to the hospital, though first he called for someone to complete his delivery.)

It was all a little risky, and not just the snake through city traffic. When he quit Goldman at age twenty-six Park hadn't held a job—*any* job—for very long. He had no clue how to build a Web site, let alone a business. But Park did have one thing going for him. He'd intuitively mastered the exciting new emotional style of business. Indeed, Park would become a poster boy for the passionate new tone of business. A CEO, Park said, had "to be really passionate." And show it. Which he felt was one of his assets. He bragged that others could "feel the passion" when he talked about Kozmo, which he'd say he loved. Literally. "Kozmo is my baby," he said protectively. He once said he might never have any *other* kids.

Park's passion paid off. One day he fished a tie—a tie borrowed from his PR agent—out of a pile of rumpled clothes. "Does this go?" he asked an employee, and held a yellow tie up to his blue shirt. Then he headed to a studio to pose for the cover of *Industry Standard* magazine. The magazine named Joseph Park Internet CEO of the Year and described him celebrating at a bar by climbing onto a baby grand piano. Park, a cigar in one small hand, a pink Cosmopolitan nearby, shouted passionately to his employees, "I . . . P . . . Ohhhhh!"

I had no doubt that Park was in a position to tell me all I needed to know. His success wasn't the result of cutthroat insider shenanigans. He hadn't pumped and dumped. Frankly, Kozmo didn't seem capable of that kind of rigorous execution. Not long before, Park had missed a payroll. No, to me, likeable and passionate Joe Park seemed proof that business was within everyone's reach.

I'd read about Park and seen him on TV; later, I'd see the fine documentary about him, *edreams*. If I could only get him to tweak my idea, my presentation, then I'd really have something, I thought. "How did you do it?" I wanted to ask.

Soon, of course, Park would be rich. Kozmo had recently filed to sell its stock to the public. Three short years after quitting Goldman, Park would be worth $150 million, if everything went according to plan. The figure took your breath away—Park's, too, for that matter. "It's a little embarrassing to talk about," said Park.

One of my advisory board members knew Park and agreed to make a call. I made a follow-up call. And, with all my new energy, called again and again. Just now, exuberant Park was in a quiet period, the required media silence before the public offering. Park, though, was something of a talker. (His fellow execs couldn't actually shut him up.) Apparently the silence was killing him. He said he'd be happy to meet with me. I was as excited as could be.

Chapter Twelve

Passion's Profit

IT WAS THE SPRING of 2000, five months into my business adventure when Consigliere and I headed to Kozmo's Wall Street office, headquarters to what was now a four-thousand-employee operation. Fifteen months ago there'd been ten. Consigliere had cobbled together a presentation based on my business plan and his spreadsheet. The cover mentioned KNation—people couldn't reliably pronounce KaraokeNation—though he listed our parent company as Throwing Elbows LLC, our private joke. Consigliere added a tagline, "Something to Sing About." I marked the whole thing "Confidential."

I was excited, nervous. A meeting like this, anything could happen. I found myself believing someone like Park might seize on our idea, pick up his phone. Perhaps he'd want to get in early, take a strong ownership position. As Consigliere and I waited in a small lobby, I couldn't help but think that something good was about to happen. "You never know," Consigliere agreed. He usually did. (It hadn't then occurred to me that Park didn't really have any money. He was a salaried employee living in a corporate hostel, an apartment with four bedrooms, half a dozen rotating roommates and, according to one visitor, a single working lightbulb.)

Unfortunately, Consigliere was sick in the most cartoonish way. He had a sturdy constitution, and yet at times he seemed to tick with ill health. There was gout, acute toe pain that sometimes forced him to go shoeless at work. He suffered occasional sleeplessness. There was something with his back as well; a pinched nerve was mentioned. He had jaw pain. He juggled meds. He'd had that heart attack, and had required some complicated surgery. And of course, he was trying to lose a few pounds. Now, in Kozmo's charmless lobby, Consigliere looked as pale as the chalky walls. "I didn't want to let you down," he said touchingly. Still, by the time Park walked in a few minutes past 8:30, Consigliere's head had collapsed into his hands— the act of inhaling seemed to nauseate him. He could barely shake Park's hand.

Not that Park noticed. He was short, wide-bodied, overbuilt, like a pint-sized action hero in khakis and button-down shirt. He had a round, wrinkleless face, long, narrow sideburns, and one of those hairdos that only TV adolescents can pull off: His dark hair was short except in the front where it stuck straight out over his forehead. He had apparently combed in some kind of goo, which made it seem as if he'd stepped straight from the shower. Clearly, he was a morning person. He was full of pep. He grabbed our hands one after the other and led the way.

In my brief experience, I'd learned that executives generally enjoyed a crowd. They pulled people into meetings, and then, quietly slipped away themselves. They liked to remind you that, though delighted to see you, they had many pressing engagements. Park wasn't like that. He hadn't always had an assistant. Later a staffer would join our meeting, but at first it was just the three of us in an oppressively low-ceilinged conference room that with a start, I recognized from TV. (Like everyone else, I'd become a business fan.) It was here that Park had suggested to his management team, "We're going to have an Amazonian market cap." It was a glorious prediction, though now that I was in the room, I was more struck by the company's drab surroundings than its exciting future. An air vent wheezed; the entire room seemed to breathe. I thought I saw skid marks on the walls, none of which, come to think of it, appeared very substantial. I sensed that a well-placed smack would level the place.

Park took a chair, placed a giant Starbucks coffee cup on one of the half-dozen folding tables that were shoved together in the center of the room. (For the right to market in Starbucks stores, Park had recently promised that company $150 million he didn't have, a move he referred to as "confidence.") I suddenly thought how Park had stared down banker's respectability and come out the other side. Not that I could imagine Park grave or anxious or, even, really, very serious. He had a quick and unusually raucous laugh, a bumping *hah-hah-hah* that seemed to go off with almost no prompting. (Imagine a pickup truck carrying cinder blocks over speed bumps. That was the sound of Park's laugh.)

Right away, I let Park know that I'd long loved karaoke.

"Karaoke?" he repeated, pronouncing it Asian-style with a long final *a*.

"Yes," I said firmly. For emphasis, I drilled a finger into the table. I might have been planting seeds. Karaoke had been a family thing for me. "Since childhood, really," I suggested. By now, I knew that exaggeration was permissible, even expected, in business. Project confidence. Sound positive. Let others know you believe in yourself. As Consigliere alerted me, "Everything is sales." It was a piece of information I hadn't taken as altogether happy. After all, he'd illustrated the thought by punching himself in the face.

Still, I'd felt I needed a bold opening statement. Perhaps I wasn't going to reverse colonialism. But the singing-is-my-life theme seemed more compelling than, you know, I drank too much one night and, luckily, ended up at a karaoke bar.

"We really think," I told Park and immediately regretted the word "really," "karaoke is an unrecognized form of mainstream entertainment." Though I didn't have Clemente—he was at his home base in California—I had his impressive survey numbers. I added that Hollywood had already sniffed out the karaoke trend, making a karaoke movie, *Duets*. Gwyneth Paltrow starred. She sang. "Not badly," I said, though I hadn't seen it.

"Get out, get out!" said Park in amazement. I noticed that when excited he tended to say things more than once.

"And MTV has a daily karaoke show," I added excitedly.

"Really," said Park.

As the presentation built, so did my enthusiasm. I was on a roll. I gestured, a bit wildly perhaps. My fingers might have been forming the edge of a pie crust. Once I'd seen a clip of Park making a presentation. Afterward, Park confided, "While I was going through the story I was like, 'This sounds really impressive.'" I felt the same. Except that my conviction, so fervent, and applied to such a specific idea, momentarily struck me as a fundamentally funny thing. I let out a small unexpected laugh of my own. Park didn't seem to mind. I glanced at Consigliere. He was sick and tilted from side to side in his chair.

"Karaoke," I continued, gathering myself, "is an online brand waiting to be claimed." People loved to sing karaoke. I simply had to provide them the means to do it online. That was my argument. (Or, as my consultant had suggested, I simply had to devise a way to charge them to do it online.)

Park grasped the idea pretty quickly—"the demand side," he said. I was elated. I'd actually worked a ton on this. I realized that because occasionally I performed a thought experiment. I imagined doing the research again—knowing already how one question led to a second and then a third—and, each time, I felt as beat-up as that salesman Consigliere mentioned, the one taking it in the face. I'd interviewed every karaoke machine maker in the country, almost all the karaoke music manufacturers, and most of the karaoke music sellers. I now subscribed to karaoke magazines; they were stacked in my office. Toothy singers stared at me from their covers. I intended to read them. I thought proudly that I'd gathered the most comprehensive figures on karaoke sales in the country. I'd learned to draw colorful graphs using the data. "You're getting good at that," Consigliere had said, never missing an opportunity to encourage me.

"I would say you almost provided too much information," Park commented, which I, at first, took as a compliment. Then he laughed that counterintuitive laugh of his.

Consigliere looked off. He was suffering and couldn't do much good. Still, his presence calmed me. I knew he'd been through this before. ("Half a Consigliere is better than no Consigliere," Clemente agreed.)

I showed Park a list of the different products we'd conjured up, things we expected people to use at our Web site—karaoke jukebox, karaoke virtual bar, karaoke party game, karaoke e-mails, karaoke duets—each of which I repeated in slightly different language to suggest that it was also a revenue stream.

Suddenly Park interrupted. He emitted a sharp, humpbacked laugh, then said he had an idea for us. *Just what I'd been waiting for!* Perhaps he'd roll up sleeves and pitch in, or better yet, gather us close and say, *Let me tell you how the thing is done.*

Instead, Joe Park spoke three emphatic words. "Go to Japan," he said.

I thought he was joking. For once, though, he didn't laugh. His features were curiously immobile, which made him appear sad.

"Okay," I nodded tentatively. I looked at Park as if he were a bratty kid, the kind you couldn't really blame, and still couldn't bring yourself to like. He couldn't possibly mean that I should go to Japan.

He did. Park thought we might be missing the real revenue boat by restricting ourselves to America. In Japan, he said, karaoke was as popular as baseball was here. Karaoke was a $6-billion-a-year industry in Japan. Of course, I knew that. I'd been on the phone with the head of the All-Japan Karaoke Industrial Society in Tokyo who, after some unpleasantness—he acted as if I were after trade secrets—sent me his annual report *in Japanese.* (I'd had Ilan look it over.)

Okay, everyone admired big-thinking. I'd read about the CEO who mortgaged his home to pay for an ad on the Super Bowl. Should I take out a loan and head to Tokyo? I couldn't imagine whom I'd speak to. The prickly head of the All-Japan Karaoke Industrial Society?

The conference room sounded noisier than ever; the vent seemed to pant. "Listen," I started to say, but Park wasn't to be interrupted. Apparently *he* was on a roll now. Park also thought we needed a good technology partner. The best.

"Lock in the technology," he said, his eyes as big as seashells. He had another word for me *"Sony,"* he said with such drama I wrote it down. He thought Sony might be an answer to both the Japan and the technology issues.

I'd once heard Park explain that the Internet businesses were "a momentum play," which sometimes confused outsiders, most of whom figured they had an intuitive grasp of business. Your income in selling something had to be greater than your cost in producing it, that was how most people assumed business worked. The Internet didn't always operate on that assumption. You needed a credible account of how you'd reach profitability. But until then, what counted was that you convincingly show you had the momentum to get there. To irascible old-economy folks this was a little like saying that the measure of good city government wasn't clean streets or low crime or a balanced budget, but parades, bonhomie, and stopping jaywalkers.

Still, most Internet people believed that momentum mattered immensely. The beauty of this belief was that until you arrived in the promised land of profit, you could lose truckloads of money. "No one cared how much money you lost," Park once pointed out. Which was fortunate since one recent year he'd lost $27 million on revenues of $3 million. Kozmo, in fact, lost money on almost every delivery it made. (Though of course it lost *more* money *not* making deliveries.)

Kozmo's hoped-for path to profitability wasn't complicated. Once you ordered a video from Kozmo, Park figured he had you as a customer. He owned "the customer relationship," which might not seem a thing that could be owned, but apparently was. Videos were his Trojan horse. They got him in your door. But he really wanted to sell you stuff with big profit margins, like CD players or aspirin or eventually downloadable movies. For Kozmo to break even, the average customer had to pay about $25 per order, and he was moving in that direction, though at the moment the average order was closer to $10.

Park didn't care. What worried him—and investors, too—was momentum, which suggested that profitability was attainable. Several things could indicate momentum, among them: losing less money each year, gaining market share, signing partners. The day Kozmo signed Starbucks—even if the deal cost Kozmo $150 million it didn't have—Park received frantic calls from investors who suddenly wanted in.

The momentum play was, in a sense, the one that Park applied to all Internet businesses. It was the one he, perhaps unconsciously, fastened onto my slim venture. What would create momentum for KNation? Why, of course. A deal with Sony.

Park had several other comments, each of which he introduced with that bumpy laugh of his. He said we needed to work on our business model. (Actually, he may have said that we needed to *get* a business model.) "Really focus on how you're making money," he said. "Like right now, I would say, if you asked me 'What is KNation trying to do?' I have like six or seven different ideas." *"Hah-hah-hah-hah."* He continued "The challenge for you is to focus on one or two and just build that piece out and do that really, really, really well." He wasn't finished. "Make sure you're the leader in that space," he added. "Once you gain that type of dominance then you start leveraging what hopefully will be a really strong brand into other categories."

I suddenly wished Clemente were here to appreciate Park. He took a real interest in this kind of talk, and I just knew he could throw in some fancy touches of his own. So could Consigliere if he'd felt up to it. (Though later, I got the impression he might have taken Park on if he'd been healthier. "Cosmopolitans? Hah!" Consigliere would snort. It was a derisive reference to an aspect of Park's branding strategy, the part where he named his company, in part, for his favorite cocktail.)

For my part, I was enchanted. Park seemed to me a giggly maharishi, one to whom I owed allegiance for merely hinting that KNation could be a household name, a category leader. Suddenly I pictured KNation a strong brand, one whose employees wore colorful jackets, just like Kozmo delivery guys. I took his suggestions as a roadmap, and was eager to get to work.

So, then, to summarize, though Park had, I felt, generally been encouraging, he highlighted a few areas for further consideration, namely technology, partners, markets, business model—and, before we left, he wanted to mention one more quick thing.

"The key is to have the right people who are completely committed," he said, and let out another laugh. "Maybe you want to get an entrepreneur," Park suggested. "Someone who's going to spend every single waking moment building this business." Park thought I needed a CEO.

Perhaps *I* shouldn't be so eager to get to work. "A CEO?" I said, a bit hurt that he hadn't noticed my executive potential.

"Someone with passion," said Park, the kind he said was demonstrated by a commitment of the 24-7 variety. Park was off. This was clearly a favorite theme. "I believe that was one of the successes I had with Kozmo, with all the business partners that we've been able to sign up, and all the capital that we've raised. Every time we talk about Kozmo," he said, "you see the passion." I was sure that was true.

Consigliere suddenly seemed really sick, like he might have to dash from the room, a possibility that I found myself hoping might suggest the kind of passion to impress Park.

So, okay, I added one more item to the list. Management. I wasn't put off. I couldn't really account for it. Somehow, in the midst of what would later seem a long list of essential defects that ought to be addressed simultaneously, I was unflappable, which I counted a plus.

"So, do you think," I persisted, "someone would invest to build the KNation site?"

Park momentarily looked around the room. His eyes seemed to rest on a dark scuff mark. My eyes followed his. The air vent made asthmatic sounds. "There's definitely an opportunity here," he said slowly and then picking up speed and, I thought, enthusiasm, he looked me in the eye. "Raising money to start the business itself is something I think, definitely, there are people out there who would invest," he said.

"Wonderful," I said.

Then he added, "Good luck," and let out a last wild, endearing tripod of a laugh.

"Thanks," I said, and left accompanied by Park's late-arriving assistant who nervously took us aside. He wondered how serious I was. Karaoke had thrown him.

"Of course I'm serious!" I shouted, and almost grabbed him. Perhaps this venture had once struck me as a fun thing to do with friends, a parlor game to spice up, as Park would have said, a boring life. Lately, I found I cared. I wanted karaoke to succeed. It was a real complication. What was there to do? I knew people who went overboard. One young start-up CEO invested his inheritance to develop software to aid stereo salesmen, an important initiative for all I know. "Next week I have to decide whether to sell my car," he said. So karaoke wasn't particularly worthy. Was strawberry milk? Was *Buffy the Vampire Slayer*? And what was so laudable about a bicycle messenger service that lost money on every delivery? I, too, had crossed some line.

What a remarkable turn of events. On certain days, I believed hip-hop karaoke a good idea, a moneymaker. I believed this with passion. And passion, I was about to learn, is a dangerous thing.

Chapter Thirteen

The New World of Work and the Culture of Self-Fulfillment

NOT LONG AGO, I came across a new, and to me, shocking business magazine. *Fast Company* said it covered the new business world, and so I eagerly leafed through its pages. After all, I was continually on the lookout for a guide to the strange, new businessland in which I lately found myself. I mean passion and commitment (even nice massages), frankly, those sounded to me like dating terms. And how about rooftop research, casual clothes, fun, youth, endless hours? Didn't those strike *you* as unusual elements on which to build a serious-minded business culture? *Fast Company,* just a few years old, was one of the era's most successful new magazines. Clearly, it had struck a nerve. It had been selected outstanding magazine of the year by the American Society of Managing Editors—the most prestigious award in magazines—as well as by *Advertising Age.* In just a few years it had amassed 700,000 subscribers, not far behind the circulation of *Fortune* or *Forbes.* (This was the kind of number that prompted Gruner + Jahr to shell out a reported $350 million for the publication, an astounding figure.)

And yet, after spending a short time with this extraordinarily successful business publication, I was surprised to learn that my hoped-for guide to the new business world didn't really cover business, not in a way that suggested that actual events took place. *Forbes, Fortune,*

BusinessWeek—or Internet magazines like *Industry Standard* and *Silicon Alley Reporter*—those publications were stuffed with news. God knows there'd been enough business news in recent years, what with the economy roaring and the future bearing down on all of us. On the covers of *Forbes* and *Fortune* and *BusinessWeek,* companies tilted at one another or at the government or at the future. In issue after issue, it was the clash of capitalism, serious stuff, often illustrated by a photograph of a man's determined head as big as a TV.

Fast Company, by contrast, featured bright colors on its covers, the kind that might actually glow in the dark, and bold, cartoony graphics. I couldn't really picture self-respecting businesspeople toting the thing into meetings. One featured a yellow butterfly, another a variation of a giant smiley face. Plus, *Fast Company* appeared almost timeless. It seemed that month after month the magazine ran slightly different versions of the same story. One typical cover story asked: "To get rich, do you have to be miserable?" Another read: "I gotta get a life." And then again, "Money! Power! Fame! (and other ways to self-destruct)." A year later, a cover featuring that bright yellow butterfly explored—or, reexplored—the theme "How to Design a Life That Works." Which isn't much different from another cover the same year: "Betrayed By Work? Or Inspired."

Fast Company used to say it wanted to be the *Rolling Stone* magazine of business. It wanted to be very revolutionary, just like that famous music magazine born in the sixties. And *Fast Company* did obediently employ some of that era's choice jargon. "Break the Rules" was one bit of period sloganeering that *Fast Company* dropped into what it called, with its usual light touch, a "manifesto." But I hardly believed that *Fast Company* had unearthed a deeply rebellious new capitalist. John S. Reed, when CEO of Citicorp, had said, "I am a revolutionary," adding impishly, "as you may know," but let's face it, the notion that the CEO of Citicorp was a revolutionary would make a self-respecting revolutionary's skin crawl. (The John S. Reed who wrote *Ten Days that Shook the World,* about the Russian Revolution, and led the Communist Labor Party in the United States, and is buried inside the Kremlin wall—*he* was a revolutionary.)

After all, there was this difference: Those sixties radicals (like the earlier Reed) wanted to *overthrow* the capitalist system, rather than make it more profitable, which was an implicit promise of the *Fast Company* "revolution."

Still, this was no put-down. *Fast Company* was built on a remarkable insight. If business had not transformed itself, in point of fact, into a bomb-making clinic of the sort that the Weather Underground and Citicorp execs would enjoy (along with a low-cal beverage), nonetheless, just looking at these covers suggested that *Fast Company* had unearthed some radically new concerns in the world of work.

In *Fast Company*, businesspeople didn't seem to worry all that much about a company's return on investment or market penetration or any of the more irritating details of corporate competition. The new-world-of-work—*Fast Company* often deployed the term as if it were hyphenated—worried mostly about, well, you. (In case, somehow, the point wasn't clear, early on *Fast Company* ran a story headlined "Project: You.") And to judge from those magazine covers, it wasn't all aspects of you. Work was principally concerned with your fragile inner state; indeed, it was supposed to make you happy.

So *Fast Company* was no manual for revolution. It seemed to me something just as provocative: a guide for the individual seeking, as *Fast Company* said, "fulfillment . . . at work." Which hadn't always been a place known to promote, or even care about, such things.

$ $ $

You didn't have to be the child of an Organization Man to know that, boarding the 7:42 out of suburbia, he wasn't thinking that work ought to cater to his potential for happiness. No, that "good corporate citizen," who sometimes seemed the standard bearer for all modern businessmen, proudly said, "I'm a company man." He offered the firm long years of service, thirty or forty in some cases, not that this was any strain.

There's debate about how contented these company men really felt, or, in fact, how numerous were their ranks. But in prevailing lore, this fellow had sharply delineated concerns. He worried about security, income stability, things the corporation could provide. Conformity hadn't seemed such a noose to him. A man rose on his own talents, but only as the company advanced. In the fifties, want ads in the Sunday *New York Times* business section made this abundantly clear. Individual progress was subsumed in company progress. "You will grow as Sperry grows," brightly promised a Sperry Corporation ad in 1957. Burroughs Corporation offered "long term job stability." Ambition was valued, but mainly as it benefited the employer. As another ad from 1957 boasted, quoting the words of one happy employee, "I . . . enjoy many opportunities to see my ideas used in the finished products of General Motors."

From the employee's viewpoint, the object was to climb the corporate ladder. Once a person secured a spot up the ladder, his job was to push the productivity of those below him. In this generation's view, ideas came from the top and went forth as directives. Many managers of the era subscribed to Theory X, which assumed that if you turned your back on employees, they'd never get anything done. This tough-minded manager applied systems, controls, processes, bureaucratic tools derived from accounting and engineering. The great confidence of the era—and it was a profoundly confident era— came from a belief in method that relied on "a chain of causes and effects." The Organization Man was a sensible, rational, business adult. As *Life* magazine concluded at the time, "From now on the country would have to rely less on amateurism and experimentation and more on professionally organized expertise."

Efficiency was a key workplace goal for this professional. Through the fifties, anyone skimming the business section would have noticed jobs for "methods and time study engineers," as one ad called the position. The job was "to set standards and be responsible for methods improvements." Frederick W. Taylor was the father of these engineers, but perhaps the most popular representative of the type was Frank Gilbreth, subject of the fifties best-seller *Cheaper by the Dozen,* which also became a popular movie, one of two about the family. Gilbreth, an early time-study engineer, worked in factories, though what really marked him in the public mind was that he applied his self-assured methods to his dozen kids. Gilbreth seemed a loveable Lucille Ball of efficiency. He took movies of his kids washing dishes, part of a program to eliminate wasted motion. On the living room floor, he demonstrated how to bathe more quickly, no doubt important with fourteen bathers.

By the seventies, many offspring of this corporate man wanted no part of his efficiency trip, no matter how zany Gilbreth made it seem. They, or rather we, had gotten something else in our heads. As *Esquire* magazine declared in 1983, we signed up for nothing less than "a new self."

The architect of this latest selfhood, according to the magazine, was Abraham Maslow, a short, likeable, Brooklyn-born psychologist with perpetually raised eyebrows, a thick mustache, and a head of hair like a shoe brush. Maslow, born in 1908 to uneducated Russian immigrants, had a childhood that hardly prepared him for his later mission. He was a lonely, depressed, unhappy, neurotic kid. "Have you ever seen anyone uglier than Abe?" his father once asked. His mother wasn't particularly supportive either. "Pretty but not nice," Maslow said, adding. "With my childhood, it's a wonder I'm not psychotic." Plus, he was jarringly shy. Smitten by a first cousin, he was too petrified to kiss her until her sister literally shoved the two together.

And yet, at a time when much of psychology focused on pathology, Maslow valued—some would say, *over*valued—possibilities. To explain his views, Maslow liked to coin his own words. "I like my phrasing," he'd say, and then introduce something like "hierarchy of needs," which Maslow suggested everyone had. At the bottom of the hierarchy Maslow located basic needs like food, shelter, and safety. Belongingness, the Organization Man's bread and butter, was up the pyramid, just under esteem, and at the very top, he placed another of his terms, "self-actualization." This referred, as Maslow put it, "to man's desire for self-fulfillment, namely to the tendency for [a person] to become actually what he is potentially." Maslow's notions weren't based on much evidence. He met a few well-adjusted people, read about others, declared them self-actualizing, and then came to conclusions about what self-actualization entailed. Maslow knew the limitations of his work—he had a soaring IQ, 195 at one test—but saw a chance to explore. He liked to think of himself "as a Daniel Boone, a reconnaissance man."

Chance sometimes favored Maslow. Later, he and his wife—he married the cousin with the insistent sister—were driving Route 1 in California as evening approached. They pulled off the road, looking for a place to spend the night, and wandered into what they thought was a motel, and what would become the Esalen Institute. At Esalen, so the story goes, Maslow happened into people eagerly reading his latest book. From that moment, shy Abe Maslow seemed like the Chaplin character who, walking along, discovers a parade has crept up behind him and, lo and behold, finds he is positioned as its leader.

We all knew people involved with the human potential movement, the one with which Maslow (and Esalen) would be identified. Some plunked down a few hundred dollars for one seminar or another—est, Arica, Sylvan Mind Control, rolfing, Scientology, Zen, TM were some familiar names. Courses like these didn't share any particular dogma, just a penchant for "self-realization" or "self-fulfillment," or "self-actualization"—which replaced self-denial and self-sacrifice, I could hear my parents say—and which often started with an amount of self-destruction. ("You're here because your life doesn't work," est attendees were told.) I hadn't taken these courses and yet I recognized their emphasis. Who didn't?

The Organization Man had *shared* feelings; he was, by definition, *part* of something. Members of succeeding generations thought of themselves as individuals, each with a buried, authentic, creative self to "unblock," get to know, express, realize, transform. After Maslow, people who had no familiarity with this shy professor seemed to work on themselves, trying to "keep growing," not as parent, earner, community member, but as human being. We were all raw material that had to be carefully explored, discovered, realized; in a sense, invented. Everyone had his or her own dreams to fulfill. Happiness, soon to be a predominating American concern, suddenly had none but individual, internal referents. Success became a personal thing. For anyone who has come of age since about 1970, these are the terms of adulthood.

Self-actualization represented one of those tidal shifts in American culture. By the end of the seventies, "as much as 80 percent of the population" was involved in a search for self-fulfillment, reported Yankelovich, who had for years conducted surveys of American attitudes. The new Maslovian self seemed to inform nearly all our actions.

With one notable exception: business. American business had just two problems with personal fulfillment. Personal. And fulfillment. For the traditional business guy, the smug language of personal transformation, what with its circular intimations of secret knowledge, made his hair stand on end.

"Did you *get it?*" "Get it" was a term used in est.

"How do I know if I *got it?*" the beginner asked.

"You'll know you *got it* when you *get it,*" came the galling answer.

Every now and then, a human resources program experimented with human potential techniques—in the abstract, employee potential didn't seem a bad thing to work on. In the eighties, Werner Erhard, who'd founded est in 1971, influenced in large part by Maslow, even ventured into the corporate training business. But the business culture seemed to balk. Before long the press was dotted with headlines like this one from a 1987 *New York Times,* "Gurus"— a distinctly unflattering title in the eighties—"Hired to Motivate Workers Are Raising Fears of Mind Control," or this even blunter one from a 1987 *Newsweek,* "Corporate Mind Control." Employees claimed they were being brainwashed, their belief systems infringed, their personal lives invaded. Some sued their employers. Businesspeople, it seemed, were more comfortable with the Organization Man's steadying beliefs, with calculations of five-year liquidity cycles or analyses of cash flow than with fuzzy notions of personal growth.

By the mid-nineties, as anyone who picked up a *Fast Company* would immediately recognize, all that had changed. *Fast Company* editors delighted in bashing the uptight, straitlaced Organization Man. It might seem odd that a nineties magazine railed against this dusty old fifties figure. But, culturally, *Fast Company* was another of the Organization Man's rebellious kids and, as such, had to stand up to this tough-minded dad. Management thinker Tom Peters, one of the magazine's influential voices, put it this way: "I don't want to go in the same door to work, Monday through Friday, for forty-one years, like my dad did. I think his work life stunk. (Sorry, Dad.)"

For the *Fast Company* crowd, the mentality of faithful service had spoiled the culture of business. The Organization Man might be a dependable adult, a gifted rationalist, but in the service of what? A dreary campaign for corporate profit—just the kind that turned off a young Joe Park. That good corporate citizen didn't *get it,* never could. And so *Fast Company* disdained the flannel-suited representative of the fifties who, poor fellow, sometimes seemed to have been created as a straw man. (*Fast Company* seemed to directly poke fun at him in this cover: "Raise Your Hand If Your CEO Gets It.") Luckily, the situation was well in hand. "*The Organization Man,* William H. Whyte's take on corporate America in the Age of Conformity," wrote the exuberant *Fast Company* editors, "has been turned upside down."

In this topsy-turvy world, not only did *Fast Company* readers, like self-actualizers before them, revolt against the same irredeemable fifties square, they applied the same solution. Maslow had encouraged the seventies individual to "become everything that one is capable of becoming." Allan Webber, one of the magazine's founding editors, said, "What you really want to do [in business] is take the risk of being what only you can be."

In *Fast Company,* the boundless Maslovian self, the one that had been so active everywhere else, finally came of age at work. Thus, a new generation of businesspeople no longer flagged their goal as doing better than their parents who'd struggled to give them a chance, or working for their kids who deserved a break. Now business seemed to offer a path to personal satisfaction, to self-fulfillment. "Jobs are not just jobs, nor are they simply a means to a paycheck,"

Fast Company's co-editors told readers. "They absorb and challenge us. They offer fulfillment." The language could have been lifted straight from Maslow.

Here was one way to understand the strange new world of work I'd stumbled into. It was, I realized with a twinge of familiarity, as if someone had spliced the DNA of the seventies into the newly receptive business organism of the nineties. Suddenly, everywhere I looked I noticed old-timey values, *my* old-timey values, popped up in a business context, where they thrived.

Most traditional business magazines, as Webber pointed out, reported from the point of view of the corporation. Thus, *Fortune* noticed that work "is not about paying the rent; it's about self-fulfillment," but seemed to suggest that employers were just going to have to stomach such brattiness in times of low unemployment. "They [these new employees] want to make money, move fast, have fun, find themselves, and do what they please. And they want all that now," added *Fortune*, as if describing an obnoxious phase of adolescence. But the good economy/spoiled kid argument didn't work. In 1998, when the *Fortune* article appeared, the jobless rate was 4.7 percent. In 1956, the year *The Organization Man* was published, unemployment stood at 4.1 percent. (In 1955 it had been 4.4 percent and in 1957 4.3 percent.) And yet those company men dressed like adults and didn't bring pets to the office. A nice massage? Take the risk of being what only you can be? I don't think so. "Tell me what the job is, and let's get on with it," that was their attitude as *Fortune* put it, one derived from the military, an experience many shared.

Fast Company shifted its viewpoint. Webber, previously editor of the *Harvard Business Review*, explained the change. "At the world of the Harvard Business School," he said, "what you analyze is the company, the firm. What does the firm do in competition?" *Fast Company*, he said, focused on what it called the "unit-of-one." (*Fast Company*, too, had a mania for inventing terms.) "The real name of the game, from our point of view, is a unit-of-one economy," said Webber. "The worldview of *Fast Company* is you ... it's no longer the company. It's the individual." It's the self in self-fulfillment.

The Organization Man hoped to do his duty, pull his weight. "We aspire to authenticity," said the *Fast Company* editors, which was the possibility of being who you really were. In the *Fast Company* calculus, foregoing job security, which corporations no longer provided, made the authenticity project more real—at least, perhaps, it *felt* more real. In one issue, writer Dan Pink reported that he'd "gladly swapped the false promise of security for the personal pledge of authenticity."

Solid, logical, cool, tough-minded, those had once been elements of the valued business personality. Of course in the quest for business self-fulfillment, the Maslovian one, emotions were the raw material to be explored, freed, built upon. Fastidious engineering and accounting methods were fine as far as they went, but what really mattered—what really *worked*—was what was in your gut. In business, the rational suddenly seemed like so much baggage. *Fast Company* quoted business leaders approvingly as saying things like, "I'm not so sure what two plus two is, but I feel better anyway—because I don't think that finite answers matter so much." These kinds of snippets—straight out of the scorned Me Decade of the seventies—ran through the magazine.

The building blocks of business success were now all those emotions that self-fulfillers had once kept locked inside like, for instance, a little J. Park passion, a dose of which suddenly, and a bit improbably, seemed the mark you would succeed in business. (Good thing, of course, since a lot of the new businessmen didn't know much about systems.) "The best companies in any field are motivated by passion," *Fast Company*'s editors quoted a businessman as saying. (He, you'd have to say, *got it*.)

Fortunately, passion appeared bottled-up inside just about everyone. Carl Rogers, one of Maslow's colleagues, had sought to "unblock" feelings. Similarly, the trick now was to "tap into" or "unleash" your passion. "The cultural revolution of the internet . . . was about unleashing passion," was how venture capitalist Jerry Colonna put it.

A previous business generation conformed. Now, of course, creativity, that ultimate seventies thing, was the definitive business value. Sometimes I couldn't help but wonder where all the tough-minded managers had gone. And why didn't they knock some sense into these mushy heads? It was one thing, after all, for exuberant college kids to spout this stuff. Now, even as bottom-line a figure as Jack Welch, the former CEO of GE—once known as "Neutron Jack" because he kept the buildings and fired the people—had been re-outfitted as New Age messenger. "None of this is about squeezing anything at all," he said. "it is about tapping an ocean of creativity, passion, and energy."

Business had once focused on efficiency, productivity, process. Now "work, more and more," as the *Fast Company* editors put it, "is about the lessons we learn: where to find inspiration, how to make sense of ambiguity, how to take risks, what makes a career grow."

From what I could tell, these editors—and, apparently, much of the business world—was on a touchy-feely bender not unlike those Maslow-inspired human potential courses. Can *you* distinguish which of the following paragraphs is from, *The Book of est,* an account of an est training, and which is from a *Fast Company* article on corporate consulting?

> This night the trainees are asked to bring into our center two people, one male and one female, whom we wish to be in close touch with, and to create each person from head to foot with our hands as a sculptor might.

> In a soothing voice, [he] instructs me to choose a vehicle that will carry me from the present into the future. It can be a fantasy vehicle or a real vehicle.

> In the second long process . . . we spread out throughout the room on the floor. Eyes closed, we are guided in creating for ourselves a "center," a safe space anywhere in the world where we can retreat and simply be with our selves.

[He] asks me to imagine that I encounter a "wild card"—an event whose probability of happening is low but whose impact, should it occur, would be great. Wild cards can be deeply personal (I give birth to quadruplets), totally cosmic (an asteroid hits Earth), or something in between.*

Previous generations might have viewed work as instrumental, as a way to put food on the table. Since then, business, as even *Fast Company* admitted, had grown more competitive, more warlike, indeed, more businesslike than ever. And yet, business, in the pages of *Fast Company,* sounded nearly therapeutic, as if a course of it, properly administered, was just what the stodgy soul required. This was, of course, a story lifted straight from Maslow.

"Work actually becomes part of the self," Maslow said of the self-actualized, "part of the individual's definition of himself."

Fast Company thoughts exactly. As *Fast Company* explained, "People want to bring their whole selves to the job—all of their skills, interests, values."

Maslow also said that for self-actualized people, "the work they do might better be called mission, calling, duty, vocation."

Just so, said *Fast Company.* "For everyone in *Fast Company,* work is a mission. Most of the folks that we write about don't go to work to make a living," said Webber who, tellingly, changed pronouns, "... We go to work to do something that we care about. We go to work to do something that represents our best effort, to be true to who we are, to bring everything about our minds, our character, our background, our education, our values into the world of work and to put it on the line to do something that really matters to us."

The great themes of the new-world-of-work would be: the need for an individual to grow and learn (rather than to climb the hierarchy), the search to realize potential (rather than the craving for stability), the prospect of creativity (and not its evil cousin conformity).

*Paragraphs one and three are from an est training.

These, needless to say, were classic Maslovian themes retooled, but only slightly, as business imperatives.

It was no small irony that by the late nineties, the military, the Peace Corps, and the new-world-of-work spoke the same language, the Maslovian one that now seemed to inform just about every contemporary aspiration.

"How far are you willing to go to make a difference?" asked Peace Corps ads.

"Talented people want . . . to do work that makes a difference," wrote *Fast Company*.

"Today's youth want to feel empowered to make a difference individually and as a group," the Secretary of the Army said in explaining its recent campaign.

Fast Company promised that its newfound business values, if properly applied, or better yet, "unleashed," would create a bold new business self. One capable of just about anything. You could, as *Fast Company* suggested, "reinvent yourself," which seemed an explicit promise of the new world of work. Or you could transform others. As someone *Fast Company* identified as a "creativity guru" said, "If you can change your mind, you can change the world." Guru, of course, was no longer a term of derision, as in that eighties headline. In fact, in *Fast Company*, just about everyone seemed to be gurus. There was a negotiation guru, a management guru, a strategy guru, a golf guru. Indeed, in the logic of *Fast Company*, everyone *could* be a guru. The magazine's Web site linked you to something called guru.com, which, once you filled out the form, counted you a guru, too.

And, of course, gurus regularly consulted for business now, without getting sued by employees. The Landmark Forum was the successor to est. Not only did it have clients from Reebok to Agency.com, but it was favorably chronicled in the *Harvard Business Review*.

This boundless new business self was idealized in the entrepreneur, in whom the magazine seemed to locate super business powers. "It is the . . . individual with a computer, a hookup to the Internet, a telephone, an airplane ticket, a fax, a modem that has the power to create a new company or overturn an old industry using their knowledge and their Rolodex," *Fast Company* explained.

I couldn't help but wonder what would happen to this powerful business individual once he or she hit the work world. Wasn't it possible that the fusty old corporation, set in its ways, would stand in the path of the self-actualizing business individual? Harriet Rubin took up this problem in a long article for *Inc.* magazine. (Harriet would later become a *Fast Company* writer.) Harriet had left a job in publishing—she'd founded a business book imprint, Doubleday's Currency—to become, as she called it, "a soloist." (The *Fast Company* term was "free agent;" the Internet term "entrepreneur"; the IRS term "self-employed.") Actually, Harriet said she aspired to be a "girl guru"—though, since she appeared to be in her forties, both girl and guru were apparently aspirations.

In any case, she was now headed back into the corporate world to take a job at iVillage, the Internet community for women. This was a bind. After all, Harriet had pretty fixed views of the corporation. Bureaucratic systems, forced smiles, endless meetings, the discouraging need to clear things with the powers-that-be—it was the Organization Man's paternalistic paradise.

Her editor at *Inc.* magazine framed the problem nicely. "The great achievement of the past few decades is that we've learned everything necessary to create businesses that grow," he confidently wrote. "But will we ever design businesses that grow us?" Harriet wanted to grow. But as she put it, "Going back to a job is like moving in with your parents." For Harriet, the parent metaphor seemed to hold special power. After all, Harriet recalled her teens—during the seventies, presumably—as full of possibility. "All those dreams we abandoned in the 1980s when we first put on a suit are coming back with a vengeance," she wrote. "A second puberty is heading our way." Harriet felt—*felt and felt,* one sensed—"Work is about your dreams." Indeed, for Harriet, as for many these days, the struggle to earn a living was largely a "quest for identity." (No wonder emotions seemed so intense at work!) In Harriet's world, as in *Fast Company's,* people trotted off to work to find meaning in their lives—the meaning that business, by the way, was once said to kill. "You're not building a company," she reminded herself, and might have added, or a list of solid accomplishments or dependable income or sturdy future. "You're building you." And so, as Harriet pointed out, "You design a business based on your life." Apparently what this most demanded was courage. "Dare to be an original," she urged herself, taking comfort in this Maslovian insight, "which we all are."

` Ultimately, Harriet would resolve her reentry into dread corporate life by deciding to retain her soloist's mindset. The right attitude, she seemed to feel, would protect her from all the fakeness and bureaucracy. It may be difficult to believe that a large organization was so susceptible to a willful self, but in the *Fast Company* universe this seemed an article of faith. Change your mind and you can change the world, that creativity guru had said.

The truth was that Harriet needn't have gotten so worked up. She had allies everywhere in the new business world.

The Internet, to start, seemed uncannily well-suited to the New Age propositions *Fast Company* put before readers. The Internet was the dreamy place where you didn't need credentials or expertise, mere extensions of your rational self. Be creative, latch onto an idea, unleash passion, and then hightail it over to the copy shop to print up some business cards. "Be your own CEO," *Fast Company* invited readers. (Talk about self-actualizing!) In the magazine, the Internet often seemed the preferred vehicle for personal transformation. "I could have played it safe," recalled one executive profiled by *Fast Company*. He had been at an international conglomerate before deciding in favor of the CEO job at a three-month-old dot-com with no revenue, few employees, and no chance of profits any time soon. The reason for this leap seemed to be that inside he wasn't a play-it-safe kind of guy. Rather, he'd always felt more of a fulfillment-seeking risk-taker. In *Fast Company*, people who jumped from big corporate ships invariably did so because it was only in more precarious Internet conveyances that they had a shot at being the exciting people they'd always intended to be.

The Internet, finally, should probably not be understood as a culture of business achievement, though it would eventually be judged against that standard. Rather, for people interested in realizing their ideas and, not incidentally, themselves, the Internet offered a culture of personal aspiration.

Not only did the Internet welcome the aspirant but, as Harriet no doubt discovered, the corporate world, too, seemed solicitous of the business self-fulfiller. Forty years ago Maslow worried that management tended "to be hard-headed," evaluating success in criteria like "smaller labor turnover." "They neglect," he said, "the whole personal development side." These days, big business often presented itself as a kind of personal development seminar.

Just take a peek at a new generation of display ads in the *New York Times* Sunday business section. Fifty years ago, these ads enticed employees with the prospect of security in the workplace and lifestyle outside of it. In 1998, PricewaterhouseCoopers, the largest worldwide professional services consultancy, appealed to future employees with this headline: "When you know where you're going, you want an open road." Eleven words, three of them "you." It might as well have said, "Project: You." At this company with 140,000 employees, as many people as live in Kansas City, Kansas, "Your individuality will be recognized," insisted the company Web site. Here was the unspoken idea that the corporation didn't really offer income or security, but rather an open-ended adventure for the self.

By the late nineties, nearly every business—it didn't matter the field—now seemed to believe that people (not systems or technology) were the basis for success. And not for their education or experience or big brains but, it would seem, mainly for their spirit, their capacity for personal growth, which these ads solicited. Aramark, in an ad for Food & Beverage Facility and Service Management professionals, said it was looking for people who want to "take their dreams as far as they will go." In its ad, American Express offered a "work environment where you have the freedom to implement change." Work at American Express, a corporation with nearly $17 billion in annual revenues, bigger than that of some countries, was apparently about freedom—*your* freedom—and possibilities—*your* possibilities.

Chase, the nation's largest financial institution, was also interested in the developing self of the potential employee. You might think that an ad for the company's Internal Audit Control Partnership would seek a stickler for the rules. Not so. "If you're interested in a company that's interested in the way you think," then Chase audit control might be the place for you.

It seemed, as *Fast Company* said, a world turned upside down. I thought fleetingly of that administration building we'd taken over in college, when I'd briefly imagined myself a revolutionary, as you may know. What were we after back then if not to make our voices heard, our individuality count? If the administration—if *someone*—had only been interested in the way we thought! Now, it turned out, business was interested. No company appeared able to bear top-down bureaucracies anymore—in these ads they hardly seemed to exist. Hierarchies had an icky, undemocratic feel. (In part perhaps—and here I thought of Harriet—because they smacked of the original tyranny of family.) Instead every employee appeared powerful; everyone a decision maker. The world of work presented in these ads wasn't about company goals. PaineWebber, which advertised for stockbrokers for northern or central New Jersey, said that it was the place where "You have the power to shape your future." Compuware, a $2 billion company with 13,000 employees, brought Taylorist efficiency to other businesses. Still, the company's ad didn't seek efficiency experts with a background in "time study methods." Company ads focused instead on the personal growth it could offer you, the future employee. "Are you ready for a career without limits?" asked Compuware in an ad mainly seeking salespeople. Thousands of employees, and you wouldn't be another number required to carry an ID just to get in the bathroom. Instead, every individual was a leader, a hierarchy of one, as *Fast Company* (or the Peace Corps or the army) might put it. Compuware offered you a "chance to lead. To explore." The ad featured an illustration of a guy inexplicably holding a bicycle over his head. Perhaps it was a reference to the "without limits" concept that served as a kind of company motto, though of course "without limits" (or the interchangeable "break away" or "open road") could have been the motto for most of these companies. Inevitably, Compuware, like all these giant corporations, like the Peace Corps and the army as well, offered something other than "maximum enjoyment for living." "Imagine yourself working in an environment that gives people plenty of room to make a difference," said Compuware.

Fifty years ago Sperry Corporation had promised "You will grow as Sperry grows." Sperry, though, had been folded into Unisys. And Unisys wanted you to know that your growth wasn't indexed to the company's. "Instead," the company said, "building skills and gaining a variety of experiences are what count," skills and experiences that would be useful for your next job. No one wanted to spend forty years with a company any more—people sometimes changed jobs every year or two. Accommodatingly, the company created what it called Unisys University, which offered courses to help "your career development." Don't worry about helping us, seemed the message, let us help you. It was in this spirit that Netscape suggested that what you learned at Netscape was "knowledge you could take with you wherever you go," like, you know, to your next job.

The square, controlling, efficiency-obsessed, hierarchy climbing, pitching-in-for-the-company business guy, the one with the deadened spirit and the bus to catch, had been overrun by seekers' values, those which in *Fast Company's* words emphasized the "potential for personal growth." A job in business was now supposed to test your limits, invigorate you, make you grow. Far from soulless, business now seemed good for the soul. These ads presented a new business guy, a hip, bike-riding, learning, feeling, growing, adventuring, self-actualizing one on his own success trip. He wasn't bringing home the bacon; he was after fulfillment, or as those *Fast Company* covers indicated, happiness.

By 2000, it should come as no surprise that long dead Abe Maslow was back in fashion. Almost forty years earlier he'd spent a summer walking around a corporation, Non-Linear Systems, a plant in southern California producing volt meters, with a tape recorder in hand. In 1965 he'd published his thoughts under the title he'd insisted on, *Eupsychian Management: A Journal*. Eupsychian was one of his loopy terms that meant, more or less, self-actualized. The original book had a small following and, by the time he dropped dead of a heart attack, had been remaindered.

Four decades later, however, his dictated journal entries were reissued. Suddenly, they seemed to burst with insights. Readers apparently couldn't get enough, so publishers issued a second volume, *The Maslow Business Reader*. Obviously, the text hadn't changed. But this time around business types found Maslow's concept of self-actualization undeniable. "Maybe . . . our minds are now ready for Maslow's profound medicine," said noted business thinker Warren Bennis. They sure are, *Fast Company* would no doubt say.

Chapter Fourteen

I Need a CEO

EARLY ONE RAINY FRIDAY EVENING, I called a meeting of *team karaoke,* as I liked to think of us. We were to convene in the lobby of the Giraffe, a small hotel on Park Avenue South where Clemente stayed when in town. (He lived in Palm Springs, California.) Clemente favored this hotel because it was small and private. I liked its European sophistication, a quality it demonstrated by supplying wine and cheese *for free* every afternoon. In my view, wine and cheese brighten a business meeting.

I arrived first and grabbed a hunk of Brie and a corner table facing a picture window. I noticed my reflection. Or *a* reflection. Bizarrely, I didn't immediately recognize myself. Then I remembered. For this meeting, I'd wanted something a little extra and had combed my hair straight back with some cream. I'd thought of Michael Douglas's hairstyle in *Wall Street,* and how commanding he'd been in that film. Commanding might not be so bad this evening, I'd thought.

Recently, you see, I worried that KNation was losing momentum. Of course business was an emotional roller-coaster. I knew that. And each morning I awoke with new ideas to get to work on. I phone-called, faxed, e-mailed, and, hustled off to meetings, many of them very positive.

Recently, I'd had a very encouraging meeting with Jan Horsfall, CEO of phonefree, whose technology enabled Internet telephone service computer-to-computer. Sound quality wasn't all that good.

Still, he told me he expected to "take AT&T down." As he said that, I noticed his shoes. They were flip-flops. Apparently he expected to take AT&T down in flip-flops. Karaoke immediately intrigued him. He thought it might be a way to recruit new subscribers. "There have to be some synergies here," Horsfall said. I told him I saw them too.

I'd also had a very encouraging meeting with Kidrin, CEO of Worlds.com, creator of 3D computer environments. At the Warwick Hotel, he asked the value of my company. The question stumped me at first. What did I have? A concept, some market numbers and deployment schemes, the beginnings of a team. That had to be worth something, I'd worked so hard. Three million dollars, I thought. A nice number, but not braggy. Then I thought of some advice I'd been given: Say the biggest number you can without laughing.

"Six million," I told Kidrin, which didn't prove any more difficult to get out than three million. I offered Kidrin 5 percent if he'd build me a 3D-karaoke prototype.

"If people say you gave away too much, tell them, 'You weren't there,'" he said, and offered me his freckled hand.

And yet, despite these promising developments, lately I felt frantic. My enthusiasms, so precious to me, seemed increasingly fragile. I'd been at this for half a dozen months and the other day the market collapsed into a bucket—a sheer 14 percent drop that literally took people's breath away. Mine included. Plus, the flip-flopped Horsfall soon stopped returning my calls. (Synergy my ass.) And Kidrin peeked at the features I wanted in my prototype—"your 'wish list,'" he called it. I couldn't get him to start work.

In a panic, I'd phoned Consigliere. "But business is fun, right?" I'd asked.

He patiently explained the business cycle and the sales cycle and certain micro and macro considerations, before I cut him off. "But it's fun, right?"

There was a pause. I thought I heard typing. "Oh, yeah," he said blandly.

"Great," I said, a little more barky than I'd wanted.

Of course, I was determined to push ahead. You had to be. Every entrepreneur said so. There were *always* going to be setbacks. What could be more entrepreneurial than setbacks?

And yet as I waited for the rest of team karaoke to arrive, I thought: KaraokeNation could use a break.

I'd lately started to think in terms of that J. Park "To-Do" list—he'd ticked off quite a few items. Occasionally, I counted them on my fingers, as if the act of inventory might make them more manageable. Recently, I'd resolved to focus on management. Park had made a fuss about it. "If you get a CEO or entrepreneur," he'd begun—like most people, he used those titles interchangeably—"[he's] going to spend 24/7, every single waking moment building this business. Then venture capitalists are going to look at that and say, I like the idea and really like the person *who's building this thing.*"

So okay, I told myself, I need a CEO, one with passion and commitment. (It was a remarkable need for me, I occasionally recalled. A few short months ago, I'd made a list of needs. *Change ink cartridge in printer* was number one, followed by an exclamation point.) One way or another, at this meeting, I had to spur Consigliere and Clemente to action on the CEO front. Wouldn't it be great if need and nervousness turned out to be winning qualities?

I knew other entrepreneurs who'd rallied their teams. Scott Rompala, COO of eComplaints, told me that after everyone at his firm agreed to a 50 percent pay cut he'd said, "Let's give it our best shot even if we go down with the ship," or words to that effect, and topped it off with a round of high fives. Joe Park had once told his troops, "I hate to lose," which also seemed to go over well. I contemplated employing these arguments with Consigliere and Clemente, though as I looked at the reflection of my slicked-back hair, I momentarily imagined a more forceful approach, like the one Michael Douglas had directed at his competition in *Wall Street.* "When I get a hold of the son of a bitch," Douglas had said, "I'm gonna tear his eyeballs out and suck his fucking skull!" (My wife sometimes used that line to good effect.)

Through the window I noticed Consigliere crossing the street in his favorite brown suede jacket; he wore it rain or shine. He seemed to move lumpily, as if he'd distributed weight unevenly in his pockets. Watching him, I wondered, Who should be my entrepreneur? Who among us, any of us, had what it takes *to build this thing?*

$ $ $

Once it was believed that entrepreneurs were like curveball hitters—born, not made. In the eighties, I'd worked for *Success!* magazine and we periodically ran quizzes to help readers learn if deep down they might be entrepreneurs. Did you climb more than a single stair at a time? Did you hate to wait in line? Were you impatient, pushy, eager to get ahead? Here were symptoms, we suggested, of latent entrepreneurship. (Treatable these days, it occurred to me, with Ritalin.) At that time, urging people to learn if an entrepreneur lurked inside wasn't always popular. It's easy to forget, but in the seventies and eighties, people, particularly those with money, culture, or credentials, didn't always want to know such unpleasant truths. "In the 1970s and 1980s, people would have laughed at the idea that . . . starting a company of your own was more laudable than working for a *Fortune* 500 Corporation," wrote Paulina Borsook in *Cyberselfish*. Prestige was in. Corporate perks were big, things like windowed offices and expense-account champagne. Investment houses had begun to recruit at top schools.

Entrepreneurs, by contrast, were the gritty outsiders who couldn't stomach authority. They were aggressive loners. The entrepreneur's risk-taking, his telltale optimism—his *unfounded* optimism—made him effective. That was the hallmark of the eighties entrepreneur. He was the person who could "produce results," Peter Drucker said at the time. But what a price he paid! The eighties entrepreneur often seemed uncouth, pushy, obnoxious, sweaty. He refused to take no for an answer, but so did stalkers. The eighties entrepreneur wasn't charming, likeable, charismatic, or particularly articulate. (Was Ross Perot?) To most people, the eighties entrepreneur seemed in the grips of dysfunction, albeit a productive one.

George Gilder would later be known as a technology evangelist.

Gilder didn't actually believe anyone could be more hyperbolically optimistic, more "cornucopian," as he put it, than he about the computer, which he covered in his 1989 *Microcosm,* or, about the Internet, discussed in his 1996 *Telecosm.* Long before either of these books, though, Gilder had been a prophet of entrepreneurship. In 1981, his *Wealth and Poverty* sold a million copies by suggesting that the entrepreneur was the engine—or, since his language was quasi-religious, the savior—of the economy. Further, he thought entrepreneurship in effect a social program, the cure for poverty. Thus, in characteristic eighties fashion, he recommended it as an especially promising pursuit for those with great need, great drive, and few credentials, especially, he said, minorities and immigrants. "Every successful ethnic group in our history rose up," he said, ". . . with a vanguard of men in entrepreneurial roles." And, he added, "Entrepreneurs are fighting America's only serious war against poverty."

In Gilder's view, which again was characteristic of the eighties, entrepreneurship sounded like war. Entrepreneurs ought to be "bullheaded" and "hardheaded" and show a "willingness to plunge into the unknown." "To take the hill, someone must dare first to charge the enemy bunker," he said. "Heroism," he figured, was necessary. Gilder would prove naive about economics—once wealthy, he'd end up with a lien against his own house. What Gilder had right, though, was that eighties entrepreneurship seemed both difficult and a little déclassé, appealing to those who often had fewer options for getting ahead. No wonder the entrepreneur was seen storming the gates; generally, he was locked out. And if that was the case, well, no wonder the Princeton kid went for investment banking in the eighties, which, after all, came with car service.

The nineties reinvented the entrepreneur. The updated model was still driven, but not nearly so desperate, and never disturbed. The class pathos had vanished. Entrepreneurs lately had options, fall-back plans. Park said that if his business failed, it would still look impressive on his business school application. Often enough, the nineties entrepreneur seemed an endearing, idealistic, Ivy League polymath who played well with others. This bunch thought they might as well give entrepreneurship a try. Why not? Their friends and families now pitched in to fund them. Jeff Bezos, founder of Amazon.com, was a Princeton grad who quit his finance job to start Amazon.com with $300,000 from his parents.

By the end of the nineties, entrepreneurial talent was no longer monopolized by a few rude souls. "One of the oft-repeated maxims of the adult world says that entrepreneurs are born, not made. Bullshit," said Ron Lieber bluntly in *Upstart Start-Ups!* a 1998 book that hoped to encourage young entrepreneurs. To Lieber's mind, anyone could be an entrepreneur. It didn't even really seem that an interest in entrepreneurship mattered, not a previously demonstrated interest, in any case. "Just because you didn't grow up peddling newspapers or making barrettes to sell to your friends doesn't mean that you lack the necessary entrepreneurial instinct," continued *Upstart Start-Ups*. In fact, by the late nineties, entrepreneurship seemed a club that just about anyone could join. *The Harvard Entrepreneurs Club Guide to Starting Your Own Business* gave an indication of just how popular the club might be when it addressed itself to "current college students and recent graduates, hereafter referred to as young entrepreneurs."

Now it was as if everyone had an inner entrepreneur waiting to emerge. We were, all of us, CEOs-in-the-making. No wonder everywhere I went people slapped those three letters—C-E-O—onto business cards. I even heard them on a couple of home answering machines. (I considered putting them on my own.)

By now, results weren't the trademark of the entrepreneur. Entrepreneurship was better described as a set of behaviors or a style, one that, as Park suggested, emphasized passion, commitment, creativity, initiative. (And since the go-getter entrepreneurial style could just as easily be demonstrated within a large corporation, entrepreneurship seemed to exist there too.)

By the late nineties, Gilder had turned his evangelistic ardor to technology. But a belief in entrepreneurship persisted. Soon, even he seemed to fall in with the nineties notion that entrepreneurship wasn't so difficult or entrepreneurs so pig-headed or annoying. In *Telecosm* he talked as if entrepreneurship, like bandwidth, was now available to all.

Indeed, one advantage Gilder saw to the Internet was that it freed all of us to be entrepreneurs. Storming the gates, charging the hill, bull-headed, hardheaded, all that was fine for the eighties. At the end of *Telecosm* Gilder offered a view of a Jetsons-like family of the near future. While fifties gender roles seemed in force, employment had changed. Now, it seemed as if everyone—or at least every man—might be a self-employed entrepreneur, working easily, productively, and in "the next room." Entrepreneurship, once like war, sounded in the nineties as painless and convenient as the Internet itself.

The shift was stunning and, given my current task, hopeful. Intuitively, I suppose I'd long understood how deep the current entrepreneurial pool might be. After all, at various points, I'd found myself offering (sometimes inadvertently) the position of KaraokeNation CEO to people I spoke with. I'd dangled it in front of Mary, the red-headed business consultant who'd flopped in bonds. *There's room at the top,* I let her know. When she ignored me, I called business schools looking for a bright MBA student. I needed someone to roll up his sleeves and, I suggested, help me *build this thing,* which was, I later realized, Joe Park's phrase. Unfortunately, just about every business school student seemed to have his or her own entrepreneurial venture under way.

At one point I thought *I* might have to take up the job. Was it so farfetched? If everyone could be CEO, why not me? Okay, Joe Park might have overlooked my qualifications, but my business-plan consultant—he'd signed on for a promise of shares—called karaoke my "brainchild," which suggested important CEO qualities, like caring and creativity, though also, I feared, a certain quirkiness. Like I might forget to turn off the stove before leaving the room. Also, I didn't seem to get passion just right. Not long ago, I brought a fist down on a conference room table to emphasize the revolutionary potential of karaoke as a music marketing tool—a concept that, I hinted, I might patent. The thud was louder than I'd anticipated. People giggled, apparently misinterpreting my passion.

So recently I'd come to the bittersweet conclusion that my CEO had to be another member of team karaoke. Consigliere or Clemente,

one of them had to step up to the plate, as I'd recently heard a businessman say.

Consigliere arrived first. The rain had stamped his brown suede
coat with leopard-like markings. He circled to the refreshment stand
where he grabbed a bottle of Merlot. (The Giraffe's version of European sophistication was self-service.) He, of course, had been my
immediate choice for CEO. He'd flirted with the idea. "If you raise
$10 million," Consigliere told me once, "why wouldn't I take a
shot?" (I'd almost put my elbows to my sides.) He could do the job,
too. He possessed a biting intelligence, presence to spare, and a freak-
ishly acute memory—he could recite the scores of all thirty-five
Super Bowl games forward *and* backward.

Not long ago, I'd managed to rope him into meeting with a
prospective KNation partner. I'd introduced him as my intended
CEO, thinking that perhaps he'd get confused and believe he *was*
CEO. In a business context, Consigliere could be captivating. He
might concoct a story on the spot—as an analyst he'd charmed an
audience with the tale of a run-in with a New York Knick in a men's
room. (In this story, fabricated, it turned out, the superstar athlete was
supposedly fascinated not by slam dunks, but by all this new media he
was hearing about.) Or maybe he'd curse or say something off-color,
you know, just between us girls. At our meeting, his foot had tapped
out good cheer, then he put it to the CEO of a company that just
that month had raised $42 million, "Who doesn't get at least half a
chub over karaoke?" I'd thought the presentation very convincing,
though after that the prospect wouldn't take my phone calls.

I knew Consigliere loved KNation, though I occasionally suspected it was the caper aspect he found irresistible. "Are you having
fun?" he'd sometimes ask. Then he'd suggest we contact Prince.
Prince would be *perfect* for KNation, he thought.

"Let's get *him* involved," he said.

Frankly, business was more fun when Consig was around.

Recently, though, he'd called me from a private spot at work, one
with a door. He wanted to let me in on his plans. Consigliere was a
handsome guy and made a fine, serious impression in business coat

and tie. Still, as hard as he tried, he sometimes struck me as a misfit. He had a business act. But his heart was set on a writer's future. He had a novel circulating at publishing houses. Occasionally, I knew, he wandered up Fifth Avenue in cutoff overalls, no shirt, pierced nipples, one red sneaker, one blue sneaker, and happy as a clam.

Consigliere had called to let me know he'd made a decision. "For Consigliere Inc., what makes sense is the track I'm on," he told me over the phone. (He occasionally referred to himself as Consigliere these days.) He was hoping to get married soon. If the market ever came back, there was venture capital work for him to do. Just now, Consigliere made clear, he preferred a job, a paycheck, a secure path.

He wasn't going to disappoint KNation, however.

"We'll hammer Clemente into doing it," Consigliere said over the phone.

Okay, great. Then Clemente would be my CEO. I admired Clemente tremendously. His dedication was striking. I'd been to the New York apartment where he sometimes stayed for weeks at a time. *Empty.* I don't mean *relatively* empty. A subway station had more furniture. In three rooms, there was a bed, a lamp, and a row of hard-spined business books.

"You don't have a phone," I'd pointed out.

He'd motioned toward the wall where I noticed a line for the Internet.

Sometimes I found myself trying to imitate Clemente. He knew all the concepts, all the terms, and on occasion I repeated a phrase I'd heard him use. Once I'd identified myself as an "Internet evangelist," as Clemente liked to identify himself. And of course I attempted his self-assured tone, though I didn't always pull it off. I'd bluffly told one music industry lawyer, "A music revolution is upon us." I didn't know how he'd take such upsetting news. Clemente was usually able to entice people, as if including them in on a secret. I, unfortunately, came off as impatient, smug, like a healthy young person visiting a sick elderly one.

Clemente possessed another strength: optimism. The unblinking kind that someone like me—and Consigliere, too, I suspected—

couldn't always count on. I'd seen it at work. Clemente figured personalized radio was on its way; he had ideas to save the imperiled music-sharing company Napster, strategies to help CDNow survive.

"What the hell are you talking about?" I could hear Consigliere rib him about any one of these ideas. "They won't last."

Clemente, of course, rarely budged. He put faith in effort. "If I do anything, I do it a hundred-ten percent," he'd tell me. I didn't know many people who said that sort of thing. But, then I didn't know many people who stayed up nights in an empty apartment plotting to revolutionize the music business.

If Consigliere occasionally seemed of two minds, wanting in *and* wanting out—he still at times toyed with changing his name to Harold—Clemente identified with his job, his mission. He didn't hide his successes or tell them for a laugh. He knew that one year he'd been quoted in the press 417 times, an impressive number. He also knew what he wanted. "I want those three letters after my name," he'd once confided. He meant C-E-O.

I'd be honored to have Clemente as my CEO. This seemed a good deal for me, for KaraokeNation, and according to Consigliere, for Clemente, too.

Clemente had a slightly different take. He arrived at the Giraffe in a black jacket, two small round gold earrings, and, and despite the rain, dark sunglasses. It looked as if his inner Hells Angel was struggling to the surface—if, of course, bikers favored Calvin Klein. A nondrinker, Clemente grabbed a bottle of club soda.

"Nice hair," he said to me, which I took as a compliment. He was something of a hair expert.

Then he took a seat, removed his glasses, and made a statement he seemed to have prepared. Clemente spoke in a breathy voice. I never learned whether this was a conscious trick, but it was very effective. Consigliere and I inched forward attentively.

"Consigliere ought to be CEO of KNation," said Clemente.

Not long ago Clemente had taken me aside. He worried about Consigliere, whom he found depressed. Lately, I had to agree, Consigliere seemed overwhelmed at work. I'd received one e-mail: "People standing in cubicle, phones ringing, yaaaaaaaaaaa." The note was signed, "out of breath." The secure path was apparently taking its toll. Now, Clemente was convinced, bless him, that if only Consigliere would bail on his steady job and run KNation, he'd be fine.

"That's the reason I got involved with KNation," Clemente said. He sat shovel-straight, looking very formal, even with that ragged hair. He had those two cave-deep wisdom lines near his mouth. (He *must* know, they made me think, or else he's really eighty years old.) Clemente twisted the bottle of club soda; he seemed put out.

Consigliere said nothing at first. He adjusted his rectangular black glasses, the shape of storm windows. He poured another glass of wine, ran a hand through his dark hair. He looked at me, then focused on Clemente, his head shifting slightly, but with terrific speed.

"*You* should be CEO," he said, as if in response. "It's a great opportunity."

"You guys," I said with a little chuckle. This is terrific, I thought. I hadn't had to make a speech, to say I refused to lose or would go down with the ship or anything else I had an iffy chance of pulling off. On a wet Friday evening, I had two CEO candidates. I wasn't counting Consigliere out quite yet.

Unfortunately, each saw the merits of the other's cause.

"Think about leaving the analyst business," Consigliere told Clemente. A CEO just wanted one or two numbers from an analyst like Clemente, Consigliere once said.

Personality-wise, they were as different as could be. Clemente, the overachieving Republican drummer, seemed to have a wild past, but didn't. He may be the only rock 'n' roll musician who'd never tried marijuana. Consigliere marched along a straight corporate path, but enjoyed letting loose. At one company off-site, he'd ended up in the pool, drunk, his underwear on his head.

Still, they'd been friends for ten years, since Clemente went to work under him. Clemente still looked up to Consigliere. Lately, though, he seemed to feel he knew what was best for Consigliere.

"You've got to get out of *there*," Clemente responded. By there, he meant Consigliere's job.

Recently, Clemente had said to me, "I want him to believe in KNation the way I do." His voice was plaintive, the thought completely sincere. And, of course, ridiculous. In the believing department, no one could touch Clemente. Consigliere had once remarked, "We're all searching for something to believe in." (Amen, brother, I almost said.) Clemente, though, had a talent for believing *in general*. Whatever he focused on, it didn't matter. I sometimes wondered if it was a muscle he developed in those late-night sessions, or if he simply had an extra matchtip of adrenaline. People got it wrong. Life wasn't arduous, there was no struggle, hardly any. You almost never needed courage, and you didn't need hope. But belief, belief turned the key. In the Internet, it sometimes seemed the real competition was over who could believe the hardest. And so Clemente had an edge. "Most businesspeople believe their own bullshit like seventy-five percent," said one businessperson. "Clemente believes his one hundred percent." Which was meant as a compliment.

Sadly, Clemente insisted that he was loyal to Cyber Dialogue in part because his employer had recently filed to go public. Clemente, an early employee, was in line for several million dollars—a complicating, though to Consigliere's mind not insurmountable factor.

"You need an entrepreneurial experience," Consigliere told Clemente. "It makes you grow."

The two sometimes were a brotherly pair. Consigliere had served as a mentor, encouraging the late-starting Clemente to make the leap from researcher to analyst. Clemente, in turn, had been sure entrepreneur Consigliere would be an early Internet millionaire. Invariably they circled affectionately until, eventually, one bumped the other, and then there was a scrap.

"You should leave the analyst business," said Consigliere sharply. "You're about where I was when I left." An analyst, Consigliere pointed out, was someone who'd never done it—it being business.

Clemente wasn't biting (nor giving up his millions). Instead, he had a counterproposal. If Consigliere wasn't going to take over KNation, then Clemente wanted him to interview for CEO of Oddcast, a technology company he'd recently met. Clemente had been talking up Consigliere.

"They'll be out of business in six months," said Consigliere reflexively.

"Take the meeting," said Clemente firmly.

Consigliere seemed to consider it, a touch annoyed. Then Clemente pointed out that Oddcast might be a great company to build an online karaoke product. Clemente even imagined that with Consigliere as CEO, KNation could be part of Oddcast, a division.

"Okay," said Consigliere gruffly. He'd take the meeting. I didn't think he was interested in the CEO position. He said, "I'll pitch KNation real hard."

So I hadn't exited our meeting with a CEO. Still, I was hopeful. (It was becoming a personality disorder with me.) We really were all in this together. We had a next step, a plan, and I felt, against all odds, that I still had Clemente on the hook, maybe even Consigliere. I almost started a round of high-fives.

"And refresh your résumé," Clemente told Consigliere.

"What's wrong with my résumé?" said Consigliere.

Digging it out of his briefcase, he handed me a copy.

It was perfect, especially the beginning. "Not a poet trying to pass," it began.

Chapter Fifteen

It's a Science-Fiction World

I ARRIVED AT ODDCAST at about noon, lugging my laptop. It contained a short animated presentation and traveled everywhere with me nowadays, as did my peculiarly durable expectations of business. Among them, for some reason, I anticipated that business would occur in upscale settings. I pictured expensive furniture, people in dress clothes and well-appointed rooms, which, I realized, was pretty much how business looked when I'd visited my father's office in the Pan Am building—now the Met Life building. He'd had a launchpad view of Manhattan, and as a boy I'd pressed my face to his office window, as hundreds of feet below yellow cabs nosed for advantage. He had real furniture; his secretary had real furniture!

Oddcast's headquarters, by contrast, had the feel of a bicycle messenger shop. The room itself—there was just one—was a large, open rectangle, with a dull gray cement floor— *several* carefully layered shades of dull gray, I'd later learn. The furniture consisted mostly of door-sized boards on sawhorses, one for each of about twenty employees. The space had no overhead lights. There were windows, but most faced the Port Authority Bus Terminal, which seemed to emit little more than a dim half-light. That first visit, I thought Oddcast looked foggy. A couple hundred dollars' worth of plants, I noted, were slowly dying.

Oddcast, like many Internet offices, was an unconscious rebellion against that conventional office, the one of status and inaccessibility. *Who has time? We're building the future.* That was the Oddcast vibe. Though I thought that the company might profitably consider a waiting room or, at the very least, a receptionist. Since it had neither, on stepping from the elevator, I waved and tried to catch someone's eye.

Fortunately, I soon spotted Consigliere huddled in a far corner with Adi Sideman, Oddcast's current chief. They were talking about the CEO job, and ever-loyal Consigliere was pitching KNation, I knew. I'd later learn that he'd managed to intimate that KNation would soon have an important announcement about its own CEO hire. He was still betting that Clemente would come around.

"Yes, a CEO is very important," Adi would tell Consigliere mysteriously.

In a minute, Consigliere and Adi finished up and came toward me.

Later, when I knew Adi better—when I knew, for instance, that he'd been a documentary filmmaker and a paratrooper—I'd look at him and think, He's a wild man. (The kind who, for no particular reason, tore the heads off tiny beached fish, then ate them whole, a feat I'd have occasion to witness.) But at my initial encounter, another impression prevailed. Adi appeared as serene as a boiled ham.

He introduced himself simply, almost blandly. "Adi," was all he said, emphasis on the second syllable. He was a thirty-year-old Israeli, with short, receding hair, rimless glasses, and an odd concavity on one temple that made his head appear slightly lopsided. Adi wore a flowery polyester shirt—cruisewear, I thought—and brown leather pants. After a quick handshake, he stood perfectly still, his arms hanging bulkily at his sides. He smiled briefly, then fell silent, except for a buggy noise I'd never really heard before. "Ihhh," he said which I took to indicate thought.

"I hope your meeting went well," I said clumsily.

"We hope all meetings go well," Adi said mystically, "Ihhh." Perhaps he really *felt* serene. (Or else, I thought fleetingly, he's drunk.)

Lately, I should note, I'd gotten over my franticness. Like all my business feelings it had proved short-lived, cyclical. I hadn't yet received a break; still, most days I managed to believe that the phone call I was making or the meeting I was in, or the next or, surely, the one after, would yield the hoped-for result. I hadn't signed a CEO, but with Consigliere working on Clemente, I found myself believing that such an event wasn't far off. In the meantime, I'd bumped technology to the top of my J. Park To-Do List. If I could only get something built, I was sure other elements would fall into place, including perhaps a CEO. Recently, I'd started to think of Oddcast as my best shot; perhaps, I sometimes thought, my last. After all, I'd been through a number of other possibilities.

I'd called Sony, as per Joe Park. A new media guy there—I quickly appointed him to my advisory board—put me in touch with another person, nice enough on the phone. I was waiting for a return call. Why wait? I'd asked myself. The Internet, I'd been repeatedly told, was a can-do place. Almost anything was possible. Of course I knew that. Possibility was the Internet's principal theme.

In this vein, I'd sometimes imagined—indeed, I was offering—a virtual room where people could meet online and sing to one another.

Russell had been impressed by that possibility. "You can do that?" he'd nearly shouted, paying attention for once.

"Of course," I'd responded. Which wasn't quite true. I mean I'd seen it done. I'd visited the mtv.com Web site, which hosted a small online karaoke room. I'd listened in as one by one people took turns singing. The sound quality was glitchy, and there was little accompanying music. Still, the first time I sat at my desk and a voice sang "Purple Haze" through the tinny speakers I'd recently acquired, and I knew there was a person somewhere out there, well, a moment like that made me recall that before all the business hustle, the Internet existed as a thing of wonder.

An MTV exec had confided that the company wasn't going to push the application, though he was surprised that someone else hadn't tried to make a business out of it.

"So am I," I'd said coyly.

When I'd asked Consigliere about putting together a virtual karaoke bar like MTV's, he'd assured me, "It's possible." Though Con-

sigliere didn't always think his job interesting enough to talk about—
"I do math all day," he said indifferently—he knew technology.

"What if," I'd continued, "users were able to create their own animated characters and move them to a stage?"

"Possible," he'd said.

"And dress them however they wanted?"

"Sure."

Later, pressed to put a price tag on my virtual karaoke room,
Consigliere might inform me, "That sounds like a million-dollar
piece of intelligence," but most of the time it seemed as if all I had to
do was hunt up a single person, practically a kid. "You need a really
bright twenty-five-year old programmer," a guy from idealabs! had
confirmed over pizza—these friendly Internet offices seemed to
constantly serve food. That was the thing about technology. From the
outside, it appeared effortless. In fact, it seemed as if programmers had
these applications up their sleeves, and could shake them out at will.
And all I needed was one programmer, I told myself.

For a while, I thought I knew just the kind, too. Ten years ago, I'd
written about programmers. Of course back then it was like talking
to battered women. I'd met one programmer who told me that in
sixth grade he'd decided "I didn't do well at Mr. Athletic or Mr. Personality." Instead he read fifty books every six weeks—a record for
the 4.0 club—until he'd literally read his way through the local
library. He did have one date in high school; took her to miniature
golf where all went fine until he asked about her "schema" for life.
Another programmer said romance confused him, and so he used a
spreadsheet program "to do a statistical correlation" of the most
important qualities in a relationship.

These poor souls had developmental gaps wide enough to drive
trucks through. And yet when it came to computers, a predilection
for schemas and correlations proved advantageous. "The computer is,
in a sense, heaven on earth," I'd been told by the speed reader. Soon
enough, everyone seemed to believe that. Indeed, the future, that
American treasure, was lately entrusted to programmers, nerdish guys
who in the nineties got reformatted. They became *smart guys* who

calmly turned the future into products, *productized* it, was the term I heard.

There was, I'd once felt sure, some clever business arrangement to make with a guy like this, one that would encourage "a technology partner," as I'd call him, to devote many hours to building me a prototype. And for a good price, one I preferred not depend on cash. (Since I didn't have any left.) I thought of "win-win scenarios"—I'd become partial to them—and was suddenly filled with optimism. (It seemed to have a life of its own.) I told myself that smart guys didn't build stuff to sidestep a patent or replace people with machines or even, despite recent reports, to make boatloads of money. "Our interest was not how incredibly useful it was going to be to business," I'd been told by the programmer who wrote Microsoft Excel, one of the first spreadsheet programs. Deep down, programmers didn't really care if things sold; as far as they were concerned, the public *was* stupid. Mainly, they wanted to write clever programs for neat stuff. Like, I couldn't help but think, for a karaoke application.

Before showing up on Oddcast's doorstep, I'd turned to a member of my jam-packed advisory board who'd helped build "massively multiplayer" games—that was the technical term—that could be played online by thousands at once. He called himself Reverend Luke; it said so on his business card. Naturally he was ordained online. More important, he'd liked karaoke's Internet possibilities and recommended a programmer who was also a musician, an appealing combination for a karaoke product.

Our meeting took place at a small bar where the musician-programmer was to perform later that evening. I had no trouble picking him out. He was the one with the silver bull's-eye painted on his forehead. "To be a bit scarier," he explained. Also, apparently for the same reason, during his show he'd swing a bare lightbulb over his head. We chatted and he expressed mild interest, though, frankly, he seemed more intrigued by the book I was reading. I'd placed my copy of *Lolita* on the bar—my book group's current selection. Apparently he had a teenage girlfriend waiting for him in Eastern Europe, where, I learned, he was soon headed.

I'd returned to Reverend Luke, who was preparing to perform his first marriage, his boss's. He suggested another programmer. "This guy," Luke said, "writes genius code."

David Moxon, twenty-six, had oversized eyes, a narrow face, and a hesitant, infrequent smile. Of course, he was rail thin. He looked, I initially thought, like the star of a hostage video. He, too, was into music. He preferred electronic music, which in an uninflected voice, he described as expressing "the joy that is machine-made." He had his own band, though he wasn't crazy about the word "band." He preferred "analogue stage show."

I was more a Clash fan myself. But who cared? We met at alt.coffee, an East Village coffee house hazy with AA-levels of cigarette smoke. There was a sofa, the guts of which, I noticed, popped out the arms. Then the genius programmer uttered these enchanting words, "Yeah, I could build you a prototype."

I'd become acquainted with technical challenges like sound latency and synchronization. "Solvable," he said in a tone that made me think of that famous old smoker with the mechanical voice box.

"You could be CTO," I said to David. I meant it as encouragement. Every young company needed a Chief Technology Officer. And David seemed encouraged, though at our next meeting, he appeared even less comfortable. His eyelids, I noticed, doubleclutched before opening. Unfortunately, he'd received an offer from MTV— $120 an hour. (That was $250,000 a year for a forty-hour week.) And though he'd like to do KNation, he'd need, he said, $15,000 for the first month, up front, which I got the feeling wouldn't cover much.

It occurred to me that after all the other possibilities, I shouldn't let this one slip away. Be like LBJ, I told myself. (I'd just read a biography.) LBJ was the ultimate arm-twister. He moved close to his man, entered his personal space.

Maybe it was different when you were president.

I leaned forward; David turned away.

I decided to hook him on our shared vision of the future.

"What would you like to be doing in three years?" I asked, and directed a hopeful thumb toward his pigeon chest.

"Composing music for video games," he said in that automatic voice, at which point I got up and walked away.

$ $ $

And so there was peaceful Adi in leather chaps and busy cruisewear. People warned me that a technology company would claim to own what it built. I hardly paused. I didn't even ask Adi to sign an NDA—he'd come through a friend. Mainly I thought of my need, which seemed as big as a globe.

Adi conducted Consigliere and me on a quick tour of his dumpy office. He took small, tense steps, like an old person, and came up quietly behind one or another of the ardent young programmers. Each gazed for all he was worth at a computer screen. Some wore earphones as they typed, seemingly lost in their own worlds. (For elite work, programming looked very secretarial.) Adi placed a hand on the shoulder of one and said in a deep, soothing tone, "What are you working on?"

Oddcast's lead product was the VideoMixer—Adi had created a prototype in grad school. One of his people demonstrated it for us. By clicking the mouse you could edit your own videos, incorporating film, cartoons, stills, and a variety of special effects. It was terrific and had even been selected for inclusion in a show at the American Museum of the Moving Image.

The company had also developed a Beat Sensor, which made characters move in time with the beat. Another young programmer demonstrated a Virtual Host. The company had created an animated interactive figure (kind of sexy, really) whose lips moved as she talked to you. Her words were triggered by what you did on a site.

"You guys can do anything," I said excitedly.

"It's a science-fiction world," Adi responded indifferently. It seemed a response he might give to any number of questions.

Still, I thought, How perfect. And because this was the slim channel of my thinking these days, what I meant was, for karaoke. Oddcast could build complicated stuff online. Plus their applications looked great. Also, as Adi mentioned, they were developed for an

Internet where people used ordinary phone connections. You didn't need to wait for fast broadband, still years away.

Adi led us to a conference table rescued, I was told, from an attorney's discard pile. He seated us, then asked in a low voice so vacant I was convinced he had no idea what we were to discuss, "What do you want?"

What *did* I want? Of course, businesspeople preferred someone who could state in a precise few words what he wanted. Dithering wasn't their thing, though, sometimes, it was mine. What *did* I want from this faraway character? My focus took off like a getaway car. *What bad timing!* After all, I had a strong sense—as strong as my peculiarly recidivist commitment to KNation—that Oddcast had to be the one. How, really, did karaoke fit with a phone company? A 3D company? I fit here. A make-your-own-video product fit with a sing-your-own-song product. I actually liked the Oddcast offices. Momentum *was* important. This one had to go.

And then, as Adi, settling his chin into the palm of his hand, fixed me with a snowy gaze, something happened. Did a synapse slip its firing pattern? I don't know. But at that once-remaindered table, I suddenly connected the feeling of *want* with the *idea* of karaoke, and it was as wonderful to me as anything, as the weather or the Internet itself. I experienced—and how excellent was the timing—a breezy surge of confidence. Perhaps I had little but a $6 million concept. Still, at certain moments—and perhaps this was one—I was a fellow entrepreneur, a Rockefeller, building some essential thing. How dull was everything else!

With my emotions enchantingly consolidated, I fired up my flash animation—finally, someone was going to sit still for it. I started to expand on my whole elaborate karaoke plan, which suddenly seemed, yes, expansive.

Later Consigliere would say, "You had his eyes dancing," though I couldn't tell by looking at Adi. It was like he'd become part of a still life: the bric-a-brac desks, the dying plants, the gray-on-gray floor, and Adi, who gazed past us, saying nothing. For all I knew he'd gone mystic and was pining for the end. The only sound was the willowy traffic that floated in an open window. Then there was his buggy noise—*ihhh*. It was two-toned this time like a car horn going around a corner, a preamble, it turned out.

"*NO,*" he said in a definitive tone, apparently finishing some internal dialogue, then added, "I see it. It's a great fit. We could take you to our music clients. They would love it."

Adi wanted to work together. We had details to work out, but this one was a go, I just felt certain, wonderful in and of itself.

Chapter Sixteen

Rock Stars

THE DAY I MET David Beal, CEO of Sputnik7.com, he had professionally spotted black and orange hair.

"Orange?" asked his second-in-command offhandedly.

"Orange," answered Beal in exactly the same tone.

Apparently, it had recently been green.

Sputnik7 had wonderful, often quirky animation, short films, music—the day we met, Beal seemed particularly taken with a short film about a guy who eats wood—and no chance of making money any time soon. Still, Beal let me know that once he raised $12 million in venture capital, it seemed every traditional businessman on a couple of continents wanted to work with someone of Beal's obvious creativity.

Perhaps KaraokeNation sounded flaky. A little money would fix that, I figured. Then Clemente might hop on board. Consigliere too. (What a team I'd have!) Music rights would fall into place. Oddcast would build me an application. Russell and I might even chat via cell phone. If I closed my eyes, I could almost see the enterprise's shrubby outlines coming into focus.

And so I thought of Flatiron Partners, which had become synonymous with venture capital in New York. To get in the door at Flatiron, most start-ups sent business plans. But those odds were long. Flatiron received five to ten thousand business plans a year, and only met with a few entrepreneurs a week. (I'd heard of one entrepreneur who, hoping to stand out, delivered his plan in a pizza box.) So when Michael Prichinello, a PR exec with just the right combination of smarts, charm, and connections, offered to call Flatiron CEO Jerry Colonna, I was delighted. Flatiron usually funded ventures farther along than mine, and then for millions of dollars. As a favor, Jerry—there was only one Jerry in the New York Internet—agreed to see us.

Flatiron was housed with Chase Capital Partners, its corporate parent, on Park Avenue South, and upon entering its offices seven months into this project I had the congenial feeling of walking into wealth. The carpet was plush, volume-absorbing. There were curved glass walls, sweeping urban views, a $20,000 flat-screen TV. Several young people attended to visitors, making sure they were comfortable, fetching them drinks. The hurly-burly of the Internet seemed far removed.

In a way, it was Consigliere's description of a VC meeting that had initially gotten me interested in business. Lately I realized he'd probably been describing a meeting with Flatiron. He'd been here before. "In that conference room," he said, nodding at the room to which an eager assistant now led us. In Consigliere's telling a meeting like this was a bit of theater. One guy in an Armani suit, Consigliere once explained, had to be the flash, the visionary; another guy, the button-down, adult, banker-type; a third slightly knowing, a celebrity would be helpful. For months, that scenario had lived in my imagination. Lately, I'd cast the parts.

Clemente had to be my Armani guy. He might look like a pirate with the Bon Jovi hair and the hoop earrings, but he wore the expensive suit, a gray-green Calvin Klein today with dark tie, and—I was glad of this—the white (not the black) shirt, which hid his barbed-wire tattoo. Plus, as I knew, he had the vision.

Despite his longish hair, Consigliere was my button-down guy. He wore a tie and sports coat, not pinstripes exactly, but he was experienced, calm, with nothing to prove. Flatiron had almost funded Consigliere's previous venture.

And then there was me. A friend recently said, "I understand what everyone does . . . except you. Why do they need you?" Lately,

I'd taken to imagining myself the MC, the host. I planned to do the introductions, move things along.

Then as we waited in Flatiron's glass-walled conference room, Jerry, perhaps New York's most powerful VC, strolled into view, upsetting my preconceived notions. Consigliere, I realized, hadn't described the venture capitalist, and I'd assumed that he'd be, well, a banker-type. I had in mind lanky and gray-haired, the kind to project moneyed respectability. He'd have a hint of the patrician, down to the hand-stitched buttonholes in his expensive suit, the jacket of which, with practiced nonchalance, he'd toss over a chair. And yet here was Jerry in jeans, a flannel shirt, sneakers. (He owned, I'd later read, all of three suits.) At thirty-five, Jerry, who may have timed the stock market boom as well as anyone in America, seemed kind of roly-poly. He had a big square head, a scruffy beard. And he entered talking, with a higher voice than I'd expected. Actually, my first impression was that he shouted, though that probably wasn't true. Was this, I suddenly wondered, the banker with his hand in a $500 million till? In these preened surroundings, Jerry looked like a member of the grounds crew.

$ $ $

The truth was that venture capital in New York had until recently—until say six years ago—been just another insular branch of banking. VCs had been bet-hedgers, cautious, settled. They spent a good portion of their days poring over the fine print on East European metal parts deals. You weren't likely to read about them in the glossy magazines. Or bump into them at a social event, or, if you did, understand what the hell they were going on about. In 1996, when the *New York Times* business section announced the launch of Flatiron it felt obligated to include a laborious explanation—a thirty-two-word explanation—of just what VCs did, including the words "yield big payoffs." Of course, the explanation probably helped Jerry's family, none of whom understood what he proposed to do when, one day, he arrived home and announced he was going into venture capital.

The Internet didn't take long to transform what New Yorkers understood about venture capitalists, or what venture capitalists understood about themselves. "VCs are the new rock stars," said Stephen Brotman, a partner in Silicon Alley Venture Partners, a $14 million fund. This was just the kind of thing prematurely graying guys from Jersey were permitted to believe for a time. Brotman, a prematurely graying guy from Jersey, claimed he was hounded not only by entrepreneurs—he received about a thousand pitches a year—but by marriage proposals.

Perhaps there was something to it. At one Internet conference, I'd sat in on a panel of six venture capitalists. The instant the session concluded, a couple hundred attendees rushed the small stage. They circled individual panelists each of whom moved toward an exit, dragging along a collection of hopeful entrepreneurs. From a distance, each group looked like a swirling solar system. One after another, the entrepreneurs, CEOs a lot of them, pitched their businesses in a few seconds, trying to get a VC's card in return.

"You see people's dreams," one of the VCs confided to me, though he was evidently weary of people's dreams. Slapping his pockets, he told entrepreneurs he'd run out of business cards.

If VCs were rock stars, few were bigger than Jerry. Indeed, at a certain moment the media couldn't seem to get enough of him. Jerry was a father of three who lived in an unassuming four-bedroom colonial in Long Island. Yet every minute of his day suddenly seemed of interest. One magazine offered readers an intimate glimpse of Jerry at home—it was 7:30 A.M.—working off a few pounds with his personal trainer, whose first name we learned was Emmanuel.

"You're doing great!" barked Emmanuel.

Jerry, we read, did push-ups, sit-ups. There was some high-stepping, and a treadmill. I found myself imagining Jerry's meaty head turning a butcher block red.

"How do you feel?" asked Emmanuel.

"Terrible!" Jerry responded, the magazine revealed.

W magazine even showed up to do—was it possible?—a photo spread on fashions of the Internet. (Imagine the tone of suppressed excitement as the correspondent peeked into Jerry's closet: *Look!* He has *three* suits!)

There was something amusing about the media delicately picking its way through Jerry's very ordinary life. (Jerry was amused.) And
yet, Jerry's background, his approach, his very ordinariness, did represent a new style, and one that would come to be the style of the New
York Internet VC.

To start with, Jerry's background wasn't fussily business-heavy.
One day *USA Today* called to ask Jerry's opinion on the devaluation
of the Indonesian currency. How absurd! Jerry didn't have a background in economics. He didn't have an MBA. He didn't really have
what were traditionally considered venture capitalist qualifications. In
fact, he didn't, at one point, seem a likely candidate to be a capitalist
at all. Jerry grew up in a working-class family—his father was a
proofreader in the printing business. As a young man he'd participated in Socialist Workers Party marches. He received a BA from
Queens College, the one in Queens, New York. It was in English literature. Jerry still loved to read, and also to point out that he loved to
read. As a rule, bankers didn't shoot you excited e-mails about the latest Jules Verne translation, which Jerry did. (Or name a daughter after
a character out of Flaubert, which Jerry also did.) "I'll warrant I'm
the most literate VC you'll ever meet," he'd tell me, which seemed a
knock on that older, more parochial banker's style.

Jerry's first job out of college had been in journalism, working for
a trade publication, which is not the top of the journalism heap. But
(even then) Jerry had a knack for timing. In 1986, as the personal
computer age built steam, Jerry went to work for *Information Week*—
he'd spend three years as its editor.

Jerry familiarized himself with technology, got comfortable with
it, another aspect of the new VC's style. Bankers used to learn just
enough to fake it in front of a client. Once the elevator doors
swooshed shut, they'd lapse into pleasant chat about the weekend
place in Connecticut. These days, VCs were techies. Jerry told a story
of nearly coming to blows over which was the better cell-phone
battery.

That old starched-collar banker wanted business to run smoothly,
to produce an acceptable profit, and to not piss people off. To that

banker—and in fact, to Jerry at the start—the Internet hardly seemed a tool to shake up business. In 1996, when Jerry—him, too—printed up business cards at Kinko's and launched Flatiron, he recalled "The expectations were that [the Internet] was going to be an iterative, incremental, evolutionary improvement in the core business processes." At the outset, the Internet was going to be a slightly better fax machine.

"Along the way the potential for greater and greater change took hold," Jerry would explain. Soon, the past wasn't prologue. The future seemed at hand. (Perhaps Jules Verne would be helpful.) The play of ideas soon seemed as important as the crunching of numbers.

For the new VC, it was as if the real subject of business, indeed, its real interest, was change. "It"—business—"is not about money," Jerry insisted, and he was often insistent, which I took as another element of the new VC style. "It's about creating the next great thing." For a time, everywhere Jerry looked he saw a "passion about changing the way things are done; sometimes," he said, "for the mere sake of change."

Like so many of these new VCs, Jerry was of the Internet, not a sober, bankerly presence riding herd on it. The new New York VC no longer huddled over depreciation schedules or charts of return on capital. He didn't seem to venerate established institutions. (For Jerry, maybe it was because one of those institutions had fired his dad on Christmas Eve after thirty-one years on the job.) Jerry preferred change, and in that regard he opted to go with his gut. If he had a rap on himself, it was that he was "too instinctual."

To a great extent, it was Jerry's style, his brash, confident, enthusiastic, casual, incautious style, that made so many want to join the VC ranks—in 1999, for the first time, more Harvard MBAs became VCs than investment bankers. That, and, oh yes, the profits. Of course, for most of the public, the defining characteristic of the new VC style was his touch. He had the Midas touch.

VCs hadn't ever done badly—even those East European prospectus readers had returned roughly 35 percent. Shortly after Jerry came online, however, it was possible to think about profits on the scale of

1000 percent. For investors, the Internet represented the greatest legal creation of wealth in history. Flatiron, with a dozen employees, would amass roughly $1 billion in gains. The civic-minded threw fits about such things—it *was* undeserved. But capital has never had strong feelings for citizenship. It seeks the greatest return.

And so, suddenly Internet capital was like sunlight in those countries where the sun never sets. "I could pick up my phone—honestly, this is true—and in thirty minutes finance a company," said one VC, meaning he could raise millions on a phone call. Institutional money abounded. Flatiron's initial pot had been $50 million; it swelled to $500 million. Smaller groups raised $5 or $10 or $14 million. And for a time no north Jersey stockbroker or Long Island dentist with an extra $100,000 wanted to miss out on this Internet thing. I knew one Jersey guy who owned a small helicopter shuttle company. Suddenly he was deciding whether to invest in a business that provided customer service via the Internet—and which would be run out of India.

For a lot of these guys, venture investments were pyramid schemes—in fact, all venture investments resembled pyramid schemes. Idealists like Jerry hated that kind of talk. And, of course, VCs batted around important ideas about the future of technology. And they really wanted to build revenue-generating businesses. But "a successful exit," to use Jerry's term, wasn't based on nailing the future or building a business. Instead, as in a pyramid scheme, profits came when an early investment was bought out many times over by other investors who believed there would be even greater payoffs later—ideally, within two years.

Most VCs accepted the logic of the pyramid scheme—even if they shunned the terminology—and, thus, they knew that the winning play, particularly for smaller investors, was to get the jump on the other money. "If the Internet is a pyramid scheme," as one writer explained, "then the only time to get in is at the start." If not, then you're shopping at upscale Saks instead of discount Loehmann's for the same merchandise.

One result, as I soon learned, was that while entrepreneurs hunted money, money chased deals. So every harebrained proposal that came through the door had to be examined—the germ of the next big thing, or next big payoff, might be buried there. In Jerry's view, many of the newer investors had little idea what they were doing. So, a second result, as Jerry complained, was that "there's shit getting funded that shouldn't."

Personally, I found both of these results encouraging. Consigliere had mentioned that the VC pitch was the biggest moment in an entrepreneur's life. Before waltzing into the biggest VC's office, I'd wanted some practice talking to the new breed of VC. The new climate certainly didn't hurt my chances of getting attention.

$ $ $

One of the earliest-stage VCs was the incubator, which supplied money as well as office space, phones, and business skills to fledgling entrepreneurs. In 2000, there were supposedly 800 of these around the country, sponsoring almost 15,000 businesses. Steven Massarsky, who ran Business Incubation Group in Tribeca, had a graying beard, a shiny bald head, and an impressive habit of standing perfectly still. He'd previously made money in the music business—he'd launched the career of Cyndi Lauper—and the comic-book business. Gold records hung on his office walls. To talk, he took me into his special room. It had twisty lamps with giant lightbulbs and beanbag chairs. He said he liked "to spin" in here, which apparently meant to think.

He read my business plan very carefully, then counseled me "Follow your passion."

So I asked him for $50,000.

"That's easy," he scoffed, which I knew meant no money would be forthcoming.

Another early-stage VC agreed to see me one spring afternoon. He said he'd come to my apartment. His office was tied up. How I enjoyed telling people, "No, sorry, I can't today. You see, I've got a venture capitalist stopping by *my apartment!*" Unfortunately, the afternoon he arrived was unexpectedly hot. The temperature shot into the nineties. I thought my apartment might burst from the heat, which, in a rash moment, I'd decided to circulate with a noisy fan.

Michael Oster of Grand Central Holdings didn't seem to mind. Oster, who appeared dressed for a Dockers commercial, took a seat at my kitchen counter as I hurried through the presentation. I had to hurry, sweat puddled on his top lip. It didn't spoil his mood, though.

"You could see people using it," he said. "It's like turning your computer into a nightclub." He had a couple of ideas, things I ought to do, and a couple of people I ought to contact. Then, he said if things progressed, "I might toss in a few dollars." He made investing sound as effortless as a game of horseshoes. Which was just what I wanted to hear. I needed a shot of confidence to ready me for Jerry.

$ $ $

Consigliere took a minute to chitchat with Jerry, recalling shared old times, no bitterness now. In a moment, Jerry turned to the matter at hand.

"I'm sorry, this is a karaoke play?" Jerry began with an unsettling pause between karaoke and play.

I laughed weakly, as if in on the joke. Of course I still sometimes recalled that karaoke was funny. But if we could just have a moment of Jerry's considered attention, I was certain the possibilities would intrigue him.

Jerry, though, bristled with an unusually emphatic energy. I attempted to introduce the unrecognized karaoke trend, the one we'd uncovered, by mentioning Gwyneth Paltrow's recent karaoke movie.

Jerry was not impressed. "I don't care about the movies," he said.

"You don't?" I said, thrown off. Didn't everyone care about the movies?

"Taxi cabs are in the movies," he said. I knew people liked Jerry, though I suddenly couldn't imagine why.

"It's a movie *about* karaoke," I said.

Jerry stared at me as if taking in a bit of spoiled meat. I handed Jerry a copy of our research. Unfortunately I'd spilled the water provided by Jerry's kind assistant. The sheets were wet, the print had run. Jerry didn't mind. "Can I drill down?" he said. "Drill down" was clearly a favorite expression. Jerry studied the sheets for a minute. "I'll challenge you," Jerry said merrily. His attitude seemed oppositional, a descriptive usually applied to disruptive children.

We claimed that 11 million adult Americans currently on the Internet either owned a karaoke machine or had been to a karaoke bar in the past three months.

"Based on your definition that includes me," Jerry said. "My kid got one at Christmas and we did it twice."

Consigliere, playing senior statesman, interjected. "Jerry's good because he bothers to understand this kind of research and a lot of guys don't." I figured Consigliere could have continued, perhaps dominated, but gave others a shot. I would have liked to jump in, Mitty-like, consort with the powerful. But suddenly, I was shy. So I let Clemente have a go. Weeks ago he'd thanked me for including him in the meeting—like I'd ever imagine it without him. Now, he seemed eager to test himself, to try out the role of businessman-on-the-line.

"This isn't a family member doing it," said Clemente. "This is you. We surveyed online adults eighteen and over. They're the ones spending money."

"Having one doesn't mean I'm a fan," said Jerry. He could, it seemed, disagree with everything you said. Still, I got the feeling he might like you to prove him wrong.

"Critical is interest in using," said Clemente. Fourteen million people have said they'd be interested in using a karaoke site—that was our other outstanding number. Clemente explained where he got that number. "That's a viable market," he concluded. Clemente was going all out. I thought for a moment he was about to stand up.

"It's *the* market," said Jerry dismissively. "I don't know if it's viable." I suddenly imagined Jerry coming to blows over a cell-phone battery.

Clemente was as relentless as Jerry. Plus he got, as Consigliere would later point out, to make those big CEO-ish assertions, the unprovable kind that people like Jerry want to hear. "These numbers say to us that people online are interested in being interactive, they're interested in getting more control over their consumption of entertainment, including music. And that includes being able to sing along in a community with their friends."

"This isn't about music, it's about community," snapped Jerry.

"It's about music, but it's also about community," answered Clemente.

You just sensed that these two were bound to get along.

Jerry might not be persuaded by karaoke, but he seemed to buy that we'd identified an untapped market, and perhaps a big one. Still, in a conference room like this, the real intrigue was hardly the future of Internet karaoke. It was money—profane, alive, and kind of thrilling. And Jerry cut to it. "I don't believe that people would pay for this," he said. Jerry's problem, which would prove to be one of the Internet's principal business problems, and indeed, a challenge for many of Jerry's businesses, was this: There might be lots of identifiable online interests or markets, but few, so far, had translated into much revenue.

Clemente maintained that there was a mass market of niches. Jerry didn't talk of niches, but of community, of shared lifestyles, of affinity, which seemed a related concept. Jerry's working theory, and one that appeared to connect many of his content-heavy businesses, was that you could attract people with the same interests or needs, then sell them stuff or advertise to them. Sometimes Jerry gave an example from the hit TV show *Seinfeld*. "The interesting thing is that you laughed out loud," said Jerry. "Do you care that it's on NBC? You couldn't give a rat's ass. It has nothing to do with the brand, the network. On the Internet, affinity is everything." Jerry appeared to see the potential in creating online communities, usually around interesting, focused content. He backed GeoCities.com (a local content site), StarMedia (a Latin site), UBO (a black site), PlanetOut (a gay site). He liked targeted news organizations. He funded Inside.com, which aimed at publishing interests, and The Street.com, which targeted financial interests.

By Jerry's lights, what we had in KaraokeNation was a link to a karaoke community. "What you're asserting is that this is a lifestyle and you could possibly exploit the lifestyle," he said.

Was there really *a karaoke lifestyle?* I wondered. It sounded mysterious. *Karaoke* friends? *Karaoke* dating? *Karaoke* clothes?

Jerry turned to me. "He's your strongest component," he said and pointed at Clemente, "because this is all about data."

Jerry focused on Clemente. "You seem pretty jazzed," he said. "Or else you're a really good actor." Jerry didn't wait for a laugh. He wasn't the type.

"I am," said Clemente sincerely. I hadn't necessarily known that.

Then Jerry turned to me. "You alone can't do this," he told me then. "But you and Clemente sounds good. And him"—he pointed to Consigliere—"I know already, and a prior relationship, that's always valuable. So are we talking about a package?"

The question hung in that conference room, all of us mum for once.

Chapter Seventeen

CEO Seeking Intimacy/Marriage

HAVE YOU PEEKED at the personals lately? You know, those relationship ads in newspapers and magazines: man-seeks-woman, woman-seeks-man. The personals are a stunningly revealing genre. A person sums up what he or she believes most attractive, most interesting, in him- or herself. When I looked at *New York* magazine's personals* in the late nineties, I noticed that many people found a business connection very attractive. "Entrepreneur, MBA, Private Pilot," was how one suitor introduced himself. "Bright, Successful, Spontaneous—Entrepreneur," said another, the dash apparently indicating some equivalency. A business connection seemed to dress up an intriguing number of these romantic resumes. "Handsome, successful business owner" was one; "physician/entrepreneur" another. (Apparently physician alone didn't cut it anymore. Nor, by the way, did attorney or college professor. "Attorney, investor," was how one lawyer described himself. "Successful executive and college professor," said another.)

CEO, of course, stood alone. "CEO Seeking Intimacy/Marriage," said one passionate businessman. I had to admire his straightforwardness, his confidence, his businesslike approach. He sought intimacy. Eventually, he might offer marriage—the punctuation seemed to indicate some staging.

---

*I sampled the personal ads in *New York* magazine from 1995 to 2000, looking at one week per quarter.

In the meantime, he, like all his fellow business suitors, offered a taste of success. Few made any bones about it. As one ad said, "You only pass this way once, why not do it in style." For the business-oriented—and these ads seemed to set the tone for the personal advertiser generally—success seduced. Specifically, one version of success, the one that yielded a "luxe" or a "glamorous life," as two ads put it, including, as one ad spelled out, "the Hamptons, limos and fine dining . . ." ("Hamptons Weekends All Year" was a variation on the theme.) "I have built a successful Internet business," said one entrepreneur, stating an important qualification. Now he wanted a woman who enjoyed "the finer things in life, including spontaneous weekends away, dining out." That attorney/investor helpfully inventoried the finer things: "arts, restaurants, travel, theater, film, cabarets, horses, Europe."

People in these ads didn't seem to go in for candlelight dining; instead there were meals at "the best restaurants," perhaps on other continents. That's what one advertiser seemed to suggest by offering this trio: "fine dining, wine, world travel." Personal advertisers didn't take cozy car trips to the shore; rather there was travel, a grander undertaking, sometimes, as one ad specified "to Europe." One advertiser neatly summed up the current romantic style, saying he sought "companion for world travel by early retirement entrepreneur." Another romantic candidate, not to be outdone, provided transportation. He was "pilot of own plane."

Of course people have often understood success as a set of financial rewards. (And no doubt a man's access to material goods has long seduced a woman.) And yet for the past fifty years, success hadn't been so narrowly focused, so single-minded. Alternatives thrived—was it the one put forward by the bohemian, the hippie, the poet, the idealist, the intellectual? How about the ill-dressed but well-credentialed scientist? You could once shun money and choose interest. Remember? Lately, as those personal ads suggested, money was like the fat old lady in the tub, crowding out other versions of success.

And so, I suspected that, in addition to all the other reasons to hurry into business—its idealism, its fun, its excitement—the recent insistence on one strain of success also had something to do with the great popularity of the business urge. Perusing the personals was hardly scientific. Still, it was difficult to resist the idea that if you weren't in business, well, how would you get the girl?

$ $ $

The nineties hardly invented materialism. As my parents came of age, the average middle-class family was able to buy as never before and measured progress against a series of ownership milestones: cars, homes, college educations. My mother, though queasy in elevators, would no doubt have been tickled to know someone who flew his own plane.

And yet my parents weren't particularly acquisitive. I suspect my father enjoyed talking about money more than spending it. He was good at figures, did them in his head, and enjoyed outwitting ineffi-cient bureaucracies. He somehow calculated that one company billed customers-of-record on the fourteenth of the month. So each month, he canceled on the thirteenth, and on the fifteenth he rein-stated. He was never charged. "Serves 'em right," I could hear him say.

As far as success went, he was serious, though amiable. "Whatever you do, do it well," he liked to repeat, a formula that seemed more concerned with effort and excellence than outcome. "Success will take care of itself." As far as money went, he often said, "Rich or poor, it's nice to have money." Which I took to mean that though everyone needed money, still, it wouldn't change a person fundamentally.

My parents' generation kept up with the Joneses. Yet the goal of this contest was not to lead by ostentatious example. In the fifties, you wanted to fit in. To spend freely, indeed to *want* freely, wasn't all that acceptable. Every ambitious person sought opportunity, but con-tentment with one's lot had a place too. Their materialism was tem-pered by the suspicion that wanting too much or too avidly could result in frustration, discontent, unhappiness.

For my parents, contained spending, economizing, budgeting, saving were part and parcel of a good character and of a healthy, indeed, of a successful lifestyle. To my parents, a penny saved *was* a penny earned, just as Ben Franklin wrote.

Of course, my parents' generation went on shopping sprees; credit was widely introduced to average consumers. I grew up in a stylish home. My mother decorated the living room with a custom-made green velvet couch and thick embroidered curtains. Yet, the hedonism rampant in those personal ads would, I suspect, have dismayed them. My father wore dress shirts till his elbows poked through the sleeves. At restaurants, he usually refused to drink anything but tap water.

My family had the appliances of most upper-middle-class homes—dishwasher, vacuum cleaner, color TVs. Still, as the academic literature of the time spelled out, buying was considered a cognitive phenomenon for my parents. A product's utility struck them as its most important characteristic. Every few years my father would purchase a car. On a Saturday morning, he'd head to the dealership. He needed a vehicle with good gas mileage and room for the family. One time he came home with a station wagon, another with a VW microbus. He didn't stock them with options. We didn't always have air-conditioning or FM radio. And he was indifferent to color. The important thing was that he could drive it home that day. For years, we had a mud-colored car.

Adam Smith, the original laissez-faire capitalist, believed consumer desire a spur to commerce. If people wanted more, then industry would produce more. But even he said, "Sudden changes of fortune seldom contribute much to happiness." And, then sounding like a Beatle, he added, "The chief part of human happiness arises from the consciousness of being beloved." (Personally, Smith was partial to good conversation.)

Future marketers would press Smith's acquisition-as-engine-of-progress views on the public—his point about happiness, well, there'd be time to talk later. Among other things, this meant thrifty Franklin had to be undone. That was an explicit project as my parents came of age. "To demonstrate that the hedonistic approach to [. . .] life is a moral, not an immoral one," was how Ernest Dichter, one of the first and most influential motivational research experts, put it at the time.

And so, to generations raised on planning and saving, advertisers had to effect a kind of conversion. "To give moral permission to have fun without guilt," said Dichter. Consumers had to feel they deserved a new car every two years, a specific goal of researchers like Dichter. Purchasing what you wanted (rather than needed) had to be thought a basic right, like the right to happiness, with which it would soon be identified.

My parents didn't outline a particular success program for me. One idealistic writer of my parent's generation wanted "some honorable" profession for his children, one that "would make the best of their abilities, provide them with the satisfaction that comes with the exercise of responsibility," which seemed to jibe with my parents' outlook. (Not that they were easygoing. From his command post in the den my father issued insistent suggestions.) Still, lawyer, educator, politician, union activist, doctor, even writer, any of those would fit the bill, as far as they were concerned. I don't believe business ever came up—except, perhaps, to take over the small school they owned. They professed happiness with whatever intrigued me. Which was lucky, since I was more drawn to interest than practical advantage. (Though, at least in my mother's eyes, a person could go too far. One interest of mine at the time was to come under fire, which was where she drew the line.)

My orientation wasn't out of the ordinary (except, perhaps, the "under fire" part). My generation had headed off to college believing, remember, that devising a meaningful philosophy of life was the top priority of a young person's life. In the seventies, an astonishing 69 percent of Americans said that "a job that is interesting" was part of the good life. Youth culture informed the world and, in case you've forgotten, it was once insistently antimaterialistic. For many, "getting ahead" seemed a marginal goal. "Why does it"—getting ahead— "trouble so many? Why is it under siege?" wondered Yankelovich in 1981.

For me, a charming French film provided an answer. In *Cousin, Cousine,* nominated for three Academy Awards in 1976, the main character precipitously changed careers every few years. But how do you get ahead? he was asked. "Oh," he said, in perfect step with the times, "that doesn't interest me at all." (What would his personal ad have looked like? "Guy with amusing job(s), evolved philosophy of life, no interest in getting ahead, seeks same.") He lacked ambition, but had a keen sense of fun, of pleasure, of the moment—and in the movie, of course, he got the girl. The film seemed to argue that your choice was material success *or* happiness. That was a robust cultural opposition, one we celebrated and mostly thought we'd invented.

And yet, whatever lofty, absorbing, success-agnostic purpose we set for ourselves, by the time my generation reached the stores, a conversion was under way. Wanting was on its way to being just fine, no longer tainted by notions of too-much or not-now. We were no longer rational buyers. We had emotional shopping experiences. Indeed, we had relationships with products. For a generation bent on expressing itself, it should be no surprise that consumption quickly became another means of self-expression. Purchases could be witty, ironic, amusing, just like our personalities. "It seems an inescapable fact of modern life that we learn, define, and remind ourselves of who we are by our possessions," said one researcher.

In the seventies, I bought a Simca, a snappy French import from Chrysler. It was quite original, odd to look at, not unlike the *deux-chevaux* in which those French existentialists tooled around Paris and, according to the newspaper ad, available immediately. I shared my father's impatience with shopping, though, I'm afraid, not his nose for the sensible purchase. A Simca was perhaps the least practical car a person could buy. A year later, when my transmission blew, Chrysler was out of the Simca business. I had to jack up the car and repair it myself, an interesting experience—I used a stick of butter to set scattered ball bearings in place—though the reverse gear never worked all that well.

By the eighties, we were on our way to embracing the hedonism Dichter had hoped for us. Restraints were coming off. Soon, the academic literature would refer to hedonic consumption, purchases "pursued essentially for the pleasure they bring." Pleasure, not utility. Consumption went into high gear, unfettered by Franklin-style calculation or the desire to fit in with Jonesie.

In the nineties, someone would uncover a quiet culture of scuffed-shoe millionaires who drove late-model cars, ate leftovers, and bragged, "I am a tightwad." But if they really existed—and even proponents suggested they weren't more than 3 percent of the population—their values hardly dominated. Consumption was now an experience that, according to the research literature, started long before the moment of purchase and endured well beyond it. Consumers not only had emotions about products, they had *pre-acquisition fantasies,* said the literature. In one study, 61 percent of respondents "always have something in mind that they look forward to buying." Almost a third dreamed—at night—of participating in the "enchanted domain" of consumer culture.

Maslow had thought that once material needs were met, people would turn their attention up the hierarchy of needs towards self-actualization. These days, self-actualization happened through credit cards. "We are what we have," explained one consumer researcher, a formula that would have made little sense to Franklin, Maslow, my parents, or most previous generations, for that matter.

Even college students had come around. Indeed, I can think of no sharper generational distinction than the changed attitudes toward money and success. In the nineties, an amazing 75 percent of freshmen declared they wanted to be "very well off financially," up from 45 percent in my era. The ambivalence toward getting ahead had been cleared up, gone in a generation. Yankelovich's query—why does getting ahead trouble so many?—has the ring of a prank question today.

By the nineties, wanting had been rehabilitated. Especially wanting money, which hardly precluded wanting happiness, or interest, or fulfillment. That cultural opposition had collapsed. Now, if you believed those personal ads, they might be bound up the way jobs and job security once were.

By the end of the nineties, 69 percent of Americans told pollsters that "a lot of money" was part of "the good life"—in 1975, only 38 percent felt that way. By now, "really nice clothes" were more important to the good life—half the population wanted them—than a job with some worthwhile content, which interested a third. Now what people preferred in a job—62 percent—was that it pay more than average. "What do Americans want?" asked one Roper survey. "More than they have," concluded the analyst.

No wonder other versions of success couldn't hold their own. Now, what you did mattered less, or how well you did it, or the honor or public esteem it brought you. Lately, there was a single galvanizing measure of success. As the writer James Atlas remarked, "making it" counted, and making it meant one thing. How much money does he earn? This, said Atlas, "is the question on everybody's lips."

$ $ $

I wasn't supposed to be the type to obsess about money, which my era thought *so* bourgeois. I was of the meaningful-philosophy-of-life generation. Still, who could resist? I might imagine myself worldly, sophisticated, broadminded, discussing Plato with a tutor I hired, or exchanging Wolof greetings with the African merchant on my block. Now whatever your references, your aspirations, your interests, let's face it, the bottom line mattered. Who didn't suspect, without disdain or irony or a second thought, that the clothes, the car, the dwelling, really did make the man? Over lunch with writers we talked of book advances or movie deals. Or of the successful writer who'd sat for an admiring profile of his . . . finances. The *New York Times* respectfully reported that this best-selling author had purchased an apartment and a summer house and part of a bar. And apparently there was a boat.

"I couldn't believe he was worth so little," a friend said, a perverse dig since of course he had more than any of us.

Whatever standards of success you'd grown up with, *having* was the thing that counted now. If that fat advance or those healthy stock options didn't validate your endeavors, then who cared how very colorful your experiences were? There was an ever-so-slight but nonetheless piquant condescension attached to the poor friend, the poor relation, the one, say, whose rented summer house was, oh, how charming, *sans* washer and dryer.

At least that's what I felt. "Our kids *love* your place," I was told.

"Great," I said and paused. "We're going to swing by and," I paused again, "uh, do you mind, if we bring the laundry?"

"Of course not."

I grabbed a box of Tide and a bottle of wine—an expensive one, just to be sure—and jumped in our donated, fifteen-year-old car.

What could a few sandy towels possibly matter? I reassured myself. Why did I sense that the lack of a spin cycle reflected on my standing? Where was my haughtiness, my postmaterialist disdain, my wrinkled-nose indifference, my indignation, my nostalgia? They were like the frail elderly. And so instead I'd paused, and in the instant of that pause I'd thought, How exasperating to always be the petitioner.

Was that the reason that each summer my wife and I hunted for a vacation house, one with all the trimmings? Not that we could afford those we saw. Did the realtors suspect? Apparently not. They treated us as if we were millionaires, indulging our complaints about the color scheme the fixtures, the view.

"Well, it needs a lot of work," we said offhandedly.

How delicious to pass, even momentarily, for a grandee!

Not that I was really excluded. Let's face it, the charmed world of success let me in, let us all in, just enough. In 1999, one in eight families earned $100,000, which made this the fastest-growing income category. (In 1990 one in twelve had earned as much, on an inflation-adjusted basis.) And my wife and I did just fine. Indeed, I'd accumulated much more than seemed possible when, skipping out on Brown, I'd signed up for "the premeditated poor," as Gilder labeled those insufficiently eager to jump tax brackets. To my amazement I'd bought at exactly the right time and now lived in a fashionable section of New York. I had a new kitchen, Miele appliances. And that summer rental, though appliance-poor, served me just fine.

Plus, I had disposable income, and could be an enthusiastic consumer. One gloomy afternoon, in need of a pick-me-up, I bicycled to Comme des Garcons' chic Chelsea address, the one you entered through a curved, swinging door and an arched tunnel—talk about pre-acquisition fantasy. I purchased the least expensive shirt in the store, just something to brighten my day.

And yet however harmless, however fun a shopping excursion might prove, it was also true that money seemed less a privilege than a necessity. Once—and this seems almost incomprehensible to me now—I'd felt provided for, as if a living would always come my way. What did I need? I can remember asking myself. The amount seemed inconsequential. Lately, I found myself walking city streets, totaling my bills, mortgage and electric and phone, insurance, repairs, medical—like my father, I did the figures in my head. Then, idiosyncratically, I'd forget the sum so that every few blocks, I had to start over. I wandered for blocks in an anxious loop of debt. Why shouldn't I be anxious? What my parents financed on one salary I had trouble imagining on two. College for three kids? A house with four bedrooms? It cost a whole lot more to be rich—or poor—these days.

What's more, by a strange, seemingly ineluctable process (the one Dichter favored), there appeared no end to the conversion of luxuries to needs. More than a quarter of those families earning at least $100,000 said they couldn't afford everything they *really needed*. It was like being a shopaholic who, paradoxically, couldn't quite afford the essentials. Was this so unusual? Whose expectations, whose tastes could resist the constant ratcheting up? The most familiar elements of the American dream had expanded. Families got smaller but new homes were by now 40 percent larger than in the seventies, 100 percent larger than in the fifties. In the seventies, 17 percent of people said they needed a second car; in the nineties that more than doubled. And one home wasn't necessarily enough either; 43 percent of adults considered a vacation home part of the good life. (You could tally the longing, since only 3 percent of Americans had one.)

Lately, I found myself attending parties just to inspect the host's redone loft, his high-end appurtenances. At one party, a male friend and I gawked at the Viking stove, cleverly vented in the rear. We talked about the tasteful Artemide lighting, the hand-plastered walls.

"Six coats," my friend said, referring to the walls.

"Six!" I almost shouted and wondered what it might cost to get such a lustrous finish for myself. (Here was contemporary boy talk. Not gadgets and sports, but appliances and square footage.)

I didn't try to keep up with the Joneses. How quaint that suburban phrase sounded! The Joneses had lived next door. My Joneses were all over the city and all over the newsstand. They were the people in *Vanity Fair* and on MTV. As a journalist, I probably came into closer contact than most. I interviewed one stock trader while he smoked a $76 cigar. "From Switzerland," he informed me, then climbed into his Rolls.

And yet no difference the job a person did, it was almost impossible to overemphasize the familiarity we felt with the material lives of sports stars, movie stars, music stars. Whatever else the famous did, they were heroes of consumption. And this was the real pinch: No matter that you kept your distance from these high-rolling lives, you couldn't help but be aware, hyperaware, of their presence. Perhaps I forced my nose in it, examining the glossies, which, whatever their stated subject, inevitably chronicled the new bourgeoisie, the one I'd once thought to *epater*. I flipped through an article about Shaquille O'Neal in *The New Yorker*. His California mansion had room for hundreds of guests and fifteen cars, including a silver Mercedes whose headlights he'd engraved with the Superman logo. I studied a photo spread of Josh Harris, the clever Internet entrepreneur who founded Pseudo.com. In *New York* magazine he was also the eccentric millionaire who wired his 4,000 square feet SoHo loft as a TV studio, plugging cameras and mikes into a $150,000 electrical skeleton.

Perhaps greed was now good. How about envy? "But do I have enough?" was how James Atlas expressed that emblematic contemporary feeling. Atlas was an interesting case. He wrote for distinguished magazines, authored important biographies. His opinion mattered. Plus he was settled comfortably in the upper middle class. He was an admirable success; my parents would have thought him one. (I'm sure his parents did.) And yet Atlas hadn't experienced what a successful person was supposed to these days: a big pay day. And so old-fashioned Atlas, his brand of success unratified, didn't *feel* like a success.

In a chilling article in *The New Yorker*, the pleasures that researchers once located in participating, even fleetingly, in the enchanted realm of affluence, seemed to elude poor James Atlas. He had a summer house and a fine apartment in a nice neighborhood and kids in private schools. And yet he seemed constantly reminded of what he couldn't afford, and thus, of who he wasn't. Indeed, he seemed to endlessly rehearse his disappointment. In one particularly unsettling scene, he recounted how his family sat around discussing what each would purchase if he or she had the money. Atlas sometimes rented a car—a lowly Corsica, he recalled. It frustrated him to not own. Not just any car, mind you. He told his family he wanted a Range Rover.

Who these days could resist wanting what you didn't have? And why should you? Almost two-thirds of people strolled around with wish lists in their heads—6.3 items on the average one, said the research. Astonishingly, people mostly had the same items on their lists—a fancy car, like the one Atlas wanted, appeared on 42 percent. Even in our fantasy lives, we represented ourselves—our best selves—through our high-end purchases. In the nineties, we were all like those personal-ad writers. We couldn't really imagine an alternative.

In response, moralists urged courage. Resist the monolithic standard of success, went their argument. Adjust your expectations, align them with your values, your philosophies of life, the ones you hatched in college. But where was the societal echo? It wasn't just the rush for money that tyrannized, but the concurrent collapse of alternatives. Who really valued the quiet, the diligent, the earnest? Who really cared about the tightwad millionaire? The appliance-less? The eccentric? The creative? The bookish? The Olympic athlete who wasn't on his way to becoming a millionaire athlete? The attorney who wasn't also a businessman? The patched-elbow member of the meritocracy who once had everything going for him? Did it really matter that in my book group we argued like cats and dogs about the meaning of love in *The Red and the Black?* (Those few hours seemed parenthetical.) Who could contend, with a straight face, that there was virtue in a modest existence? (Virtue was your own foundation doling out grants.) Public display of poverty seemed faintly ridiculous. Like the Halloween costume worn day after day by the insistent child.

Mostly, money whistled and we came running. All of us. Like those incoming freshmen, we strove to be well off financially, very well off. Still, the moneymaking culture, so inviting, so promising, left us, many of us, feeling winded, iffy, a bit excluded. And yet what was the alternative? Be a struggling novelist? Sharp in a tan corduroy jacket? *Please!* Who would you date?

No wonder business now had us delivering our dreams to venture capitalists, sometimes in a pizza box. The new business culture built on some of our best notions—our sense of our own possibilities, idealisms, even our individuality. But also it appealed to our deep-felt insecurities. Money wasn't only a treat, a fantasy, a means to an end. It was the only thing that mattered. And the success culture, once ironic, now avid, suggested that what we had wasn't quite enough, didn't measure up, and maybe, if we headed into business, well, we might do better. And get the girl as well.

Chapter Eighteen

To Advance the KNation Cause

THE EAST VILLAGE ADDRESS I'd been given led to a brick tenement next to an awning marked "Precision Body Piercing." The tenement's front door was made of reinforced steel which, nonetheless, pushed open easily. I entered a short, stingingly bright corridor. There, two signs begged visitors to secure the door behind them. Crime, I sensed, might be seconds away. Fortunately, Adi poked his head into the hall. I followed him into his apartment, and couldn't believe my eyes. It was as if walking a seedy urban street I'd turned a corner and suddenly, found myself in a nightclub.

Adi's apartment had two sweeping floors. The lower one featured a stage. Adi mentioned that Blue Man Group had once rehearsed here, though these days, in keeping with the nightclub feel, it was often used for parties. There were two huge stacks of speakers and a DJ setup. There was also a Ping-Pong table, a movie screen, a card table, a bar, and a large metal pyramid that was either an ornate candleholder or the largest bong the Mideast had ever produced.

The apartment's expanse was impressive, though on closer inspection, what struck me most was the unusual decorating sensibility. Bare red lightbulbs poked from a smoky black ceiling. One wall had been painted a pale blue and stuccoed. Someone had affixed an unsmiling, white eight-foot-tall mask, in the style of a death mask, to one wall. I spotted a spider web of string, a piece of art perhaps. Another piece, a canvas, featured right-angled braces, wire mesh, screws. Ivy grew in through one window and ran down a brick wall. On second thought, the place seemed less like a nightclub than a college dorm where the kids had, on the spur of the moment, decided to throw an S&M night.

Clemente said he too had been impressed by his first visit, though he remarked on a faint odor.

"Beer," he said, a bit disgusted.

My first impression was more acrid. I thought the beer smelled like urine.

I put odors out of my mind. I was here on business. Since our meeting, Adi and I had engaged in several follow-up discussions. We'd spoken of ways to work together, and seemed to agree on many points, perhaps most. I'd sent Adi a list of features I'd like to see in a karaoke application. I'd asked for the moon. Adi considered it thoroughly, even had it evaluated by a technical person, before dismissing it out of hand. I'd decided to push for a scaled-back version, a demonstration model, something I could at least show to Russell's people or anyone else interested in my karaoke vision.

The other day Clemente, a member of Adi's advisory board, had told me confidentially, "Adi says karaoke is a million-dollar idea."

By now, I knew how long that kind of enthusiasm would last. Like everyone else, I might feign indifference to the economy. But Nasdaq's dip—it had begun another decline—meant time was running short. (I'd heard unsettling rumors of layoffs at Russell's 360hiphop.)

Adi had once warned, "If you don't have a strong position, go find leverage." Sadly, leverage and I were, as yet, unacquainted. Still, I couldn't wait much longer. So, some eight months into my venture, I'd arrived with an offer, a fair one, and the antique notion that fairness mattered. It might be S&M night; I needed a commitment. I had to get Oddcast on board.

Adi was happy to hear me out, though distracted. (I occasionally suspected that a strong breeze could distract him.) Downstairs at a bar area, he served some store-bought Middle Eastern food that he proudly ate with his hands. "Israelis are animals," he mentioned with a laugh. Then he marched upstairs and settled us into a sitting area with a worn chair whose insides poked through the arms and two beat-up couches, most of the apartment's furniture as far as I could tell. I sat on the longer couch, the one covered with a blanket. Adi settled on the shorter, stained one.

Adi poured us glasses of Glenfiddich, a gift from fellow Israelis who breezed in and out of a door at the far end of the apartment. Each time Adi spotted one, he pointed with his chin and mentioned a military rank. "Captain," he said. Or else, he said, "The unit, but he won't tell you that." It was apparently an Israeli commando unit. Another was in naval intelligence. Adi had spent three years in the army's special forces, the red-booted paratroop unit. Adi, I knew by now, was unimpressed by many things. "Normal, normal," I'd heard him respond to tales of business treachery. But clearly Israeli soldiers stirred him.

Casually, to break the ice, which I couldn't ever seem to leave intact, I wondered if Adi favored peace with the Arabs. Adi sneered. He had quite a toothy sneer. "The only people who aren't for peace," he said, "are those who never had to beat women and children," as I gathered he had.

"And," I thought, "we haven't even *started* talking business."

$ $ $

I sometimes thought of Adi as the archetypal Internet CEO. He didn't have a business background, any obvious business skills, nor, in fact, much initial business interest. "I didn't want to be an entrepreneur," he once told me, adding, "I had no idea *what* an entrepreneur was."

Every family has its folklore. In Adi's, his older brother was the genius. This was apparently undisputed—he'd been in product development for Scitex, a public company based in Israel. Adi's sister had been a beauty queen—Junior Miss Israel—and later a lawyer.

And Adi? "I was the wild card," Adi explained. He'd gotten into trouble in high school—he was a thief; among his misdeeds, he stole some exams—and had been forced to leave. The secret of Adi's military career was that, as a result of his youthful crimes, he could have avoided dangerous service. Instead, he campaigned for admission to the special forces. He was glad he had. He loved the army and was a highly regarded soldier.

After the military, Adi thought he might want to be an actor. "That's not serious," his father, a scientist, had told him. Instead, his father suggested film school, which apparently was serious and not incompatible with Adi's theatrical inclination.

"I didn't know who Scorsese was," Adi pointed out. Nonetheless, three days after leaving the Israeli Defense Forces, Adi joined New York University's undergraduate film class of 1995. As a sophomore, Adi heard a sociology professor discuss the North American Man-Boy Love Association. Many people would later be familiar with NAMBLA and, as far as I can tell, that's largely due to *Chicken Hawk,* Adi's 1994 documentary about this tiny exotic group of pederasts. Financed with $9,000 earned moving furniture, his film, though banned in Israel, showed in fifteen American states and won the New York Underground Film Festival.

Adi might have pursued a film career—inquiries came from Hollywood. He had three-quarters of a screenplay in a drawer, but described himself as "too shy" to pursue the matter. Plus this was the mid-nineties, and soon Adi would hit upon the insight that struck many creative New Yorkers at about the same time. Every medium was, really, a digital package. If you had digital skills, so the thinking went, you could command the media. "It's all going to come together," Adi told his hopeful father as he enrolled in New York University's Interactive Telecommunications Program. ITP blends technology and art, the former in service of the latter. Graduates tend to call themselves "interactive artists." One student created a laser harp, another Jello that talked.

In 1999 Adi formed Oddcast with two others, one an ITP grad. "We wanted to run a company," was how he described their first slight impulse. As an office, they used the stage floor; Adi's desk faced the giant white mask. To make money, they wrote programs for the likes of Marilyn Manson and Nine Inch Nails. But, as Adi explained, "Content was our passion." Of course, content was *everyone's* passion at the time. That wasn't difficult, since content was, more or less, anything. It was words, pictures, music, a fourth-grader's poem, *Chicken Hawk*.

New York had long attracted painters, writers, filmmakers, the traditional providers of interesting content. By the mid-nineties, many of these artists saw the Internet as *the* place to pursue their creative urges. After all, off-line you might be a hopeful screenwriter, a left-leaning filmmaker; on the Internet, if you had digital skills, you could be Fox TV. At least that was the promise.

Occasionally, I looked at Adi and thought, any day now he'll be an old man. I knew he worked long hours and six-day weeks; often, he seemed exhausted. I couldn't always imagine him running, or being slapped on the back. He sometimes spoke deliberately, as if weighing each thought, and filled pauses with that wacky aeronautical sound. Lately, though, I'd learned that Adi also operated in emphatic mode. It came out of nowhere, arising midsentence, even midword. He'd shriek and sometimes snap his fingers in the air, as if cycling through the high end of a mood disorder. "*THIS* is my dream come *TRUE*," he'd told me. "The pipes are there in *EVERYBODY'S HOUSE* and we all have access to *SHOVE* stuff in." With his programming skills and the Internet, he could make his point to the neighborhood or the world.

Inevitably, Adi's point was a subversive one. He connected with someone who called himself the Media Attacker—he shouted at politicians, hoping to expose them. In one memorable exchange, the Attacker, a white liberal New Yorker, called a talk show on which Senator Jesse Helms appeared. In a fake Southern drawl he thanked Helms for "helping to keep the nigger down," a phony compliment that Helms responded to with a salute. Adi loved the Media Attacker and gave him a "show" on the Oddcast site. He also had a show for Witness, the musician Peter Gabriel's spotlight on human rights abuses. Another called OTV featured rap songs constructed from politicians' speeches. (My favorite was a wondrous group rap by Al Gore, Bob Dole, and Bill Bradley.)

Creative content like this would draw tons of users. Money would roll in (though exactly how wasn't clear). Content was going to be king, that's what Oddcast thought. That's what *everyone* thought for, by my calculation, about four months. In truth, content could only be successful if popular—popularity was fungible. Sadly, the Media Attacker didn't command much audience share.

By the evening I visited Adi's apartment, Oddcast, like most every other content provider, had moved on. ("We don't say 'content' anymore," was how one CEO delivered the news to me.) It hadn't been a difficult decision. Oddcast's content never made money, but the software programs it wrote to manipulate other people's content did. One application in particular seemed promising. For his master's project, Adi had created a CD-ROM application that allowed users to edit their own videos. Oddcast spent months turning it into an online editing application.

Soon, Adi flew to the West Coast to pitch Macromedia, a public software company creating an entertainment site. The dozen people at the meeting gave the VideoMixer an ovation, then asked for Adi's terms.

"Terms?" Adi thought, as if he'd never heard a thing so ridiculous. "You're Macromedia. What do *you* want?" Eventually, Adi asked for $3 million for a lifetime license. When that didn't fly, he asked for $60,000 for a one-year license, which Macromedia turned down after its engineers looked under the hood. They didn't believe Oddcast technology could support Macromedia's thousands of simultaneous users.

Not long after, Adi convinced his brother to apply his genius to Oddcast's "toys," as his brother called them. His job? "To make them industrial strength," said Adi.

Why would his brother accept the offer?

"To save his little brother," Adi explained.

Eventually Oddcast would license a VideoMixer for as much as $250,000.

Adi had at first assumed that one of his cofounders would be CEO. They were American and presumably understood the business system. Plus, as a friend explained, "Adi is an artist," which seemed a way to describe not only his creative inclinations, but his sensitive spirit. When, early on, a friend had been forced out, Adi had seemed disheartened, near a breakdown. After hearing this story I'd asked Adi if he liked business. He paused for five seconds—I counted—which is a long time in conversation. "I like the results of it," he said in a tone so cheerless it made me think of his dying office plants. Then he paused for five more seconds. "It's a necessary evil," he added.

Internet business once seemed a big tent under which every creative intention could thrive. Not so, it turned out. At some point you had to come to terms with business's inflexible purpose. Creativity was lovely. It got you in the tent. But what kept you there was an unshakable desire to wring profit from it all. And so, however sensitive, rebellious, independent, however fine, artistic, or freaky your bent—and Adi really did seem to experience fewer constraints than most—at some point you would, if you chose business, spend much of your waking life asking yourself this question: How do I make money?

Adi had signed on as CEO when no one else really seemed to want the job. Then an Israeli businessman Adi knew invested $1 million in Oddcast, and his management responsibilities were solidified. At some point, Adi embraced the role. "You have to hurt some feelings to do business," Adi would eventually tell me. "I didn't understand that equation at first."

Of course, Adi had previously discovered toughness in himself. He'd spent much of his army life patrolling the West Bank. Once I asked him to name the most mentally or emotionally difficult thing he'd had to do in the army. He paused for twenty-three seconds, an eternity, then said, "I'm not sure." I got the impression the competition was stiff.

In any case, by the time I met him, Adi seemed to have nurtured an instinct, even an appetite, for power. He might not want to be CEO—he hoped to hire a CEO. Still, he now believed, "A business has to return some value to shareholders. If emotions get hurt in the process, well, you try to do the best. But a business is not a social service. There's a price for everything."

Within six months of opening, Oddcast had received buy-out

offers. Adi was told to jot a business plan, anything, on the back of an envelope. A company put seven figures on the table, a significant fraction of which would go to Adi. "It's a crazy time in history," said Adi, who didn't take a salary at the start. He would have been a millionaire—on paper at least. (The deal was for stock.) Oddcast turned it down. "I'll wait for eight figures," Adi said.

$ $ $

We were pretty far into the Glenfiddich by now, Adi, as usual, farther than me. At the other end of the apartment—a pitcher's mound away—Israeli troops seemed to be doing some kind of maneuvers. Adi, who felt under the weather, had pulled on a furry black hat, a girlfriend's pink sweater-coat, knit slippers. Normally, I like an evening's entertaining moments. I enjoyed thinking about Adi's army days, his business progress, his swagger. But anxiety had started to set in. Doubly so because I sensed that anxiety, usually so energizing, wasn't going to do the trick. *He'd turned down a million dollars,* I found myself thinking. Gazing at Adi, I'd started to wonder what kind of kook I had on my hands.

Through back channels I knew that Adi believed karaoke a promising idea. I had to take the initiative. "You know Oddcast needs another product," I suggested, trying an indulgent tone.

Adi was unmoved. "I could make a business out of the VideoMixer alone," he said in what I thought of as his blank mahatma voice. Then he abruptly changed the subject.

"What else are you doing?" he asked offhandedly. "What are you writing?" This was a trap, I knew. Over the course of meetings people asked a variety of qualifying questions: Who is your CEO? How much money have you raised? However, no qualification was more basic than the one that gauged your commitment. There might be gentlemen farmers who devoted weekends to their fields, inventors who tinkered in basements. Business was lately an endurance contest. I'd recently heard of three Internet entrepreneurs who'd died on the job, driven to their deaths, it was assumed, by their commitment. It was tragic, and just right.

"Sadly," I said, "I am doing KNation."

"I recommend you don't do it," said Adi. He flashed a rectangular smile that in an instant disappeared. His pep seemed to be running down.

I wasn't going to fall for it. I knew Oddcast could use meetings with potential clients. Meetings were a kind of capital in the Internet. I'd had success scheduling meetings for KaraokeNation—pitching my catchphrase, my concept. I could set up meetings for both of us. That was my offer. Adi seemed to rouse. He wasn't going to build a full karaoke application for me; he couldn't afford to. (Consigliere had guessed about right. Oddcast really was going to run out of money in a few months.) But we could tell potential customers that if they liked karaoke, then Oddcast, developer of the VideoMixer and other terrific products, which Adi would demonstrate, was just the company to build it.

"We presell karaoke," said Adi in an oddly twangy tone. I could tell he liked the term presell. If, in the process, he happened to sell the VideoMixer, all the better. Then he'd have the funds to build me a karaoke application. Plus, Adi agreed to build me a demo, something I could show at these joint meetings.

It was a quarter step, maybe a half. "Beggars can't be choosers," Consigliere sometimes reminded me. Call it synergy. And maybe too that unlikely thing, good will. In a moment, Adi added one of those nutty, delightful sayings he still occasionally came out with. As I stared at that slight concavity on the side of his head—a result of brain surgery, I knew by now—he said somberly, "I will make it my mission to advance the KNation cause."

Later, I'd realize what a very funny thing this was to say. At the moment, though, I found the possibilities irresistible. Adi's cell phone rang. A friend, another Israeli—a captain? a lieutenant?—was on the way, and so I ducked under the spider web and the bare red lightbulbs and headed to the street.

Chapter Nineteen

Over a Barrel

THE NIGHT THINGS went wrong began innocently enough. Clemente said he had some news, which wasn't unusual. Clemente often had news. He'd received an e-mail from the CEO of Time Warner or he'd attended the Indianapolis 500 at the invitation of the CEO of Nortel. I suspected that I wasn't the perfect audience for these dispatches—I didn't, for instance, know what Nortel was. Still I did my part.

"Wow," I usually said, or something along those lines.

Tonight's news was to be delivered at a Chinese restaurant named Wo Hop, a favorite of Clemente's. Wo Hop was a sloppy, old-fashioned basement place—a holdover from before Chinatown got cuisine. The waiters had brown food stains on their shirts; they spoke a spare, martial English. Shortly after we arrived, a waiter shouted "There," and pointed us to a table.

"I love this place," said Clemente as we sat down. A stylish dresser, Clemente could be a bottom feeder when it came to nourishment. But then he had some encompassing allergy that apparently ruled out several food groups. With him, quantity seemed the most important consideration. And Wo Hop piled it on. A few minutes after we sat down, Clemente, a six footer with a thirty-inch waist, was digging into trucker-sized portions.

This evening, Clemente was dressed in jeans and a T-shirt, spotless of course—his jeans might have had a crease—though I could see his barbed-wire tattoo, the one he didn't always admit to having. As far as I was concerned, the casual Clemente constituted a genre violation. Clemente was not a casual or offhanded guy. He had the gift of seriousness, which he could confer on others and sometimes conferred on me.

In our business discussions, Clemente usually took the lead. His lips would squeeze into thin lines, and in that woolen voice of his, he'd introduced a strategy. We'd bat it around, consider it from various angles. To me, it was like we were talking about IBM. Sometimes Clemente would toss in a new word. Staying on top of Internet jargon was a demanding task. But Clemente was fluent in the exciting new language of business. Sometimes I scribbled notes, just for the pleasure the exotic word combinations gave me—*microcasting, wallet share, database charity, monetizing eyeballs, sticky applications.*

Lately, I felt I'd developed a knack with some of these terms, and the concepts that attached to them. I'd even come up with ideas about KNation's business model, the one Joe Park felt was so important to have. Clemente, I got the impression, did too.

"What are we?" I could remember him snapping as we waited for a taxi one day. We were on our way to a meeting to ask for money. Apparently he thought we should nail that down beforehand.

"A portal," Consigliere had responded with a shrug. I thought he might have said that just to appease Clemente. It did seem to settle the matter. You couldn't really argue with portal. For a while *everybody* was going to be a portal, which was an entryway to the Internet. (The idea was to attract tons of users, then sell ads.) Search engines were huge portals; Russell was going to be a hip-hop portal. There was a Baptist portal and a porn portal. NBC wanted to be an entertainment portal, so did Disney for a while. There was even, I read, a *cornflakes portal,* apparently the route all cornflakes lovers would take to the net. KNation, too, could be a portal, the one through which the karaoke lifestyle enthusiasts would pass when entering the Internet.

The portal craze, though, like the content craze, had fizzled. (You couldn't just designate yourself a portal, it turned out.) Lately,

I'd been hearing about user-generated media. Terms flew around the Internet. But I liked this one, and I got the feeling Clemente did too.

"I, too, see the value of UGM vs. a pure-play K-Portal," Clemente said in one recent email.

User-generated media or UGM simply meant that users created their own media. Chat rooms and e-mail were types of user-generated media. Clemente's Internet surveys consistently showed that some people would like to create their own entertainment as well. In that case, I was certain they'd like to sing their own songs, a user-generated application if ever there was one. Apparently, Clemente saw it my way. I expected that one reason he'd invited me to dinner was to bring some seriousness to bear on this interesting possibility.

To my dismay, however, Clemente seemed almost lighthearted, upbeat. Did he really want to gab about the Knicks? Or his daughter's new school? Clemente was spooking me.

After all, I could think of no reason for Clemente's high spirits. Things weren't going well at Cyber Dialogue. I knew he did excellent work, but on recent visits to New York, the company couldn't seem to find him a desk. "A number of issues have arisen pertaining to my role at Cyber Dialogue," he'd written in one e-mail, "and I am now in a position to more seriously consider options outside of the company." He'd signed that note, "Karaoke or Die." (Conveniently, Cyber Dialogue had withdrawn its public offering, another victim of a declining market.)

Consigliere thought all this a very positive development. I'd even had a preliminary conversation with Clemente in the back of a cab. I'd mentioned the KNation CEO spot and broached a salary figure. He'd scoffed at the number, but I'd thought of it as a discussion, the start. One that we might advance over dinner.

Clemente jabbed a chopstick at a plate of liquidy noodles. Clearly, he had something else on his mind.

"Oddcast offered me the CEO job," he said suddenly.

I was stunned. My fork dropped. (I never used chopsticks, couldn't figure them out.) Wasn't it "karaoke or die"? And weren't we friends? *But I've been to your apartment!* I nearly blurted out. *The one without furniture!*

Perhaps he'd had a couple of doubts. "Is karaoke a product or a business?" he'd asked. Okay, a couple of elements lagged. But for months, I'd simply believed Clemente would take over KNation. Lately, I'd started telling people he *already* had! I'd snuck his name into a recent version of my business plan, listing him as CEO—"I thought that was the strongest element," one advisor told me—until he got wind of it and made me take it out.

Now he'd jumped ship. And to Oddcast, a company I wasn't quite sure was in my camp. How had Adi pulled it off? It wasn't as if the two were separated at birth. Adi was a left-leaning Democrat; Clemente a rock-ribbed Republican. Clemente kept a Mercedes in his Palm Springs garage; for a time, Adi had Roller-bladed to work from his East Village apartment. Clemente was a clotheshorse; he'd sneak off to Barney's in the middle of the day. Adi scratched, he picked, he farted, and he didn't own a single suit! To me, it didn't seem likely he ever would. I'd accompanied him to a clothing store. He didn't appear to understand how it worked. He'd wandered out of the dressing room naked from the waist up. Adi could seem barely civilized and, I got the impression, kind of liked it.

Now *these two* were to join forces. Adi, I'd learned, had flown to Clemente's Palm Springs enclave, where the pool man and the lawn man came every week whether anyone was home or not. Apparently he'd made a favorable impression on Clemente's wife—she was said to have a nose for people—and then put it to Clemente. I could just imagine how he said it—"Pe-e-ter, we want you to be our CEO"— and then, I supposed, he made that buggy noise. Adi offered him a whopping share of the company; something like 20 percent was what I heard. (When Consigliere and I talked about luring Clemente aboard, Consigliere said 3 to 5 percent was standard. I was willing to go to 5. And that was of KNation!)

"But Adi's a wild man," I protested.

"He's an artist," Clemente explained to me. I should have known. Clemente was already Adi's interpreter. Clemente I learned, had even taken Adi for a first visit to Barney's. Adi had shrieked across the entire floor, *"This suit costs two thousand dollars!"* Then he purchased what looked like a Nehru jacket.

Admittedly, it all made sense. Adi was hawking some snazzy tools. Clemente had a vision of how they fit with the Internet's entertainment future. Clemente assured Adi that what Oddcast really had in the VideoMixer was a way to facilitate user-generated media, the very subject I'd been eager to explore. (Soon "User-Generated Media" would appear with a little TM indication on Oddcast's Web site.)

I felt miserable. My left eyelid had lately started to blink involuntarily. My vision occasionally went double. How could *he* do this to *me?* I wanted to say. I considered begging. Or tossing the table over. That would be a statement. Make his favorite waiters hunt for noodles on their knees. Something—*anything*—to let him know the kind of person he was trifling with.

Instead, I sighed like an adolescent forced to apologize. "Well," I managed. "Isn't this good news."

"Thank you," Clemente said politely and grinned like a catfish.

The thing had gotten its grips on him; I could feel it. There was no turning back. "I believe that there could be some tremendous synergies with a KNation/Oddcast partnership," he said, "We'll have to think this through more thoroughly." He imagined that KNation could be a division of Oddcast. Or a product line. Oh, he imagined all kinds of things. "Since early on I envisioned Oddcast as the ideal company to bring your online karaoke vision to life," he said which was true enough.

I nodded, and considered momentarily what it would be like to work for a karaoke division of Oddcast. My heart sank.

The next day I phoned Consigliere to tell him Oddcast had nabbed Clemente. *"Right out from under us,"* I sulked. There might have been a hint of blame in my voice. Consigliere put a good face on the news. For a depressive, he could be annoyingly upbeat. "This can't be bad for KNation," he said. That's not how it seemed to me. I'd started this as a fun thing to do with friends. Somewhere along the way I'd gotten hooked. On just what I couldn't say. I felt a part of it, I guess, the great business cavalcade. Perhaps it was the focus, the energy, the weird *gravitas* that slipped into my voice whenever I got going. I knew what a business model was. I had one. (Actually, I had several.) And I had a new attitude to go along with it. Occasionally, I was dismissive, commanding, a way I'd longed to be. "Yeah, but how is his business going to make money?" I'd say, a pushy new business realist.

And yet now I had needs, a ton of them, and they were terrible, insistent things. Wasn't business supposed to be easy or not hard anyway? Now, even my friends weren't quite on my side.

Sitting at my desk I suddenly wondered if maybe I didn't really need Clemente. I phoned James, my dry cleaner. Yes, I thought, James might be just the person to help me build this thing. When we'd last conferred, James had been in the missile business in the un-air-conditioned basement of the dry cleaners. Back then, I'd hesitated to reveal the nature of my own enterprise, or even its name. This time, at my kitchen counter, I showed him my business plan. I told him the name.

"KNation," I said.

"You're kidding," he said. He seemed astounded. Perhaps he felt it worth the wait. "KNation." he repeated. Apparently he'd thought of purchasing that name himself.

"James," I said, "I know you have a lot of contacts through the dry-cleaning business." His own opportunities had fallen through one after another, yet no failure seemed final. Other possibilities seemed to arise just as fast. He seemed busier than ever. "Take a look at my business plan," I urged him. I wanted him in on this.

James, though, failed to return calls, e-mails. Finally, one day, I caught up with him at the dry cleaners.

"I can't help you," he said somberly, as if consigning me to my fate.

Over the next few weeks Clemente called frequently. He wanted me to be involved. He talked about leveraging my contacts—the ones my journalism background offered. He knew about my arrangement with Adi. He wanted me to hurry and set up some meetings where we could sell both karaoke and the VideoMixer. He assured me Oddcast was working on a demo.

"I believe in Oddcast," he explained. And now, he wanted me to believe too.

Indeed, he believed so deeply that he'd borrowed money to invest in Oddcast stock, something over a half-million dollars. He seemed to believe this would save taxes when his stock options were worth tons. He could end up very disappointed, I thought. He didn't seem to think about that. "This is a culmination," he said "of everything I've done."

"Yes, yes," I said enthusiastically to whatever he proposed. I knew this much by now: Business was a bit of a con. In truth, I was over a barrel. I needed Oddcast more than ever. And I needed Clemente, too.

PART THREE

PART THREE

Chapter Twenty

Hip-Hop Is Karaoke

IT WAS A SUNNY NOONTIME in Manhattan. The sky was such a crisp clear blue it could have been poured from a paint can. A perfect day, in other words, for a New York City traffic jam. L.A. had its mysterious freeway slowdowns; D.C.'s Beltway could produce estimable rush hour delays. However, in Midtown Manhattan, just a few misbehaving cars could tie up traffic so thoroughly that pulses alone seemed to move.

I was hoping for nothing less. You see, I was in a meeting, a high-stakes karaoke meeting, in the backseat of a dark LTD that had just pulled away from the curb near Sixth Avenue and Fifty-third Street. For as long as the ride lasted, I had the ear of Chuck D, founder of Public Enemy, which was almost always described as one of hip-hop's "seminal" groups, and one of its most politically incendiary. Chuck D, the rap intellectual who took inspiration from the Black Panthers, was, I hoped, about to consider the appeal of hip-hop karaoke.

Just to arrange this meeting had taken months of anxious phone calls. (With karaoke anxiety was always close at hand.) I'd already had several false starts. Yesterday had been typical. First, I'd received good news. Chuck D was giving a speech at the Hilton, and I was told he'd be available afterward. I was to meet him at the hotel. Then, at the last possible minute—*how predictable!*—I'd received a second call. Chuck D had to scoot off to the airport immediately after his talk, it was explained. He'd have to reschedule.

Chuck had rescheduled before and each time it had been difficult to get a meeting back on track. I didn't dare let another chance slip away. So when I heard the disappointing news, I took a deep breath, closed my eyes, counted backward from ten, and let my hand float in the air, steps a doctor had once suggested to help me relax. Suddenly it came to me. "Let *me* take Chuck to the airport," I shouted at his assistant.

"No!" the assistant had shouted back, reacting as if I'd suggested carjacking her boss. Eventually, though, she'd come around. She ran the idea by three of Chuck's people, each of whom had approved.

"It's all set up," was the message the assistant left for me late last night.

Of course, as I knew by now, in business nothing was ever *all set up*. Except in the way that things are *all set up* in, say, horror movies. You know, a young good-looking but unknown actor heads toward the water for a midnight swim, waving and saying. "See you tomorrow. It's all set up." Then a little seesawing music begins and things, the ones that were *all set up*, go haywire. The actor disappears from the movie.

And so, perhaps it wasn't entirely unexpected that with things *all set up*, I casually introduced myself to a group of fussy PR functionaries at the Hilton and was immediately shooed away. They claimed to know nothing of my appointment with Chuck D.

When I protested, one PR woman, apparently the lead one, shrugged, turned away, turned back, then pointedly said, "Wait there," and motioned with a finger from her eye to a spot on the floor just in front of a bodyguard whose thick arms were crossed at his chest. Then she wandered off to kill time with her PR cronies. Apparently she'd heard the seesawing music, figured I'd soon be out of the picture.

Normally, a situation like this would discourage me; I'd have walked away. I did feel a little downhearted. But, gathering myself, which I seemed to do a lot of these days, I recalled I was a proud member of the entrepreneurial club. I should be energetic and determined. The planned meeting wasn't *for me*. It was a shot for *my* baby, for karaokenation, a venture for which I still seemed to believe I had some aptitude.

I fixed the bodyguard with what I hoped was a pleasant but gritty look. "Are you Chuck D's bodyguard?" I asked quietly, though I didn't doubt it. His biceps were the size of a car door. And yet, I thought I detected *something* agreeable in him. Just a minute ago he'd called out to a young female friend, "Lookin' good," and had quickly drawn in his breath. He waved for her to come over. When she ignored him—she clicked her tongue in his direction—he acted hurt. Apparently, he had a softer side.

"There's been a mix-up," I began evenly. I tried to speak without moving my lips, so as not to alert the PR sentries.

"What?" he responded gruffly, and leaned toward me.

"I have an appointment," I half-whispered and settled a hand over my mouth. His boss, I suggested, wouldn't want to miss me because of an oversight. "I'm afraid Chuck D doesn't know I'm here," I said. I meant here in the general sense though, for some reason, I pointed to my feet.

"Is that right?" he said, as if reading from a phrasebook. His voice was deep and perfectly dismissive. But then he said almost gently, "Wait." He pointed to the spot on the floor, the same one the PR woman had targeted, apparently a well-known spot. Then he executed a sharp military turn.

"I'll stay here," I offered to the *v*-shaped wedge of his back. I started to bounce on my toes, and daydream about Chuck D., the only person I knew to have transformed himself from powerful recording artist to pioneering Internet entrepreneur to public figure taking on the music industry. If only I could get *him* involved, I thought.

My plan was to show Chuck my karaoke demo, the one Oddcast had built. Adi and I had engaged in detailed back-and-forth though, in the end, he let me know he'd thrown something together in a few hours. Still, it looked lush, sexy, and worked, more or less. (Apparently these guys really could shake these things out of their sleeves.) The demo featured a virtual host, an animated Asian-looking woman.

"Welcome to the hiphopkaraoke lounge," she said. "I haven't seen you here before."

She could be programmed to say anything. More important, she could *look* like anyone.

What, I'd lately wondered, if she looked like Chuck D? What if the founder of Public Enemy were my hip-hop karaoke host, in ani- mated form? On the demo, you could choose a song to sing. Once you did, the host asked, "Are you ready to start singing?"

What if Chuck asked that? He could make Chuck-like com- ments, rhymes perhaps.

The "k-nation" demo, as Adi labeled it—he had trouble spelling KNation *as well* as KaraokeNation—currently allowed you to sing along with a duet by Foxy Brown and Jay-Z, though the words scrolled just a bit slower than the music. I imagined a cartoon Chuck could invite people to sing his hits, "Public Enemy No. 1," or "Don't Believe the Hype," or, *all together now,* "Burn Hollywood burn / I smell a riot going on." Users could e-mail their versions to him. He'd send them back witty, encouraging comments. I couldn't help but think that Chuck D would be perfect for karaoke.

In a minute the bodyguard returned, took up his previous spot, crossed his arms as before, and once again leaned toward me. Even his cologne was aggressive. Then, in my ear, he sang out, "You're in." Miraculously, he'd taken the matter directly to Chuck.

"Yes!" I shouted like a sportscaster.

Chuck said he would ride with me after his speech, a dispatch that turned the PR commandoes wretched—they'd been following along—until, very professionally, each one took me aside to apolo- gize.

"'S all good," I got to say, very upbeat, to one after the other.

$ $ $

This morning, Chuck's picture had appeared in the *New York Times.* He'd been photographed in Timberland boots and shorts in his char- acteristic performer's stance, a cross between a boxer's and a speed skater's. As Chuck approached the Hilton's podium, I noticed he wore the same Timberland boots, though he'd opted for long pants. Of course, the audience, several hundred college music journalists, didn't care much what he wore. They were too delighted to be in the presence of a music legend. They were Chuck's kind of crowd. Though mainly white and, from what I overheard, particularly interested in tattoos—"You got *another!*"—they, in fact, represented hip-hop's majority audience. Hip-hop, as Russell had told me, was youth music. White kids accounted for 80 percent of expenditures.

On the wide, deep stage, Chuck stood quietly for a moment. Then he announced he hadn't slept much. A hip-hop celebrity's life must be like that, I thought. (Though it would turn out that Chuck's sleep loss was largely due to driving his wife, a flight attendant, to catch a 6 A.M. plane.) Suddenly, Chuck gripped the podium with two hands, as if about to execute a gymnastic maneuver. "For years," Chuck said energetically, "corporations tied the whole fucking game up." People had to pay all that money for CDs. Why? "Behind closed doors," explained Chuck, "there ain't no real reason, other than, 'Fuck it, they'll buy it.'"

The crowd laughed appreciatively. These young journalists were sympathetic to Chuck's beef: The music labels had long misused not only the artist, but also the public. Though I suspected Chuck's word choice got them going, too. Here were well-behaved students from expensive colleges at one of New York's largest hotels, and what language! Chuck even chided himself. "I'm over my cursing quota," he said.

Chuck seemed pretty down on the music companies. For a while, he'd been pretty down in general. "The middle of the nineties was a very, very, very dark time," he said. Other rappers got involved with guns and drugs and gangs. Tupac and Notorious B.I.G. were shot down. Chuck, too, couldn't stay out of trouble. Though Chuck, being Chuck, got into a different kind of scrap. (He couldn't really keep gang names straight.) Chuck wanted to release his music digitally. When the record company said no, he was furious, and posted a song on his Web site anyway. The song was "Swindler's Lust" and it accused the record companies of stealing from black musicians.

"*Hand in my pocket / Rob me for my chocolate.*" Soon Public Enemy would stop touring.

Then came the Internet, and the way Chuck talked, it was like a mood elevator. "The start-up entrepreneur could get in the game," said Chuck. In 1999 Chuck founded his own Internet company, rapstation.com, a home for, as Russell would say, all things hip-hop.

Chuck ran a lean operation, seventeen employees and no venture capital. "You can be *that* black guy to get the money from the white venture capitalists," said Chuck. "I'm not *that* black guy." Chuck might have liked to get his hands on the millions others were blowing through. Still, not being *that* black guy freed him to do other things, like represent Napster, the company that permitted a person to copy the music on another's computer. The record companies had hauled Napster into court; they hoped to put Napster out of business.

From the podium, Chuck scoffed. "Trying to stop that shit is like trying to stop the rain," he said. If not Napster, another company would spring up. He seemed confident. "*Stop, Stop!*" he yelled, mimicking frightened record execs. He thought they'd end up where they ought to be. "Right in the motherfucking crazy house," he said.

To Chuck's mind, the Internet was like hip-hop, a challenge to power. And though hip-hop had moved comfortably into the suburban mainstream—the music industry loved hip-hop these days—Chuck, like Clemente, didn't see how anyone could stop the Internet's subversive influence. "I predict there will be more than a million artists and a million labels participating in the distribution of artists," Chuck said. "In the new realm you have to look at the public, number one *as a participant.*"

From my seat in the dark auditorium, I jotted down the word "participant," which seemed suited to my cause.

Then Chuck concluded, "It's the most exciting time in music *ever.*"

After his speech, Chuck walked through the lobby, a few steps behind his bodyguard. I nervously trailed a few steps behind Chuck. A PR person hurried to follow behind us, carrying, I was glad to see, Chuck's bag. Nobody dared approach, though Chuck occasionally yanked a business card from a bloated wallet and pressed it on someone he recognized.

At one point, eager to establish rapport, I shouted ahead to him. Unfortunately, "Nice speech," was all I could think to say.

"Lecture," Chuck corrected me. He apparently preferred the term lecture to speech.

I fell silent then and as anxious as ever. It occurred to me that Chuck could still leave me behind.

At the curb, Chuck signed an autograph for his bodyguard, said hello to his driver whom he knew by name, then ducked into the LTD. The PR person apologized to me one more time.

"Oh, don't worry," I said curtly, and propelled myself into the backseat and almost into Chuck D's lap. (I'd long ago decided that Adi and Clemente weren't going to squeeze in on this opportunity.)

And then as soon as the driver pulled away the strangest thing happened. My anxiety, gathering for hours, for weeks really, lifted. Perhaps it was simply too taxing to be anxious all the time. Or perhaps, finally, it was my gift, my only real gift, to feel at ease when circumstance gave little reason. I let go of the image of Chuck D, angry black man rapper who'd written "Welcome to the Terrordome" and "Fight the Power," and who might, I'd very recently feared, leave me at the curb. Instead, I thought of Chuck, the forty-year-old father of young kids who rose early to drive his wife to work. Chuck, the burly guy next to me, was, I told myself, kind of a square. He was a good parent, solid citizen, and he didn't smoke. Chuck was probably the only rapper to ever speak out *against* malt liquor, Nike, and marijuana. I pictured Chuck mowing his lawn in Long Island, where he still lived, chatting across a fence about appropriate influences on kids. "Well, some rap lyrics," he believed, "it's best that they don't know."

Maybe physical proximity always suggests other kinds of closeness. But here was the thing. A person could chat with Chuck. *I* could chat with Chuck, I suddenly felt sure of that. Cocooned in the backseat with seminal rap artist Chuck D, I felt, for once, completely relaxed. Oh, this was wonderful. *This* was all set up.

$ $ $

From the car Chuck waved to a construction worker, who slouched next to a jackhammer. Actually, he shot the guy a peace sign, which seemed to physically straighten him up. (Okay, so he wasn't a *typical* suburbanite.) "Done that," Chuck said referring to the jackhammer. He mentioned he'd had seventeen jobs before becoming a rapper. It seemed odd to have counted, but I thought Chuck's point was that, like anyone else, he knew about hard work.

Rap was something he'd gotten involved with because, he said, "I dug the rebelliousness of it."

"You understood rap?" I asked. It was a dumb question but I compensated by asking intently.

"I *over*stood it," Chuck said, not missing a beat.

We laughed. We were getting along swimmingly. Chuck was in no hurry to get to my concerns, but then neither was I. I was enjoying myself too much. I imagined we'd stay in touch, send jokey emails back and forth. He'd try out new lyrics on me. Maybe I'd send him one or two of my own.

If only traffic would cooperate. Where was gridlock when you needed it? Unfortunately, each traffic light we approached, magically turned green. At this rate, my meeting would be over in just a few minutes. And I needed a little time to nudge the good feeling in the direction of KaraokeNation.

Chuck didn't care. He babbled away. He was explaining some clever idea—he wanted to share *everything*—he'd come up with for Internet talent scouting. Chuck, a bit of a show-off, not that I minded, liked to toss rap wordplay into conversation. People, he said, were now "Lewis and Clarking through the thicket."

How, I wondered, did he put up with the awful record industry attacks? Chuck assured me I shouldn't worry. "I wanna be able to be a target that absorbs your industry bullets," he said bravely.

"Wow," I heard myself say, and grinned. I grinned incessantly, and nodded, attentive, encouraging until, spotting the Midtown Tunnel, my good mood stalled. The airport couldn't be more than twenty minutes away. Then Chuck, a super guy, would be out the door, my opportunity gone. The thought produced in me a jabbing abdominal pain, the kind I associated with the term stomach stapling.

"Chuck, I'd love to hear more," I thought. I actually rehearsed this speech in my head. "Almost anything from the guy who helped change a generation's music. *Fear of a Black Planet,* you know, I can't tell you, that was *such* a favorite. *Really powerful stuff.* And the bits about the coming music industry revolution. *Very interesting.*" But it was clear, as clear as the insistent pain in my belly, that I needed to find a segue. I counted backward. (I didn't dare float my hand in the air.) All I could come up with was, "You know the *really* interesting thing about *Fear of a Black Planet* and karaoke . . ." It was like being an idiot, this mental constancy.

Then as our uncanny driver swerved—he seemed able to dodge traffic—throwing me at Chuck, and proceeded into the Midtown Tunnel, this thought struck me: terrific lighting. Yes, the tunnel would provide a perfect background for a laptop demo. No time to waste. I unsheathed my computer from its carrying bag.

Chuck was saying, "I'm launching the paradigm . . ."

"So anyway, Chuck," I interrupted. "I want to show you something."

At first Chuck simply continued, ". . . for an online record label."

Then there was the familiar cascade of notes from my computer. The sound of Microsoft Windows booting up. It brought Chuck to a halt.

"Take a look at this," I said with a hint of just-occurred-to-me sincerity.

Chuck must have witnessed a fair amount in his life. Flavor Flav, his rap partner, had been in trouble with drugs, guns, the law. Still, Chuck seemed surprised at the appearance of my laptop.

I triggered the demo. Chuck looked on.

The virtual host appeared.

"Wow," said Chuck, which I took sincerely.

"She can be anybody," I said preparing the terrain. I meant the host.

"Hm-hmm."

Sometimes, for reasons that aren't clear to me, I had a tendency to imitate people. My voice took on the accents, the tones, even the words of the person I spoke to. I liked to think of this as an attempt to meet someone on his own terms. Usually, it was unobtrusive, unless I spoke to a Southerner, or once, when I'd interviewed a deaf girl, that was bad. With Chuck, I suddenly slipped into an imitative groove. My voice deepened, slowed. My *t*'s sounded *d*-ish. My *I*'s suddenly resembled *ahs*. Was I trying to do Chuck?

I'd picked up Chuck's concerns, his themes. Now I gave them back to him in his tone.

"I figure everybody loves to sing music. That's their first relationship to it. Before they're consumers, they like to participate," I said. "Participate" was Chuck's word.

"Hm-hmm," he said. The mastermind of Public Enemy seemed to be with me. If he noticed my change in diction, he didn't mention it. As I spoke, Chuck said "Uh-hunh." He said "right." I heard encouragement everywhere.

"The thing that I really like about karaoke is it's a participation mechanism," I said for emphasis.

I clicked on a button and the lyrics popped up.

Chuck may have written songs called "Fight the Power" and "Anti-Nigger Machine," but just now he loved hip-hop karaoke. I knew this because I asked.

"Chuck, what do you think? Chuck, tell me truthfully."

"Hip-hop," he said with some resolve in his deep voice, "is karaoke."

Of course it is.

"It's a virtual shower," Chuck said, a reference, I'd later figure out, to singing in the shower.

"For the next version we'll put people in a lounge, twenty people together," I said. I knew by now that was out of the question, but I couldn't help myself.

"Oh, yo, I think it's a great idea," he said.

I pointed to the animated host. "What I actually imagine is, here's Chuck D."

"Hm-hmm," he said. It was a hearty hm-hmm.

Chuck couldn't pay to get an application built. He didn't have the money. (I suddenly wished Chuck was *that* black guy the white VCs took to.) But if I could find the money then Chuck was interested in appearing as a host. Imagine! There was a value-add. "If you could work something out getting it on rapstation.com, then we could do anything," he said.

He wanted me to talk to his business partner. Then he gave me his own private e-mail address. (Maybe we would have a jokey e-mail relationship after all.) At the airport, we parted comfortable, friendly. Oh, it was terrific. Chuck and me, both participants in the coming music revolution. If only I could have refrained from shouting peppy comments at his back, things like, "Tell your business partner I'll be getting in touch," and, "Karaoke's in *our* future," and two or three other things that, in retrospect, I wish I hadn't called after the founder of one of the era's seminal music groups.

Chapter Twenty-one

Life Under the Influence of Business

NOT LONG AGO, if you examined what business thought, or better yet, felt about itself, the results were troubling. For years business seemed like an adolescent at that awkward age. It had self-esteem issues.

Start with that fifties business guy. As everyone seemed to know, he'd been a congenial bore. The sixties hardly did much for his self-image. In that decade, historian Richard Hofstadter reported that "stigmatizing" businessmen was an acceptable cultural reflex. Businessmen focused on profits, which wasn't a very creative or, really, very pleasant thing to do. Entrepreneurs were hardly on top. They were "self-devaluating," Maslow noted in the sixties.

Colleges were happy to dismiss business as not really serious, certainly not intellectual. In the seventies, Daniel Bell could survey leading thinkers, even those with a conservative bent, and conclude that "romantic or traditionalist, enlightenment or irrationalist, vitalist or naturalist, humanist or racialist, religious or atheist—in this entire range of passions and beliefs scarcely one respectable intellectual figure defended the sober, unheroic, prudential, let alone acquisitive, entrepreneurial or moneymaking pursuits of the bourgeois world."

In the eighties, business finally got a break. Instead of the dull businessman, prime-time TV offered the businessman-as-crook. The businessman swindled and cheated; he stopped at nothing, including murder. A surprising number of TV businessmen kept guns in their desk drawers. "Once you give up integrity the rest is easy," said businessman J.R. Ewing of the hit series *Dallas*. A 1986 documentary claimed that businessmen committed more crimes on TV than did any other occupational group. And the entrepreneur was singled out for a special rebuke. The entrepreneur was "the kind of guy people love to hate," said one TV writer of the era.

It was during the eighties that I'd gone to work for *Success* magazine, though we soon renamed it. *Success!* we called it, an effort, I suppose, to encourage the down-at-the-heels business guy. Yet looking back, we probably did as much as anyone to reinforce his insecurities. After all we liked to solicit advice from subcultures—the athlete, the military, the country boy, even the mafia. The unconfident businessperson, we implied, could use help from just about anyone imaginable. The mafia, as I recall, was going to teach businessmen how not to take no for an answer.

By the late 1990s business's outlook, its notions of its own worth, its appreciation for its techniques, had clearly changed. The awkwardness had disappeared. Business, you might say, got self-esteem. Suddenly business doled out advice like handbills, dispensing tips on language, on direction, on strategies for living, you name it. In fact, I couldn't help but notice that lately everywhere I turned, people seemed eager to borrow *its* charms, *its* authority, *its* explanatory power. If, for instance, you wanted to emphasize deep seriousness, then business was the language for you—even if you happened to be, say, the U.S. Secretary of Defense. "We seek to raise the cost of doing business for foreign terrorists," was how the Defense Secretary explained his plans. Of course, he planned to kill or arrest them, but, still a reference to business seemed to underscore his grave intent.

Perhaps business and war had always shared certain traits. Now, though, if you wanted to make a point about romance, business seemed to offer a framework for understanding. A friend in the dating scene explained courtship to me. "As a man you are viewed by a woman as an aspirational product," he said. "You have to enhance her brand." Sadly, he'd recently made, as he put it, "a brand presentation error." He'd been overly enthusiastic. Apparently correct positioning for the male brand was *cool*.

In the same vein, an acquaintance, referring to his recent engagement to be married, said, "We clinched the deal." The expression startled me, but probably shouldn't have. Who didn't believe, with every baby-faced new businessman, that these days the world offered us deals; we negotiated the terms. And who, thus, didn't suspect that the people most qualified to lead us were those with a demonstrated talent for the deal? New York City mayor Michael Bloomberg and New Jersey Senator Jon Corzine and even President George W. Bush were in the successful businessman mode, which suddenly seemed a much more significant qualification than, say, a deep understanding of the issues or a history of public service or intelligence or charisma, the kinds of qualities once sought in politicians. (Ten years ago, Ross Perot, a successful businessperson, had seemed mostly comical as a political contender.)

The better we felt about business, the more widely its outlook seemed to apply—and in the nineties we felt very good about business. Of course, marriage was by now a partnership. (What was a prenuptial agreement but an attempt to limit the liability of this particular business relationship?) Sex was performance-based and the object of a training industry. Relaxation was more task-oriented than ever (and usually linked to the need to pay). Play had become exercise, which was designed for efficiency, squeezed in like an end-of-the-day meeting, while stock prices played in endless loop on individualized TVs.

Family life required quality time and, one suspected, quality control. Not surprisingly, business tools often proved useful in a family setting. I read of a mother who showed her children a Microsoft PowerPoint presentation, titled "Family Matters, An Approach for Positive Change to the Wyndham Family Team." It was an effort to get the kids to do their chores. In another era, Mom might have withheld allowance or dessert. Somehow, though, the win-win spirit of business seemed the better approach. So mother Wyndham *pitched* her laggard offspring with accompanying graphics and, no doubt, an inspirational close.

These days, it seemed possible to believe that whatever challenges we faced, a business approach could help. Already a dozen years ago, Stephen Covey's incredibly successful *7 Habits of Highly Effective People* was, in part, based on the notion that business techniques ought to be applied to what were previously considered private problems. Three early chapters were subtitled "Principles of Personal Vision," "Principles of Personal Leadership," and "Principles of Personal Management." By now civic society, the one that preached responsibility to family, community, polity, seemed passé, as well as a little tax-heavy. Now what mattered was what worked, and clearly, what worked was focused, business technique. No wonder one Ohio town put welfare families through seminars that taught them to be proactive and to synergize.

As an organizing concept, family could seem a touch behind the times. As an ad for Merrill Lynch asked, "Corporations like to refer to themselves as 'families.' Shouldn't it be the other way around?" Of course it should. Maybe, then, they'd run better. As management guru Tom Peters wrote not long ago, "Business skills—literally—make us free."

Recently, it seemed that in just about every undertaking we strove to be like businesspeople, to be productive and efficient, to improve our performance, to advance our goals. Little was exempted. Not even childhood. Indeed, these days, the defining drama of a kid's life was, just as in business, the struggle to get ahead.

Have you looked at the lives of children lately? Kids worked hard these days, if not at a paying job, then at the skill-building activities preparatory to one. The work-world's emphasis on efficient use of time, diligent planning, skill-acquisition, calculated rewards, and of course busyness was now fashionable for kids, too. Competition was a framing concept of contemporary childhood—as it was for the business world—and, inevitably, the competition was very stiff. (It really was. In places like New York City, there was competition to get into elite nursery schools, those which taught your kid to sing "London Bridge Is Falling Down" in Japanese, the kind of clever trick that would get him into private kindergarten.)

Childhood, the successful one, was goal-driven. Kids had tests to pass, milestones to hit. Indeed, childhood had the feel of a cult of compulsive industry, as if these kids were already engaged in careers. Parents aided (and abetted), out of love of course, but also, as one New York parent complained, "If my kid does homework by himself, he can't compete with his classmate down the street whose parents are eagerly quizzing him on the periodic table." The more affluent teens had retinues of personal performance coaches. *Every single child* in one well-to-do New Jersey private school had a tutor—at least one. How else would they do well on their college entrance exams, which they took as early as the seventh grade?

Once, of course, kids' daily lives were informed by play, the old-fashioned kind, the chief characteristic of which was its aimlessness. American childhood—and in particular American boyhood—was supposed to be a time of idleness, high-jinks, games. Huck Finn's adventures were, in part, a rebellion against the Franklin-led cult of self-betterment that Mark Twain saw encroaching even in the nineteenth century. Later, in the forties, Willie Morris wrote about a love affair with his dog, Skip, whom he taught to play football, and yet Morris still waltzed off to Oxford University. That was the era of my parents' childhood, which, in stories I heard, seemed to involve a lot of stickball—there were no organized sports in my father's neighborhood—an after-school job, and no cello lessons. And, in the sixties, Frank Conroy's *Stop-Time* described a childhood that seemed taken up with "necking," smoking, and fooling around on piano and yo-yo.

As a kid, I'd participated in activities like Scouts, religious school, Little League, but large stretches of after-school time were unsupervised—they were free time. "I'm going out," I'd yell and race through the back door, the one we never locked. We were often kids on our own, roaming the neighborhood. Many afternoons, I did nothing more productive than toss a ball around. Recreation was often pointless—*you* explain the point of running bases. "The trouble with youth is it's wasted on the young," my father often wistfully quoted George Bernard Shaw as saying. His point—one of them—was that middle-class children were the real leisure class.

These days, industry, activity, goal-orientation, were as much signs of a successful, of a *happy* kid, as of a thriving Internet businessman. If, that is, happiness still mattered for kids. "Happy," one teacher was told by a parent, "doesn't get you into Harvard." Kids, as everyone knew, were car-pooled from one enriching activity to another. One overachieving parent wrote, "We shuttle [our children] back and forth between school and play dates, and they're almost as harried as we are, with their drama workshops, cello lessons, and French tutoring." Unstructured time—just hanging out—made some parents uncomfortable. "You can go downtown *if you have something to do there,*" I heard one parent tell her twelve-year-old.

Play dates were fun, no doubt, and yet contemporary fun didn't always *feel* like fun used to. One twelve-year-old I knew helped design a fighting robot with friends. One of the kids made a Microsoft PowerPoint presentation of new design ideas. Another created a spreadsheet to help the group evaluate those designs. Of course, one group member took notes at meetings and e-mailed them to everyone.

Soon, others wanted to join the group, which was terrific. Interviews were set up for prospective candidates. These junior-high kids somehow had the orientation of a corporate human-resources department. Each candidate was asked what experience he could bring, which usually brought an answer involving a kid's father's job. "Well, my dad's an engineer," was one response.

One particularly probing interviewer pressed ahead with more specific questions.

"Are you smart?" he asked.

"Yes."

"Do you think *I'm* smart?" he pursued.

One candidate was vetoed. "Not serious enough," was how the criticism was framed. Eventually, one of the mothers had to end the interview process. She needed to remind them that the limit had been reached. The limit of how many kids her station wagon could transport to important meetings.

All this was incredibly endearing, and pretty funny. But there was an insight here too. Some kids played pick-up basketball. It was also possible to find young teenagers playing "job interview" these days.

But then why not? These days there seemed few age-cohorts, socioeconomic groups, demographic slices, or communities of interest that couldn't, somehow, benefit from the clever application of a few of the hale, redemptive tricks that had lately made business so self-confident.

Chapter Twenty-two

I Don't Give a . . .

WE WERE AN UNLIKELY TRIO: Clemente, Adi, and me. I hoped to soon reach a written arrangement with Oddcast—my friend Clemente, now serving as Oddcast CEO, had promised as much. Everyone, really, was very positive about getting something on paper. "Can't wait." "We'll bang something out." I heard things like that. "I have no anxiety about it," Adi told me. Still, there seemed to be some ill-defined delay. I couldn't put my finger on it. In the meantime we were an informal and, to some, confusing team.

"So you're from different companies?" asked one prospect as he eyeballed us.

"It's being worked out," we assured him.

Still, I mostly felt terrific about our emerging arrangement. I set up some meetings. (I'd lately started to think of myself as very connected, like a brain cell.) Oddcast didn't take me to *its* meetings; still, I was happy to have its representatives at mine. I made a different impression with these guys at my side. Clemente would show up in a lime-green Calvin Klein or dark Hugo Boss suit, and black Prada shoes which he polished himself in that empty apartment—he'd moved in there from Palm Springs for the time being. He'd open with the vision, the one in which every user created his own media. Then Adi, dressed for recess, would demonstrate the Oddcast products. I, in what I thought of as a first-day-of-school outfit, would then show the karaoke demo. Adi might not appreciate the implied equivalence of my karaoke concept and his finished Oddcast products. But I was thrilled to have KaraokeNation in such distinguished company. Moreover, I enjoyed the repertory aspect. In fact, it sometimes seemed to me we were less a muscular business team than a community theater, and each of us might dash off to a real job as soon as the show was over.

In these settings, my optimism ran high. My whole life seemed italicized. Almost every day I experienced peaks, the intensity of which invariably took me by surprise. I wasn't accustomed to thinking of myself as that optimistic a person. But then, nearly everyone in the Internet seemed to believe, as a specific principle of contemporary life, that *anything* could happen. Moreover, that that anything could happen *now.* "That's the beautiful thing about this," Chuck D had told me. He meant the Internet. "Deals are made quickly. 'Hey let's go for it. Where can we go wrong?'" he said. Who could disagree?

I made an appointment with Danny Goldberg, a friend of Chuck D. (After the break-up of Public Enemy, Chuck had done a solo album at PolyGram, in part because Danny ran the parent company.) I liked to prepare for pitches by learning about the client, and I liked to think of an icebreaker. "It's all about getting a few laughs," said Consigliere, who, I noticed, had managed to avoid the optimism bug.

As part of my research, I'd learned that Danny had headed Atlantic Records, and later Mercury and Warner Bros. He'd managed the bands Nirvana and Led Zeppelin, as well as Bonnie Raitt. Danny had made millions and still was widely considered a good guy. Now he had his own small record label, distributing Chuck's new band, Confrontation Camp, among others. To me, it seemed inconceivable that Danny would pass on an opportunity to finance a Chuck D karaoke application. I could imagine him using Chuck's words: "Hey, let's go for it. Where can we go wrong?"

Plus, if the logic of the thing wasn't sufficient, we had a personal in. Incredibly, Danny had managed Clemente's band, Diving for Pearls.

I arrived first and spent a minute alone with Danny, who, stylistically, didn't seem to have changed in years. He had longish hair, a

button-down shirt, and jeans that didn't fit. They were baggy, though
not in the current style. It was more a saggy look. Danny's features
seemed to have a vague aspect as I said hello. I thought he might be
trying to bring me into focus.

I went for my icebreaker, and hurriedly suggested how excited
Danny would be to reconnect with Clemente.

Danny didn't recall the name.

"Peter Clemente? You were his manager," I said hopefully.

"No."

"Diving for Pearls?" I said, naming Clemente's band.

"Oh, yeah, they made one album," he said, "It did okay." I had the
feeling Danny could have recited the sales figures.

It was a minor setback. I still couldn't imagine that Danny would
fail to recognize the marketing potential of a Chuck D–hosted
karaoke application. As soon as Adi and Clemente arrived, Danny
ushered us into a nondescript conference room, basically a cubicle
with a ceiling, and then almost as soon as Clemente coaxed a recol-
lection out of him—about some musician in rehab—Danny offered
an opinion.

"I don't give a f-fuck," he said and really leaned on the f, "about
the Internet." I'd never really heard anyone dismiss the Internet
before. It wasn't a very popular thing to do. Danny threw up both
hands. He might have been starting a kung-fu maneuver. "I know it's
the future," he said, with a hint of conciliation, "but I have to sell
records today." Then he walked out of the room, showing us the
backside of his saggy jeans.

"It's a good thing he knew me," Clemente pointed out.

Other meetings went better. I focused on the urban sites, those
that had attracted millions of users with hip-hop music. They were, to
use Jerry's term, affinity sites, rallying people who had the same tastes
in music and, so the theory went, similar lifestyle interests. Now they
searched for ways to engage users, make them stick. Hip-hop karaoke
should, I figured, be a straightforward solution. So, too, should the
VideoMixer. Jerry hadn't given us money, but he did provide something valuable. Introductions, including one to Urban Box Office,

one of his portfolio companies, which would like to be a black AOL. Urban Box Office had raised more than $70 million, which bought them three hundred employees, though they were still working out some minor details of current business procedure. Like, for instance, the company's street address actually led to a small camera store around the corner.

When I found my way to UBO—the kindly storeowner had pointed in its direction—the office seemed as hectic as an air-traffic control tower. Three receptionists answered phones, put calls through, paged employees, dispatched messengers. From the waiting area, I could see almost a hundred employees. Some were jammed together elbow-to-elbow, as in a school cafeteria.

UBO's first CEO had recently died—he wasn't much past forty when he suffered a heart attack. The new CEO was Adam Kidron and, in his office, he immediately suggested ways to incorporate karaoke on his site. And he loved the VideoMixer. A question of where to get karaoke music arose, and I mentioned I was working on that, though he might want to make his own arrangements. (Despite my attorney's efforts, my deal for karaoke music rights seemed stalled.) Still, it was a great meeting and so, too, was the one at hookt.com, to which we'd been sent by Mark Lieberman, CEO of Interactive Video Technologies, and, of course, a valued member of my advisory board. (Business, I noticed, was a little like high school. If you were in with the popular kids, you were set.)

Hookt cofounder Chas Walker was a former investment banker at Lehman Brothers, where he'd been one of the most senior black employees and, by his own account, one of the more "arrogant." After being laid off, he'd spent time on his couch nursing back pain when this thought occurred to him; "The Internet is the hottest thing *ever.*" He wasn't all that big a fan of hip-hop, but he and a partner saw the opportunity to attract a youth market with the music, then sell them stuff. Chas and a partner had approached Russell and thought they were working out a deal with him. Russell, though, apparently thought otherwise, and so they'd raised $14 million to start hookt. Soon hookt had amalgamated the Web sites of two hip-hop stars,

Puff Daddy and Eminem, and garnered one of the larger slices of urban Internet traffic, hundreds of thousands of monthly visitors.

In our meeting, Walker wore sandals and seemed perfectly likeable. He had a hearty laugh and, I thought, an affable manner. (A week later, we'd end up in a chummy embrace outside his office—though, on reflection, it was possible I botched the handshake.) As our demonstration got under way, Walker gave us his full attention, which I knew because his forehead seemed to buckle over his brow. Then he started excitedly pulling people into the meeting. Soon, he had four staffers in there. He loved the applications. He may have particularly loved the VideoMixer, but he said he was ready to do karaoke, too. ("I'm ready to rock 'n' roll" was how he'd later put it.) He made passing reference to the dreaded win-win scenario, which I knew by now meant that a client didn't want to pay much, but as the meeting closed, Walker said, "Where do we go now?"

We'd left the question unanswered for the moment. But once outside I was buoyant. Adi, typically, said, "I've been in hot meetings before and nothing happened." One thing, though, did happen. Nine months into my business career, Clemente turned to Adi and said he wanted Oddcast and KNation to negotiate an official agreement.

I couldn't have asked for more.

Chapter Twenty-three

My Lawyer Pulls a Fast One

BEFORE SITTING DOWN to talk, I was determined to find a motivator—for Oddcast. Adi was the one who once counseled "Go find leverage." And I'd recently had an idea. Clemente had let me know that he was intent on raising money for Oddcast. Two and half million was the figure he mentioned. "My mission," he called it dramatically. He seemed to be working to a precise timetable. Sometimes he said he intended to secure the funds on an exact date. Then, within six months, he added, he'd raise another $20 million.

Unfortunately, circumstances had started to work against such fastidious scheduling. The stock market had lately proved as much of a roller coaster as starting a new business (though most could tell that we'd seen the top of the ride). Most of the orthodontists and stockbrokers once dying to get in on this Internet thing no longer had the stomach for it. A few still took meetings, but they tended to have unpredictable reactions. "You've got to change the name," Clemente recalled one saying. "Oddcast is a terrible name." And the larger investors were more besieged and more hesitant than ever. Even Jerry said he'd recently awakened in a sweat, not feeling such a smart guru any longer. Lately, I'd even heard talk of an "innovation glut." A backlash against innovation couldn't be a good sign.

And so it occurred to me that Clemente might feel some pressure. "Most challenging has been raising capital," he agreed over coffee one day. He sounded like a heavy smoker deprived of nicotine.

Things were going well, of course. CEO Clemente was decidedly upbeat. Other aspects of the business advanced. He and Adi had some great client meetings, intense ones—and he was excited about those I generated. Plus, I knew Clemente was whipping the sales force into shape. He'd summoned them to the hand-me-down conference table, then stood on it to rouse them to action. (This concerned me. I knew that table. It wasn't all that sturdy.) Apparently the sales force had been under the impression that they were selling clever toys. Clemente informed them that in fact they offered revenue-producing opportunities. Clients should know that the VideoMixer had slots where advertising could go, not that ads were very easy to sell these days. In any case, Clemente thought the sales team would really start producing soon. Already, he said, Oddcast had been asked to pitch a couple-million-dollar piece of business.

Clemente wasn't one to inflate possibilities, though he seemed to have a kind of night vision for them. He saw possibilities where others perceived dark, murky road. He even said that Oddcast had a company interested in karaoke, if the application recorded a person's voice.

"Of course it does," Adi had told the potential client by phone. Then he hung up and yelled across the office to a programmer, "Make it record!"

By now I knew that most, if not all, of these possibilities would never materialize. Even Clemente once privately confided that Oddcast had a fifty-fifty chance of going under. Though as soon as that dastardly admission escaped his lips, he wanted it back. He sent me a lengthy e-mail—the energy he had! He wanted to "leverage our friendship" so that I'd reconsider his snap opinion. "Oddcast WILL succeed," his e-mail said.

"Of course it will," I reassured Clemente, "once karaoke is on board."

Even with karaoke, I knew that success would come easier if Odddcast reached its money-raising goal. By my calculations, it was $1 million short and could use some help. One important function of Internet lawyers, I'd lately learned, was as a conduit to investors. And so I thought to bring Clemente and Adi to meet my corporate attorney, John Mancini, a leader of the Internet practice at Salans Hertzfeld Heilbronn Christy & Viener.

I'd been introduced to Mancini by a guy I'd known as a teenager—business really was like high school (with less hair). Over lunch, Mancini had been enthusiastic about KNation, though, perhaps, it occurred to me, he was the enthusiastic type. Now, in any case, I was proud to say that Mancini was my $375-an-hour attorney. Fortunately he'd agreed to waive his fee for a percentage of my company, once a common Internet arrangement.

Mancini, in his mid-thirties, had the dewy good looks of a much younger person, and a proprietary feeling about the Internet, which he'd taken to early. He seemed almost protective when talking about it. "That's *not* how things work in the Internet," he'd say if someone tried to wriggle out of an agreement. "Right now they're acting like businessmen," he'd add, which seemed a cut below Internet standards. (Of course, he also told a story about a successful Internet entrepreneur he knew, who enjoyed testing firearms in his apartment, which apparently didn't contravene the standards.)

Mancini didn't really blame those who didn't measure up. He talked as if they only hurt themselves. I got the impression he felt there was lots of work to do and everyone ought to pitch in. Mancini seemed to fear that people who hadn't figured this out were in danger of getting left behind. When would they learn? "Deals happen quickly in the Internet, sometimes just on a handshake," he'd say in a tone so solemn I imagined him in church or on TV.

For my part, I loved talking to Mancini. After a few minutes with him I inevitably felt that I, too, was engaged in the fast-moving issues of contemporary business. Occasionally, I'd call him at home on a Sunday. It was one of his few days to be with his family. Still he was usually eager to kick around KNation issues. Recently, we'd gone round and round: Was it better to be a division of Oddcast or a joint venture with Oddcast?

"How much control do you want to give up?" he'd say.

"Well, I don't know," I'd begin. "How *good* do you think these guys are?"

We considered the matter. Eventually, he came down on the side of a division. If I were a division of Oddcast, I'd get management, technology, he pointed out.

"Then," he said, "you can do what you do best."

I paused. I found myself waiting. I wanted him to tell me what I did best.

"Vision, creativity," he said. "That's your edge."

Right, I almost said, but stopped myself. I was afraid it would come out overenthusiastic, like a halftime cheer.

At this point, I'd started to believe that either way, as division or joint venture, it was better to be together. Much better for me. Even I had begun to fear that, given the economic climate, increasing efforts might yield diminishing returns.

Mancini said he'd be happy to meet with Oddcast, if it could help. He thought he could bring investors to Oddcast, and perhaps recruit a new client in the process. All this, he pointed out to me, would promote my cause. As Mancini explained, he couldn't go forward with Adi and Clemente until they'd wrapped up their deal with me.

I set up a meeting for a Friday evening. Mancini had graciously rearranged his schedule, and invited us to his Rockefeller Center address. I arrived a few minutes early and entered near the statue of Atlas-with-the-world-on-his-shoulders, proceeded through the dark, cool lobby that, this evening, as always in my experience, betrayed not the slightest hint of commerce. I hardly ever saw anyone hurry; actually, I rarely saw anyone at all. Usually, I rode the plush elevators alone, just as I did tonight. I took a seat in the enormous lemon-yellow waiting room. It was quiet as a library and as always, I felt as if I could spend contented hours here using the free phone or thumbing through company bulletins from exotic places like Almaty, Baku, Kyiv, or just watching the firm's attorneys descend the long carpeted interior staircase. Business at a place like this struck me as a dignified upper-crust activity, full of interest and not too much turmoil, the kind a fellow might go in for after prepping at Exeter and graduating Yale, and I was always glad to be included.

When Clemente and Adi arrived, we called Mancini. I'd never seen Mancini in anything but a suit. This evening, though, he strolled into the waiting room in casual attire—sports coat, loafers. Clemente sized him up as a fellow Republican. ("Did you see the tasseled loafers?" he'd say later. Apparently a Republican giveaway.) Clemente and he immediately hit it off.

"I'm an evangelist for the Internet," Clemente mentioned at one point.

"Me, too," Mancini deadpanned, just a bit sorry, I thought, not to have said it first.

In an intimate, sprightly voice, Mancini said, "I've managed to get us a good conference room." Then he led the way to the largest conference room I'd ever seen. It seemed about sixty feet long, maybe twenty-five feet wide, and was filled end-to-end with one huge conference table, a magnificent piece of furniture. It featured delicate work—was that inlay?—of the kind that suggested a metropole and colonies and skilled laborers working for cents an hour. There had to be almost thirty heavy chairs; footmen, it occurred to me, might be needed.

"Oh, sometimes," said Mancini nonchalantly, "it's too small." I'd never seen Mancini so blasé. Adi and Clemente were impressed. I could tell. We took up position at one end, huddling in a close bunch. Adi and Clemente sat next to one another, facing Mancini. I positioned myself behind Mancini.

Clemente, dapper as ever, seemed a bit more tired than usual, which was saying a lot. His eyelids floated half-open. Who knew when he'd last slept? Still he swung into command mode, revving up his tiny laptop.

Adi looked windblown and, I decided, slightly mad. Lately, I'd taken to cataloging his gestures. There was the one where he simultaneously pulled back both corners of his mouth; another where he poked his chin forward in a can-opener thrust and let out a noise that sounded like *eek*. Adi, too, went for his laptop.

They started their pitch, the energy of which was something particular. "We want to be the dial tone for the new economy," Clemente said almost right away. That was the vision statement, bold and, given the scrappier times, semiridiculous. Months ago, I'd met that surfer-dude CEO in flip-flops who declared he was bound to take down AT&T. You could say that kind of thing back then.

These days, the economy treated visions more harshly. And here Oddcast, a virtual startup, laid out a grand one. Some, I knew, might think of its flagship product, the VideoMixer, as a neat little online editing gadget. Clearly, Clemente and Adi felt they'd latched onto a bigger concept. The VideoMixer was going to be "a content engine," the kind anyone with film, music, or photo files could use to create an original piece of media. One day over dim sum Adi had explained as much to me, using tabletop materials to illustrate the idea. By the end, a bunch of chopsticks jutted out from saucers, resembling, I thought, a cartoon cat. It was possible that every manager would create a VideoMixer business memo or every teenager would run his own personal TV station. But recently, possibility, like content and portals, seemed a dated Internet theme.

Clemente, nonetheless, bore down. He mentioned how Oddcast's products fit in, products which were still being productized, as I now knew to say. "We've developed applications that speak directly to a huge market opportunity," said Clemente, "applications that will fundamentally change the way people communicate." No doubt the communication thought had led to the dial-tone idea. Clemente, as usual, was very convincing. Still, I couldn't help but think that he sounded a little out of breath, like someone on an ever-so-slightly accelerating treadmill.

"That's why Oddcast is and will continue to be a market leader," he said.

Is? I jotted down.

Mancini showed no hesitation. "I get it," he said, which, I'd learned, was a very Internet thing to say.

Clemente mentioned Oddcast's revenues—the company actually anticipated over $1 million in revenue. Adi chipped in, noting his own modest salary, always impressive to investors. He listed the talent he'd assembled; he had a knack for that. He bragged about his brother's background, inevitably referencing his military experience, and the company's sales force, which momentarily reminded me of Clemente atop another conference table. I'd rarely seen Adi so eager to please.

To this energy, Mancini returned restraint. He slowly crossed and uncrossed his legs, briefly dangling one tasseled loafer. He straightened a crease. He cocked his head slightly, as if listening to a birdcall. Later he'd say Oddcast's revenue projections seemed aggressive. But not at the moment. At the moment, Mancini dropped a name, told an anecdote, the kind to suggest he was part of the fraternity, the one that every new business revolutionary secretly believed dispensed opportunities.

Mancini mentioned a friend. A venture capitalist no less. This VC, said Mancini, kept a score sheet on presentations. He never gave money to anyone who rated under a nine. The unstated suggestion was clear: Mancini might help them measure up. Adi and Clemente were rapt.

Mancini was pitch perfect; authoritative, never eager. Still, I was convinced that it was the room, its vast colonial sweep that carried the day. You just had the feeling good things could happen in a setting like this. Maybe $20 million things. Or, perhaps, bigger things.

"Our aim is to grow you to a *Fortune* 50 company," Mancini said with a perfectly straight face.

Later, I'd check. To get in the *Fortune* 50, a company needed revenues of $32 billion a year!

Clemente and Adi nodded.

Mancini swung back to the issue at hand.

"I'm confident I can help you raise money," Mancini said. "At least get you in the room," which would, of course, be this room.

"This room is a nine," Adi said.

"The room works," Mancini agreed. He smiled, paused, and then, it seemed to me, moved in for the kill. His voice may have lowered a note or two. "I'd like to mention this to a few investors," Mancini said next, as if he might have them on speed dial. Then as if that weren't enough, he added, "With your permission, of course."

Clemente quickly gave permission.

"I like to line up several investors at a time," he added. "I find you always forget something in the morning and in the afternoon it's perfect," said Mancini.

Clemente made a hasty note to send Mancini a new business plan and a couple of investor kits.

Then, in a just-remarking-on-the-scenery tone, Mancini put in one last thing. "I understand," he said, "you're working on a deal with KNation," which prompted Adi to break in.

"He's *your* lawyer?" Adi asked and turned to me. His chin was forward. Did I hear the *eek?* Somehow Adi had missed that part.

"Uh, yeah," I said.

Then Mancini let them know that he, of course, couldn't really help Oddcast until they'd tidied up their business with me.

After Clemente and Adi left, I stayed behind. For a few minutes, I was alone in that grand room with Mancini, my lawyer, who said wistfully, "I wish you'd been on the management team with them." A delightful thought, which I knew he meant.

Chapter Twenty-four

Clear-Eyed Seeker
of Wisdom and Truth

THE OTHER DAY CEO Clemente described something in a hush-hush tone, not all that different, of course, from his everyday whisper. We talked by phone. I imagined Clemente speaking from a corner of Oddcast's gloomy offices. (For some reason, I always pictured that place rolling in brown fog.) Clemente was a company loyalist. As soon as he'd departed Cyber Dialogue for Oddcast, he changed his private e-mail address to OddcastPC. Yet Clemente had personal concerns as well. These days, businesspeople did. One of them, as he told me in that confidential voice, was to pay attention "to building my brand." His personal brand. The phrase struck me. I hadn't run into people who thought of themselves as brands. Clearly, though, Clemente was on to something—he usually was. And to understand the promising business world I lately found myself in, I knew I ought to pay attention.

The business culture seemed to have come up with a potent new representation of the self. We were each of us aggressive little firms. Me Incs. was a going phrase, a telling update on Me Decade, the term for the seventies. "When we try to figure out how to . . . live our lives, we figure out what hot companies do and scale it down to size," wrote the *New York Times,* explaining the contemporary impulse.

And not just *any* type of companies. Me Inc., it was important to emphasize, was primarily a marketing business. The late nineties proposed that in significant ways, people were indistinguishable from brands. This was one of the more important currents in recent business writing. Tom Peters had been the first to broach what he termed the "brand called You." Others signed on. "The idea is simply that you are a brand," said Alan Webber, coeditor of *Fast Company*. If Clemente worried about his brand, it was because he, like so many others, had been informed that a leg-up for a career was a little brand awareness campaign for the brand called You.

Peters, of course, was one of the most popular management gurus of the last quarter century. Twenty years ago, when foreign competition seemed poised to dominate American business, Peters cowrote a book telling managers what was wrong. Some of his advice could fit on a bumper sticker—*stick to the knitting* was one choice bit. (He also opposed huge hierarchies and favored engaging workers.) And yet if advising business to stay with what it knew, i.e., the knitting, didn't seem particularly complicated, Peters' timing was shrewd. After all, American business at that moment was caught up in a rush to diversify. Peters's first book, coauthored by Robert Waterman Jr., *In Search of Excellence,* sold 4 million copies.

Peters's eighth book, his 1999 *The Brand You 50: Fifty Ways to Transform Yourself from an "Employee" into a Brand That Shouts Distinction, Commitment, and Passion!,* expanded his potential readership from every manager to every employee, many of whose careers no longer seemed secure, in part because, just as Peters had suggested, business had gone on a streamlining binge.

Now Peters warned employees that quiet, diligent achievement was no longer an option. Do what you love, if you want. Still, Peters pointed out that what really mattered was how you were *perceived*. A hundred years ago, Emerson complained, "What you are shouts so loudly in my ears I cannot hear what you say." In Peters's world just the opposite seemed true. You were what you said you were. So your job was to scream your message until you were red in the face, which was Peters's style when addressing a large crowd. (The spray flew from his mouth. He was occasionally termed a spitter, not a speaker.)

According to Peters every single individual *required* marketing. "Our most important job is to be head marketer for the brand called You," said Peters.

This was quite a striking development for business. This notion, for instance, wouldn't have rung true for the self-made man of a previous era. Businessman Ben Franklin was wily and competitive. He knew the importance of connections and money and marketing. His *Poor Richard's Almanack,* the one with the famous sayings, was in part a promotional campaign for his printing business. But what he told himself, as well as everyone else, was that character counted in business and in life. As a young man, Franklin created a chart of thirteen virtues. Each week he spent time improving one of them—neatly, his program took one fiscal quarter. Be neat, work hard, don't squander your savings. Be humble, moderate, sober, sincere. The result would be unimpeachable character, and also customers. For Franklin, and for self-help writers for the next hundred years, character paid. And it paid for anyone. Indeed, success was a welcoming kingdom; implicitly, it could be entered by anyone who diligently applied the rules.

By the middle of the twentieth century the success literature had undergone a marked change. Stephen Covey, author of *The 7 Habits of Highly Effective People,* identified the change as the arrival of the Personality Ethic, though given recent developments, it might also be considered the beginning of the Personal Marketing Ethic. Dale Carnegie, Napoleon Hill, and Norman Vincent Peale were early examples. Generally, their view was that someone with a sufficiently likeable personality or a positive outlook or a burning self-confidence could win friends and influence people, as Carnegie put it, and that would lead to success. Willy Loman, Arthur Miller's midcentury creation in *Death of a Salesman,* was a famed adherent of the Personality Ethic. For salesman Willy, to be liked or better yet, to be well-liked, was the most important advantage a person could have in business and in life. ("He's liked, but not well-liked," was a Willy Loman put-down.) To Willy, and to generations of the future, a "winning image" would be a key ingredient of business success. "Look like a million so you can make a million," that was the idea as it would later be presented in *Dress for Success*. The focus was no longer on the rewards of virtue or character, as that self-made man of old had preached. Technique mattered; not character. (Covey, by the way, advocated a return to issues of character; though, a contemporary man, he sometimes pinned character on virtues like recognizing another's "individuality, separateness, and worth.")

Miller's Loman turned out tragically—Willy committed suicide—but others of the era looked at the same material and had a laugh. For a time, tweaking the overzealous self-marketer was pretty good public sport. At least everyone seemed to share in the fun behind Shepherd Mead's 1952 book, *How to Succeed in Business Without Really Trying: The Dastard's Guide to Fame and Fortune*. Mead was an exec for the advertising company Benton and Bowles when he whipped off this slim, charming send-up of the man on the make. The point, for those who missed the book, the Broadway musical, the movie, or the Broadway revival, was that anyone could succeed in business. Talent didn't matter much, nor character. "If you have education, intelligence, and ability, so much the better," said Mead flippantly, "but remember that thousands have reached the top without them." Just follow a few simple rules, counseled Mead, most intended to help the young man stand out. Not, of course, by the quality of his work, which didn't seem to count for much, but by the *appearance* of hard and good work.

By the time Peters took up the theme—really, he was the latest iteration of the Personality Ethic—personal marketing wasn't funny, with everyone in on the joke. Little in Peters's world ever seems like fun. Personal marketing, in particular, was serious stuff. In case you missed the point, Peters said it left him "scared shitless."

And yet—was it possible?—a fair portion of Peters's advice wasn't all that dissimilar from the advice Mead put forth in his happy-go-lucky satire.

Consider the similarities:

> The very keystone of modern business is the Idea. In fact, no greater praise can be given you than to be called an Idea Man.
> *How to Succeed.*

Think B-I-G. As in big ideas. You are your "big ideas."
Brand You 50.

The conscientious businessman will make every moment count.
How to Succeed.

Every moment . . . every micro-event . . . has a Message.
Brand You 50.

Attract attention. Let them know you're there—in a well-bred way of course.
How to Succeed.

You are your own P.R. 'agency.'
Brand You 50.

You will have to take their dream notions—[those of assistants]—and Whip Them into Shape, stamp them with your own brand.
How to Succeed.

Is what I'm doing right now consistent with building a brand, my brand?
Brand You 50.

It is your duty to lead the way, and you can only do this by being an expert. Be one!
How to Succeed.

You've simply got to know a lot about something of significant value to a bunch of Potential Clients.
Brand You 50.

Peters, of course, would say that the quality of a person's work mattered; Mead that it mattered not at all. And yet it's difficult to resist the impression that many of Peters's suggestions for winning at what he called, in perfect *How to Succeed* tone, "the Great Game of Business," weren't all that different from Mead's. In specifics, at least. The tone of course was starkly different. Peters uttered his advice frothy with passion, the era's choice emotion. Mead, one suspected, proffered his giggling with irony.

But then, the nineties was not a particularly ironic time. Peters, for one, didn't seem to have an ironic bone in his body. Gritting his teeth, he proposed that you grab every advantage you could. He didn't pay any mind to the negatives once implicit in marketing—like, say, that it was a lie. "I don't think brands are marketing flim-flam," said Peters. These days, what wasn't marketed or, business seemed to ask, couldn't be? Soap, cigarettes, political candidates, stock market prices, and, now, business individuals? And so, Peters looked at business and saw techniques the individual could learn from and apply. "Take a course in marketing," he suggested. Or, he added, "Construct a formal word-of-mouth marketing plan." For yourself. You had to stand out, and not necessarily by qualifications or deeds—though, if you had them, "so much the better" as Mead put it—but, in any case, by tricks of self-definition, the branding strategies that worked for Kellogg's or Nike.

Of course, satire, even when done sincerely, still smacks of satire. One can easily imagine Mead slipping Peters's most earnest advice—word for word—into his sly send-up. There is, for instance, Peters's dastardly recommendation to: "'Manage' trustworthiness. Explicitly." Or his counsel that everyone should ask himself: "What have you done . . . s-p-e-c-i-f-i-c-a-l-l-y . . . in the last twenty-four hours to enhance your . . . Image of TRUSTWORTHINESS?" (There's no accounting for Peters's deranged punctuation.)

Peters, though, is no satirist. From his determined point of view, the person intent on getting ahead really need not worry overmuch about reputation, character, or what he almost dismissively referred to as "substance." "Partly it's a matter of substance," said Peters. Though it might not be a bad idea to market yourself as having lots of substance or, given the terms of the current debate, a passionate character. Passion, clearly, was the era's primary branding strategy (except perhaps, when dating).

For Peters, the implicit message of the current business culture was clear: You were the person others took you for. The truth was what people believed. In Peters's world, reality seemed a little elusive, its challenges, for the most part, presentational.

In a now-eerie example, Peters suggested that Arthur Andersen was the kind of company an individual ought to emulate when it came to personal branding. No doubt Andersen effectively promoted itself as reliable, assiduous, honest, the precise qualities that later events would suggest it glaringly lacked. (Andersen was the auditor on duty when Enron deceived the public.) Perhaps, as some would claim, Andersen was simply a bad apple, an aberration to an otherwise rigorous business ethic. It seemed equally plausible that Andersen was an extension of Peters's branding logic, the one which suggested in ellipses, capitals (and decibels) that trustworthiness was, essentially, a marketing issue.

Peters called for every person to do "a feature-benefit analysis" of himself, the kind that could be done for any brand. He wasn't interested in worthy but, as he said, in "noteworthy." Give yourself fifteen words, said Peters, to describe what it was that made you outstanding. Then, of course, as he put it, "you still have to market the bejesus out of your brand." Clemente was hardly the most calculating person I knew—on the contrary, I found him honest, good-to-his-word— still, in a world without job security, he understood the importance of self-marketing. Fortunately, as a consultant, Clemente had plenty of accomplishments to let people know about. Plus, not everybody got to pose for *AdWeek* astride a Harley. *Easy Rider* business consultant, I'd thought. Not a bad brand-building moment.

For those less fortunate, Peters was full of ideas for raising a profile, grabbing the spotlight, promoting the self you hoped to be taken for. Some were small, practical suggestions. He thought you could write an opinion piece, even if for a local paper. That might help. He suggested joining Toastmasters, learning to be a public speaker. Or creating your own Web site.

Willy Loman's next-door neighbor was going to argue a case before the Supreme Court. "And he didn't even mention it!" said Willy. To which the young man's father replied, "He don't have to— he's gonna do it." It was a commonplace of the current business culture that accomplishments, like character, no longer spoke for themselves. And so Peters instructed all brand you-ers to create buzz about their achievements, no matter how small. Don't just sell, oversell. "Sell-the-hell-out-of-yourself," said Peters. He wanted you to sell "the sizzle"—*your* sizzle. The subtext was that you should market yourself as *already* successful—as seen, as heard, as *already* doing good and important things. "Think like the schedulers for the President of the United States," he wrote, "Every moment . . . every micro-event . . . has a Message. Adds or detracts from your Brand Image. I.e.: Become your own, conscious Spin Doctor . . ."

No doubt this approach was suited to the New Economy. Business had once emphasized results—that was what entrepreneurs used to be good at getting. Now, though, solid results were few; they'd come later. As I well knew. Meantime, entrepreneurs had ideas and plans. They had momentum. In such an environment, marketing—and the right auditors—could create perceived value.

All this, I noticed, was delivered as good news. Peters billed it as part of nothing less than a white-collar revolution, liberation from company-dependence, Dilbert-like cynicism, and the grinding routine of good corporate citizenship, the type his dad, who'd worked for the same company for forty-one years, had signed up for. And yet it didn't strike me as entirely comforting. (And indeed, Peters said over and over, "It is scary.")

Personal marketing, after all, was predicated on the idea that deserved promotions based on solid work had gone the way of job security. Further, it posited that every man or woman should be out for him- or herself. The new business ethic paid lip service to teamwork as a supposed alternative to hierarchy. But clearly these were different kinds of teams. After all, business, Peters reminded us, "requires you to act selfishly—to grow yourself, to promote yourself, to get the market to reward yourself." (Not a stance particularly conducive to teamwork.) In fact, business, in Peters's world, seemed a lonely struggle. I sometimes sensed that one message of the new entrepreneurial economy was, You're on your own.

These thoughts could make a person gloomy, which, it turned out, Peters often was. The most poignant moment in Peters's thumpingly upbeat book was the admission that he didn't *feel* upbeat. He couldn't maintain enthusiasm without a great deal of effort and a daily

Prozac, which he used "to dispel a little of the semipermanent pall."
(This in a chapter that talked about "practicing your smile.") No wonder enthusiasm seemed so important to Peters; clearly it was elusive.

I couldn't help but think that here was an insight into the real
state of the brand-you world. Not only was the world perilous for
the consumer of hyped products (or companies) but, if the product
was you, then you were in danger too. After all, a premise of the
brand-you world was that if success wasn't ratified by publicity, then
it didn't count. It wasn't much of a leap to suggest that the precious
self—the me of Me, Inc.—only existed as a reflection in the eyes of
others. "This brand-called-you demands constant feeding," said ever-
attentive Harriet Rubin in *Inc.* magazine. "Every day that you're not
out in the marketplace reminding people you exist, you disappear."
Death by lack-of-publicity.

Business claimed to offer fulfillment these days; it was touted as a
route to liberation. But, clearly, there was a darker side. (I sometimes
thought that the new gains were, really, cleverly marketed losses.)
Doing a job well, bringing to bear talent, commitment, excellence,
even passion wasn't really enough. You didn't, finally, have control.
Recognition by others was the only true measure of contemporary
success, and it was all-too-fleeting. In the virile new business culture,
the one taking over, it could seem that accomplishments were
ephemeral, marketing everlasting.

Unless, of course—and this was a wild thought—Peters was wink-
ing at us the whole time, assuming that we, like those fifties audiences,
were in on the joke. Perhaps, it momentarily occurred to me, he expected us all to join in the fun. To sing along. Maybe to a melody
pulled from Frank Loesser's musical *How to Succeed in Business Without
Really Trying.* Could Peters's excited tome be a musical? Think of the
possibilities, if you just took a Loesser lyric and rearranged it slightly:

You've got the cool, clear eyes of a seeker of wisdom and truth.
Yet there's that upturned grin reminiscent of gin and vermouth
Oh, I believe in the brand-called-you.
The brand-called-you.

Chapter Twenty-five

Gradually, Then All at Once

NEGOTIATIONS! How I loved the sound of that word! Like *deal* or *leverage* or *frequent-flyer miles,* it was resonant of business, the thing I'd set out to do all those months ago. Our negotiations were scheduled for Yakiniku, a Japanese restaurant not far from Japas, the bar where one drunken night almost a year ago I'd stumbled into karaoke.

In preparation for the evening's business, I spent some time talking to my attorney Mancini. Not long before, Mancini had asked me to sign a waiver permitting him to represent Oddcast, a paying customer, as well as KNation, a nonpaying one. (He hoped to represent Oddcast in investment-related work. But since Oddcast and KNation were working out a deal with one another, a waiver of conflict was necessary.) Mancini pointed out that the two companies weren't really in conflict, but in the appearance of conflict. Three lawyers were on the line as Mancini asked me to sign. The conversation confused me, since I thought we'd agreed that withholding Mancini's services was the leverage I had with Oddcast. Unless, perhaps, Mancini was shrewdly prepping me for negotiations, conducting a pointed clinic in business pressure. In any case, once I refused—appearance or not, I couldn't imagine why in the world I'd go along—there was no problem.

It was with our relationship in its usual pleasant state that Mancini and I discussed my approaching talks with Oddcast. I'd envisioned a lively back-and-forth with Adi and Clemente. They'd make an offer, I'd scoff. They'd get a sense of my determination, my mettle. Then we'd get down to business. Mancini didn't imagine that at all. He figured Clemente and Adi would quickly offer me a fat percentage of Oddcast in exchange for the rights to karaoke. Sometimes Mancini and I kicked around figures, back-of-the-envelope kinds of things. Oddcast had four other products. I offered a fifth. So logically, I ought to end up with about 20 percent of the company.

"Really?" I wondered aloud.

Mancini thought 20 percent sounded fair. I'd own the product, of course, which was important since it would give me control; Oddcast would build it. Then, he suggested, we could roll up our sleeves and get to work.

"Do what I do best," I said, unprompted.

If we all pitched in, who knew how far we could take this thing? Mancini, as usual, made business sound like it mainly required cooperation. I, in any case, looked forward to working together with the others. And why wouldn't I? Clemente had for so long been on my side, and he assured me Adi was too. After talking to Mancini, I thought, We'll get this done, then I can sell karaoke—*sell the hell out of it* were the words that occurred to me. The plan, my plan, was to share the revenue from sales. I'd come up with some generous revenue-split ideas. I thought Oddcast deserved about half.

Still at Yakiniku, I was nervous. A lot was riding on this meeting, let's face it. I'd been at this for nearly a year. At this point, I didn't see many alternatives to Oddcast. None, actually. Plus, I couldn't help but notice that many of my new business acquaintances were lately scurrying out of harm's way, with mixed results. In fact, the urban space was emptying. Russell Simmons had sold out. It was labeled a merger, and he still had influence, but BET.com, Web business of Black Entertainment Television, was running the show. "I've got good partners," Russell said, knowing he'd got them just in time. UBO, Jerry's entry, was on the verge of collapse (and soon would go). Hookt hung on, barely, after entering into talks to buy a VideoMixer. It was in "survival mode," as one exec put it, though not for long. AKA, an early licensee of the VideoMixer, was about to pack it in, after bragging about its robust health; 88hiphop, which appeared on Pseudo.com, would disappear even before Pseudo did.

The Internet in general had the feel of a last man standing contest. "Let them all fucking go out of business," snapped Adi one day. "Hurry up and go." Adi, who wore his brown chaps at the time, might have made an okay cowboy, I thought.

And so I wanted negotiations to go just right, an outcome I thought most likely if I appeared sharp, serious, orderly, and maybe a touch removed, the demeanor of a person tying up loose ends. Unfortunately on entering Yakiniku, a demure Japanese woman instructed me to remove my shoes. Can one be sharp and serious, can one be *businesslike* in one's socks? I thought of the story by Tolstoy, *Kreutzer Sonata*. A shoeless husband chased his wife's terrified lover from their house, then stopped. "It is ridiculous to run after one's wife's lover in one's socks," he said. In my socks I, too, felt slightly ridiculous, especially after I stopped in Yakiniku's bathroom, where the tile floor was a bit splashy.

Naturally, I'd arrived early. (Couldn't I ever have an urgent call to delay me?) Yakiniku seated diners on low benches around a wide table; under the table was a hole into which you stuck your feet. With a shiver of vulnerability, I slipped my soggy feet into the dark, unable to feel a bottom.

I decided to order a drink. Just to have it on the table when they arrived. Which I thought would demonstrate a certain poise.

The attentive Japanese waitress hurried over.

"Boilermaker," I said emphatically, indicating a shot and a beer.

She issued a deflating half-smile. Such a term was beyond her. She seemed to have no idea what I was talking about.

"Water," I said brightly.

Adi and Clemente rushed in a few minutes later—recently they seemed to travel everywhere together. Adi, of course, looked disheveled. He might, it occurred to me, have given up combing his hair. It looked like a crop that wouldn't quite take. Adi smiled and apologized lavishly for their tardiness. His smile, I noted, seemed to take a long time to prepare.

"No problem, Adi my friend," I said, just the way he'd say it. Recently, I found myself imitating Adi's speech, the long flattened *e*, even, occasionally, the electronic hum. (I was like a foreign exchange student when it came to new accents.) Lately, I noticed that Adi returned the favor.

"You're imitating me," I'd told him not long ago.

"Imitating me," he'd said.

Clemente, of course, was impeccably dressed in a black suit. With that hive of hair, he looked like a mod undertaker—except for the glasses. He wore dark sunglasses that he declined to remove.

"Conjunctivitis," he explained amiably.

Adi placed his cell phone on the table and ordered a carafe of sake for himself. Clemente lined up three cell phones in front of him. He was transitioning among phones and had a complicated system of outgoing and incoming calls. Though I'd never known him to drink, he ordered a glass of wine. Then he cleared his throat and in his shoe scrape of a voice said that he respected me and wanted me to be happy, everyone to be happy, which even then I took as a bad sign.

"I have to look out for Oddcast," he quickly added. He was Oddcast's CEO, I didn't need to be reminded. And so Clemente, who'd helped nurture KNation, who'd almost (I still liked to think) been its chief executive, set a yellow legal pad on the table. He intended to take notes, leave the negotiating to Adi.

Yakiniku is one of those restaurants where diners cook the food themselves on a small grill built into the table. Almost immediately Adi began ordering food, more attentive to quantity than type, it seemed to me. In a few minutes, the table reeked of burning meat. Adi, chief cook, deftly turned the food, parceling out sizzling morsels.

For all my resolve to be calm, definite, unemotional, I was too anxious to eat. Adi ordered another sake. Then between sake bottle one and two, or was it two and three, he stated, "I like you."

"I like you, too," I responded awkwardly. Everything would go well now. I mentioned my ideas for splitting the revenue from licensing—fifty-fifty, I smiled—and other matters of collaboration. Perhaps I was too jaunty, or went on too long. Or perhaps the sober one at the party always seems loopy. Adi cut me off with a "thank you." He held a chunk of beef with his chop sticks. He'd talked to his attorney, he said.

"My lawyer says Oddcast must own the karaoke program," he said. "My hands are tied." (Clemente stayed silent, though he'd later say this was news to him.) Adi meant for Oddcast to own the product.

I'd arrived tonight believing I finally had a technology company, a grand one, to build my product. Now, it appeared my technology company had me! *Double-crossed!* I thought. I could have shouted, and briefly considered it. *No, you won't take karaoke from me!* Something along those lines. Would that have been the right note to strike? There in the restaurant with the odors of burning meat and sticky socks? Where was Consigliere when I needed him? Working late, he'd said.

Suddenly, I was distracted. Adi stood. He towered above the table. He was shoeless, and balanced on a colorful seat cushion in socks full of holes. Adi scanned the room as if searching for something. Sometimes, I knew, his Israeli friends, fellow soldiers, dined here. Would there be troop movements upcoming? But just then, Adi focused on his shirt to which he seemed to have developed an aversion. He began to unbutton the thing—perhaps it was a little warm. Once Adi had seemed so remote I thought him in danger of flatlining. Later, I'd seen his excitable side, his hands tossing in the air like hooked fish. This appeared to be something different. Was he going to remove his shirt? (He hadn't, I knew, quite mastered the dressing-room concept. Perhaps it was the general notion of public space he found problematic.)

Clemente stopped taking notes, peered through his dark sunglasses. I stared too. Adi seemed to be shouting, as if in the grips of quite a big emotion. Then as inexplicably as he rose, Adi returned to his seat, and to our discussion.

He pointed out that karaoke was not really protectable. The technology to create the application was widely available. "Everybody will have it soon," he said. He even said that a client had asked Oddcast for karaoke—an exaggeration, I'd learn later. On occasion Adi could be a bit of an egomaniac, and yet he was right, karaoke wasn't exactly proprietary. Despite my warm feelings toward it, karaoke wasn't *really* mine. There were other karaoke applications available even now. Eatsleepmusic.com had been pushing karaoke even before I'd been to my first karaoke bar.

"This isn't fair," I said absurdly. "Not what we talked about."

By now, the food was mostly gone. Adi, often fast out of the gate, seemed done in. In fact, he fell over. Oddcast's first CEO stretched flat on his back on a hard cushion. I stared at his round belly. Clemente, Oddcast's current CEO, looked on, too.

An artist? I thought. How funny, it suddenly seemed, to envy Adi, which, of course, I did. Adi's eyes were closed. He appeared to be going through something. Maybe several things at once.

Is this how business is done? I wondered.

In a moment, Adi popped up again. This time to point out that he didn't think I should get much of Oddcast at all.

He wanted me to participate in sales of the karaoke application. He had some revenue split ideas of his own. He thought 5 to 10 percent a reasonable figure.

"You want to make me a glorified salesman," I said, sounding like someone held underwater too long.

"No, no, no," Adi and Clemente chimed together, a chorus of good intentions.

"You are our partner," Adi said soothingly. *"Ihhh."*

Then he collapsed again. A hand extended over his head, as if starting a backstroke.

"Five percent!" I shouted.

Again he sat up.

"Gross sales," he said, hooking a finger at Clemente's notebook. His one concession.

Then Adi stood a second time. This time, in his holey socks, he moved to the middle of the restaurant where he began to reenact an encounter between his friend the Media Attacker and a politician's bodyguards. Apparently the Media Attacker had been punched and held in a headlock, and still continued shouting at the politician. Adi did a pretty fair rendition of both sides of the conflict.

$ $ $

The next day I awoke with the beginnings of a cold. I moved to my cluttered desk, stacked with karaoke magazines and (still) phones galore. I drank hot tea, wore a knit cap and felt suddenly depressed by the deficiencies of my office view which mainly took in a towering brick wall.

Clemente telephoned. He wanted me to be happy, he reiterated. "It would be the worst outcome if you took this somewhere else," he said movingly, an option I felt obligated to consider. One advisory board member didn't think I should let karaoke go. People generally didn't. They made it sound as if I was giving in, giving up—not much admired in business these days. Unstinting effort, that's what you were supposed to muster. Where was my commitment? My passion? Where indeed?

I had little doubt that the Internet would make good on its promises; in ten years it would be everywhere and, like electricity, always on. It would bring convenience and personalization to the consumer—people would download movies, talk over an Internet phone, shop online as if it were the corner grocer. And some day every hopeful fifteen-year-old and every eager new VP would dial up a content engine of some sort and put out a zippy multimedia memo to his girlfriend or his staff. (I'd become something of an Internet evangelist myself.) And karaoke, too, would someday be delivered over the Internet, to bars and homes. That was obvious, and obvious *was* good in an idea.

For a time it had also been possible to believe that anyone could wander into business, start a venture, be a CEO. "I know five CEOs," Consigliere had recently remarked, though Joseph Park was no longer one. (He'd been bounced by his board.) As business drama, the

Internet had been action-adventure all the way. A few entrepreneurs with a lot of grit and a few skills, people like Adi and Clemente and even, I sometimes thought, like me, were going to battle a dark corporate elite, and hold their own. Hierarchy wasn't going to count for so much. Perhaps it was even a disadvantage just like, so the thinking went, millions of dollars of infrastructure.

Lately, of course, business didn't seem to welcome every inflamed spirit. In 2001, 210 Internet businesses collapsed, and with them $1.5 billion in investments. It wasn't just the urban sites, those I'd been involved with. Markets that once laid claim to the future—that mesmerizing term—shut down. Even Kidrin, CEO of Worlds.com and my idea of a real businessman, experienced trouble. His company's stock tumbled to about 30 cents. Recently, he'd asked *me* for help. He wanted an introduction to a customer. "How much cash do you have left?" I asked. A couple of months, he said, which I figured meant one.

It turned out that business could use newfangled digital skills. But what really came in handy, what really sustained a business, were organizational resources. When the stock market shuddered, lone Internet entrepreneurs, for the most part, went harmlessly to ground. Capitalism had its own life to lead; it had integrated new technologies before. This was an old story. A century ago, ill-prepared, underequipped entrepreneurs had lost their shirts when railroads appeared the new opportunity.

Back then, in the first part of the twentieth century, the fashion had been to laud entrepreneurs for their steady effort, persistence, thrift, moderation. And yet, the real business story of that time was the formation of large organizations. Indeed, even in the heyday of the self-made man, his wasn't the style of business success, as the scholar John Cawelti has pointed out. The self-made ethos was already nostalgia, with some preaching mixed in. "The trusts," as their critics referred to giant businesses, were the prominent economic movers. Among their advantages were financial resources, rapacious instincts, manpower, and size. And everyone knew it.

In a similar way, we all recently rooted for hierarchy to be turned upside down, bureaucracy flattened. We wanted a powerful individual actor to stride the earth. And yet, it seemed possible that even as we romanticized the struggles of one entrepreneur, we knew it to be a sentimental tale. In the competing story, the realistic one, victory went to those who commanded resources as large as a navy's or who, more wily than others, put institutional might behind their own schemes.

The Internet would find a lasting home within the large corporation. Indeed, rather than aid lonely revolutionaries to upend entire industries, the Internet mainly seemed to help existing companies wring more work from average employees. In business, the Internet would prove an efficiency tool *par excellence;* it would further Frederick Taylor's project. Remember when there were secretaries, assistants? When VPs didn't answer their own mail? When a person couldn't work on the beach?

Certainly music would soon be sold over the Internet, and in digital form, but not by hundreds of small entrepreneurs streaming code from an extra bedroom, or crafty artists cutting out the record industry. You could be sure that the handful of corporate giants who controlled the business would eventually determine an orderly process, one that wouldn't undercut their margins. Content would be king, but brand-name content. And the few who controlled it, they, really, would be royalty. The mass market had some life in it yet.

As I knew by now, the real challenge to online karaoke wasn't building an application. Wrangling the rights to use all those songs, that was the real challenge. Pelosi, my music rights attorney told me he was embarrassed that he couldn't get the deal through. But the music publishers refused to let go of those rights, not for Napster, and not for me. I knew that karaoke was really a content business. Oddcast would learn that soon enough.

Yet to note the inflated hopes of Internet businesses was not to declare the Internet a failure, though some made that mistake. The Internet changed something other than the country's economic balance of power. It would prove a "business cultural phenomenon," to use Jerry's phrase. The Internet would help popularize a new way of talking about business purpose, and about work in general. The Internet was a little like California, the place where new, slightly lunatic things seemed to take root first, before taking over.

Once, perhaps, business convinced people to invest themselves in mediocre jobs by throwing money or promotions at them or, alternatively, threatening them with unemployment. In the new century, business would make a different pitch. Business would offer itself as a platform for dreams. It wanted to be a liberator; its goal to free the dreary business soul. Not from long hours—work, after all, was longer than ever. But from the carping, the regrets, the plugging ahead, the clock-punching of the ordinary cubicle dweller. The Internet helped convince people that business was a thoroughly engaging struggle, an emotional and spiritual struggle. It made business a place where our hepped-up natures, our outsized and, perhaps, too, our best ambitions, could all be at home—perhaps the only place. In the new century business would continue to be the setting where a person's authentic self was best expressed.

Even if the entrepreneurial gold rush came up a few dollars short, this new business outlook would influence generations to come. Of that I had little doubt. Never again would the business culture appeal to the aspirant with talk of loyalty, method, systems, process, rationality, service, duty, ladder-climbing, belongingness, good corporate citizenship, or even steady income—the Organization Man's comforting beliefs. "We're not going back," one testy editor at *Fast Company* magazine told me. Not to worry, I thought. The elements that attracted people to entrepreneurship—the shot at fulfillment, at mobility, at excitement, at transformation, at making a difference—those would be defining elements of business life for a long time to come. The business culture, like the culture in general, would forevermore be framed in terms of the individual. And specifically, the individual's happiness, which, more and more, would occur at work, or not at all.

$ $ $

And yet at my desk, my knit cap pulled down against an imaginary breeze, my thoughts slipped off in another direction. I hadn't failed to notice business's surpassing idealism, nor its promise of excitement.

Indeed, I'd bought in. I'd wanted fulfillment as much as the next person, probably more. I was generationally disposed. And hadn't I gone after it? When I reviewed my anxious reminders to Clemente, my importuning what-ifs to Consigliere, my tone astounded me! Would the meeting work out? The pitch? The talks? The contract? All the hope had made my head hurt. How I'd wanted this thing! (Which was something in and of itself.) I'd lost sleep. I'd tossed, an angry man. *Angry at the fate of karaoke.* Which at various points I'd thought good, important, a moneymaker. I'd whispered revolution like the rest. *Get out of the way,* I'd thought, *the world is changing.*

And yet lately—perhaps I really had a fever coming on—I couldn't sustain the belief that in hawking karaoke I was, in fact, making a difference. It seemed a heavy load for karaoke to shoulder, or for business in general, for that matter. Something didn't work for me.

The marketplace was truth, I'd repeatedly heard from excited new business participants. What truth? Lately I couldn't avoid the suspicion that business lowered people's sights. The activity of business, when I considered it, was mostly selling, and selling was mostly drudgery. And its redeeming purpose? Selling what, after all? What was the point of all the hectic activity? What was it we all hoped to accomplish? One night, I'd listened to an AOL exec, a bright personable guy, say he was devoted to "slamming ads" into every area of the subscription service. He wore colorful pants, I recall, which suggested to more corporate types "the kind of creativity so valued around a place like AOL," he said, a deadpan send-up of this new business culture. Selling ads? Was that really creativity?

I switched to squeezed lemons, which I drank straight, like shots, and then moved onto the heavier metals, zinc and silver, which I dosed into a glass of warm water. (At the health store, a guy who claimed to be a doctor sat at a folding table and wrote me prescriptions.) I had an admission. I was sure passion was the new fuel of business, and would be for years to come. But passion in business—*for* business—seemed almost unintelligible to me. It was possible karaoke had taken me down the wrong path, allowed me to be both of it and not of it. Still, I suspected that for me the story would have reached the same point with supercaffeinated cola or online editors or a delivery-in-under-an-hour service. If fulfillment was business's fine new purpose, and I didn't doubt it, I just couldn't see how I was going to get my share.

I didn't overlook money as a source of excitement. That was how I'd first conceived of my adventure. To make a million was what I'd set out to do. One young entrepreneurial employee at Kozmo had told me, "Passion was also about getting wealthy." No one in his right mind any longer wondered if greed was good. Money wasn't grubby; it was *fascinating*. Greed was everywhere, the engine of everything, as banal as antifreeze. The good life would forever be indexed to the economy.

But I'd always wanted more than money. I'd wanted adventure. I'd wanted a team. (And where was my team these days?) I'd wanted to be entertained and have a hoot and give as good as I got. And I'd wanted to angle my way in, toward the center, where business had set up shop.

In past months, I'd had a couple hundred meetings, ten times as many phone calls—perhaps not a lot by Internet standards. For me that was a ton. Lately, it seemed that I expended great energy on an exceedingly small matter, a mismatch I'd previously associated with a suburban adolescence.

Plus, lately I couldn't avoid the feeling that I wasn't exactly what people expected. I sometimes felt like those intelligent chimps you see on TV commercials. They dress in the outfits, learn the gestures, mime the motions, and yet they're always gags. Frankly, I'd started to feel as marginalized as ever. Perhaps I was a throwback—who wasn't? I was weary. All the caring had worn me down. I could not imagine doing this day in and day out. I was tired of telling people I was *in* karaoke. I knew business had undergone a makeover. But did it really provide sufficient scope for a person's ambitions? Andrew Carnegie's line, one he said early in life, came to me: "To continue much longer overwhelmed by business cares . . . must degrade me beyond the hope of permanent recovery." I didn't see how business would make good on its promise of fulfillment.

I'd asked Consigliere if we were throwing elbows. "Yes," he said cheerfully. That was months ago. And I thought he might be humoring me anyhow. (He usually did.) After all, he was also surprised that I was still at it. What about fun, a one-time preoccupation of mine? Not long ago I caught up with Greg, who at twenty-six had announced he intended to retire at thirty. He was thirty now. We spoke on a Wednesday. On Friday his company of thirty-five employees would run out of money.

"But it's fun, right?" I insisted.

"Business is about as much fun as fistfighting," he said. He told me that an employee had complained that his company had no soul. Greg, who'd attended a graduate program in English literature, snapped, "This isn't poetry class."

I'd lived for a while on the outskirts of the Internet. Perhaps I was deficient in skills. More important, given the recent business thinking, I seemed to lack the proper buoyant attitude. I felt like Tom Peters, not pumped-up, passionate Tom who shouted from every stage, but gloomy, private Tom, the one in a semipermanent pall, cramming in exercise and sunlight, even just a few minutes, and of course, meds, anything to lift his mood.

What was it I believed? What gave weight to my activity, worth, to use an old-fashioned term? I wasn't supporting a family, bringing home the bacon. Duty didn't call. My wife had a career. We didn't yet have kids. Once work had been pitted against the rest of life. You labored so you could enjoy life outside the office, with your family. These days, entrepreneurship proposed other terms: Work ought to provide deep, abiding interest. Frankly, I was bored.

I'd wanted tales to tell, which was properly my domain. That's what I was good at. I'd always wanted to be a writer. Writing had made me climb through a window, a feat which, in retrospect, seemed almost entrepreneurial. And not incidentally, I thought that writing was rewarding. To make sense out of the weird and exciting things around me, that was an important task.

I took my cap off, felt my sweaty head. What if, I suddenly thought, I wrote a little book?

$ $ $

"I am getting out," I said aloud at my desk. And as I did, I discovered this: I wanted out. Why aren't I a millionaire? I hardly cared. I'd given enough main and might. Truth was, when the doublecross came, I was flooded with relief. Call it a case of market rationalization. Oddcast's modest offer suddenly seemed awfully good to me.

Oh, I'd miss tossing around the terrific new vocabulary—eyeballs, and stickiness, and business model. (Like I missed throwing around the terms I'd picked up during my stint at car repair. Universal joint, overhead cams. *That* was a vocabulary to reckon with.) Still, it was time to turn this thing over to someone else, someone whose belief was, yes, I thought I had the word: fundamental. Someone who believed that people were customers, customers users, and users really wanted, in measurable quantities, to create their own content. "User-generated whatever it was," said Consigliere one day. Often I felt the same. Who really desired to make music videos online? Or for that matter, to sing a song online? Let me hand this off to those who not only believed in an Internet future, but found in that belief sustenance, interest, passion. Clemente and Adi were the right people. I wanted these guys to take over KNation. They'd be better at it. Neither was a seasoned executive. And I wasn't sure their comradeship would last. (Clemente wanted to move desks around, create an organizational chart, perfect the business plan—activities that made Adi's eyes roll from concave temple to flat one.)

But Clemente was a believer. He had this Internet stuff in his bones. He'd chased me down the block and scolded me for not getting his belief quite right. He was driven—had been since he was a college rocker. I sometimes thought of him as a business monk in that spare apartment of his—if, that is, monks evangelized for the Internet. And Adi, more driven, more cutthroat than he seemed, was clearly in it for the long haul. And no less passionate. I once heard him shriek like a cockatoo at the words "user-generated media." Until, of course, those words went out of fashion, then Oddcast dropped them from its Web site.

Was business difficult? Maybe not intellectually, but putting all the elements together seemed nearly a miracle.

Our deal—that captivating word—would take months to finalize. (It wouldn't come through until almost spring 2001.) Mancini would get irate. He thought the delay an insult to Internet standards. "You don't do it that way in the Internet," he said. He sounded exasperated, like a weatherman announcing a storm.

"Everything has to be negotiated," Clemente told me at a time when I'd started going to bed with headaches. Apparently, he was reflecting on his own experience.

I would have leverage only fleetingly, just the brief hope of venture capital my lawyer represented. "I have incentive, too," Adi would tell me at one point, a reference to Mancini's promised efforts. (Eventually Mancini would set Oddcast up with a VC meeting, and in the *room,* though nothing came of it.)

Adi and I managed to blame the lawyers for miscues and delays, but I suspected it was Adi speaking through his lawyers. He was a nice fellow, an able, inspired leader, and one I still occasionally thought of as fragile. Though lately I had the feeling that he weighed his options, all of them, including perhaps the one of cutting me out. I'd get 10,000 shares of Oddcast, a percentage point or two by my calculations. And my commission of between 5 and 10 percent of gross sales, once offered for the life of the karaoke product, would last four years.

One time Adi asked me for some minor point, saying, "Pl-e-e-ease," in that bug lamp tone.

"No," I got to say with some satisfaction, my one moment.

Mostly, I just felt relieved. To those who thought I'd given up in un-entrepreneurial fashion, I thought of what Kidrin had once said. "You weren't there," I told anyone who asked.

Shortly after the deal was agreed to, Consigliere came out to celebrate. He'd been a faithful onlooker, counseling from the sideline. For old time's sake, he shifted his elbows like a battered washing machine. Then we ducked into a bar, a Japanese bar. Perhaps twenty bottles of sake hung against a back wall.

We were as jolly as could be, roared like titans, and as the evening wore on even talked, me and Consig, about another little venture.

"We should do something," he said.

"Again?"

"Yeah," he said and ordered another sake. "This time we'll do it right."

Of course we will, I thought. I didn't know why. But my mood lifted then. "Well," I started. I just couldn't help myself. "I had been considering this one thing I'd heard about at a party," I said. "A thing with gambling."

"*Gambling!*" he shouted. I could tell he liked the idea. "That would be fun," he said.

"I think it really might be fun."

Then Consigliere lamented, a bit loudly, the lack of intoxicants in our lives. Who could argue? We were fit to be tied, and started to drink our way across the back wall.

Epilogue

New York, New York

LONG AGO, I'd promised to show Russell's people my prototype. And so when Oddcast built one for the karaoke customer it had found, I decided to take the prototype to Russell, who this time waited behind his desk, rubbing a roly-poly and, as I soon learned, queasy belly with a flat, wide palm. He appeared more relaxed than the last time I saw him. I noticed a *Bhagavad-Gita* on his desk, which perhaps had some influence. Or else it was the flu. Russell was sick. "The room is fucking spinning," said Russell with that delightful soft lisp. Or perhaps his relaxation was due to the fact that he had no more Internet headaches. Unlike a lot of other people, he'd made it to safety.

As I was led in to his office, Russell was finishing up with a previous meeting, which I observed for a few minutes. It seemed to be Russell's day to receive business petitioners, a kind of entertainment for him.

"Do you know who that was?" Russell said excitedly when the young man left. "Michael Eisner's son," said Russell, answering his own question. The father ran Disney. Russell, too, was a fan of business.

The prototype of the karaoke application was installed on my laptop. Getmusic.com, a project of Vivendi Universal, would soon sign up for KaraokeStation, as Oddcast called it.

Russell looked at the application. He liked it still. He really did believe this hip-hop karaoke thing was interesting. He took the microphone I'd brought along.

Would he like to sing "New York, New York," the Frank Sinatra version, or "The Way I Am" by rapper Eminem?

"Hip-hop," said Russell, and in an instant he began to rap along as Eminem's words scrolled. "I am what I say I am," Russell sang in a drone that seemed to have something to do with his uneasy stomach.

Then Russell, as was his way, picked up a phone, hitting the speaker button. He called an executive vice president.

"I'm here with my good friend," he began, then turned to me. "What's your name?"

In a few minutes, I headed over to 360hiphop where Russell had set me up with three executives. I'd gotten a roomful of them. These were the decision makers. Finally, they'd see my prototype.

"Okay," I said, "Who would like to sing?"

Of course, in this vast KaraokeNation of ours, everyone would, almost as much as everyone would like to do business. And yet, no one offered to take the mike. I looked around. I urged someone to step forward. I recalled that as a youngster, Chuck D had suffered microphonitis—he wouldn't give the mike up. In this room, I noted, the opposite affliction seemed to have struck.

And then because I was eager, with an eagerness that still stunned me, to see this thing alive in the world, I took up the microphone, the one thing I'd promised myself I'd never do.

It was my karaoke debut. I chose the Frank Sinatra song. The words scrolled. Music played. I smiled, tapped the mike as a performer would, then sang badly and to my heart's content. *"I want to be a part of it, New York, New York . . ."*

Brief Update

ADI SIDEMAN is once again CEO of Oddcast. Peter Clemente moved to Sony Music Entertainment where he is a vice president. (He did, by the way, cut his hair and found the experience less traumatic than feared.) Consigliere is busy at his consulting job, though he still occasionally wears nipple rings under his coat and tie. He is making minor revisions to his novel which has received favorable responses from publishers. Joe Park, who once suggested that if his business failed the experience would look good on a business school application, attends Harvard Business School. Jerry Colonna plans to leave the banking business and talks about writing a book. Russell has moved on from the Internet to Broadway with a good old-fashioned show about poetry. Thom Kidrin maneuvered Worlds.com to survival and likes to think of his company as the cockroach of the Internet. After changing firms and leaving his beautiful Rockefeller Center offices, John Mancini helps run the technology group at LeBoeuf, Lamb, Greene & MacRae, where he is busier than ever. James is back behind the counter at the dry cleaners and recently seemed a little downhearted. Pat still washes windows, though he seems upbeat. He shot a dramatic series, *The New Guard*, with the digital camera earned from his cybersquatting proceeds, then showed it on RadicalZoo.com. Given his knack for publicity, it should be no surprise that the *New York Times* ran a report on the making of his film. KaraokeNation lives. Sort of. Oddcast licensed KaraokeStation to Getmusic.com and then to Warner Brothers which used the application to promote its movie *Rock Star* (though I'm still waiting for all my money).

For more information on life in our Karaoke Nation, or to sing your heart out with our karaoke product, go to www.karaokenation.com.

Acknowledgments

This book required many kinds of help. I'd especially like to thank those who participated as businesspeople, either at my side or across the table from me. At the top of that list are Adi Sideman and Peter Clemente, as well as Steve Reynolds, whom I decided to call Consigliere before I realized how difficult that was to pronounce. They're capable, bright, and fun. Each, I'm sure, will be a success on his own terms. In addition, there were dozens and dozens of helpful people willing to dispense advice or contacts or enthusiasm, even after they realized what they'd gotten into. Among them, I'd particularly like to thank Thom Kidrin, John Mancini, Greg Easley, Paul Cimino, Rick Lew, Stephen Schnall, Chas Walker, Scott Rompala, Lydia Sussek, David Hartt, Rev. Luke Murphy, Audrey Brenstein, James Ebron, David Kang, Jonathan Landreth, David Fishman, John Meserve, Mark Lieberman, Kevin Nakao, Kasaun Henry, Sheena Lester, Jeff Petterson, Norman Beil, Ron Sweeney, Darien Leung, Andrew P. Lee, Carrie Brenner, Charlie Yi, Cliff Michel, Larry Pearl, Jeff Okkonen, Mary Kallaher, Paula de la Cruz, Jasen Slutzkin, Brian Conley, Dave Brooks, Holly Taylor, Debby Solomon, Susan Murcko, Jolyn Matsumuro, and Michael Prichinello, among many others.

I lucked into a series of very good researchers and assistants, among them Jimmy Wong, Kareem Fahim, Elizabeth Mitchell, Deepti Golash, and the outstanding Michael Donohue.

I had some terrific readers who took time away from their own projects to give me invaluable feedback on various drafts of my manuscript. I thank Robin Marantz Henig, Deborah Franklin, Laura MacDonald, David Friedman, Lenore Davis, Marion Maneker, Lilibet Foster, Steve Shainberg, Ellen Ryder, Craig Unger, Debbie Boekchin, and Mary Duenwald. Writerly support, including essential mood-coaching, came at important moments from John Marchese and David Meyer.

John Homans is a truly gifted magazine editor who, though he'd never admit it, championed the article that led to this book. Later, he made time for my book concerns in his multitasking life. Thanks also to Caroline Miller, editor-in-chief of *New York* magazine, who commissioned the original article, and then published it despite its unwieldy length. My Free Press editor, Bill Rosen, and publisher, Martha Levin, both "got it" from the start, for which I am deeply thankful. Bill's insights—sharp but respectful—helped reshape several aspects of the book and made it funnier and smarter. My deep appreciation to my agent, the goddess Lisa Bankoff at ICM.

Finally, my thanks to my wife Tina for her love, humor, and kindness.

Index

About the Author

STEVE FISHMAN is one of the more honored magazine journalists in America, with bylines everywhere from *The New York Times Magazine* to *Rolling Stone* (and including *Details, Vogue,* and *Success!*). His article on how cigarette companies target young women won the President's Award from the American Medical Association, and he has won the prestigious Best Magazine Story Award given by the American Society of Journalists and Authors an unprecedented three times. His first book, *A Bomb in the Brain,* was one of *Library Journal's* Best Books of the Year, and was excerpted or adapted for *Health, Science Digest, The New York Times Magazine,* and *Rolling Stone. The Washington Post* wrote that it was "a literary tour de force." The *Los Angeles Times* wrote "no book in a long time has had such an emotional impact on me." And *The New York Times* called it "more vivid than if it had happened to me . . . read as though a novel . . ." He lives in New York City.